Risk, Resilience, Inequality and Environmental Law

To Clive, Richard, Issy, Corin, Esther and Gregor

Risk, Resilience, Inequality and Environmental Law

Edited by

Bridget M. Hutter

Professor of Risk Regulation, Department of Sociology, London School of Economics and Political Science, UK

Edward Elgar PUBLISHING

Cheltenham, UK • Northampton, MA, USA

Published by
Edward Elgar Publishing Limited
The Lypiatts
15 Lansdown Road
Cheltenham
Glos GL50 2JA
UK

Edward Elgar Publishing, Inc.
William Pratt House
9 Dewey Court
Northampton
Massachusetts 01060
USA

A catalogue record for this book
is available from the British Library

Library of Congress Control Number: 2017931760

This book is available electronically in the **Elgar**online
Law subject collection
DOI 10.4337/9781785363801

MIX
Paper from
responsible sources
FSC® C013604

ISBN 978 1 78536 379 5 (cased)
ISBN 978 1 78536 380 1 (eBook)

Typeset by Servis Filmsetting Ltd, Stockport, Cheshire

Printed and bound by CPI Group (UK) Ltd, Croydon, CR0 4YY

Contents

PART IV GOVERNANCE

PART V CONCLUSION

Contributors

Felicia H. Barnes practices environmental law at Hunton & Williams, LLP. She regularly assists clients to navigate the intersection between science and the law. Felicia clerked for the Honorable Joseph R. Goodwin in the Southern District of West Virginia and the Honorable Mary Beck Briscoe in the Tenth Circuit Court of Appeals. Felicia graduated *cum laude* from Georgetown University Law Center and *summa cum laude* from the University of South Dakota, receiving a BSc in biology.

Dean Curran is Assistant Professor of Sociology at the University of Calgary. He has degrees in economics, philosophy of the social sciences and sociology. His key areas of research are social theory, risk and inequality. He has publications in the *British Journal of Sociology*, *Economy and Society*, the *Journal of Classical Sociology* and a (2016) book, *Risk, Power, and Inequality in the 21st Century* with Palgrave Macmillan.

Cameron Holley is Assistant Professor in the Faculty of Law and member of Connected Waters Initiative Research Centre and Global Water Institute, UNSW Australia. His main fields of interest are: water law, environmental law and natural resources law, with a focus on regulation and governance. He currently holds three Australian Research Council grants on integrating coal seam gas and water, water compliance and enforcement, and water governance. In 2014 he received the IUCN Academy of Environmental Law Junior Scholarship Award for his contribution to environmental law scholarship.

Bridget M. Hutter is Professor of Risk Regulation, Department of Sociology at the London School of Economics and Political Science and former Director of the ESRC Centre for Analysis of Risk and Regulation. She is a leading authority on risk regulation. Her books include *Regulation & Risk*; *Organizational Encounters with Risk*; *Anticipating Risks and Organizing Regulation*; *Managing Food Safety and Hygiene*; and *Regulatory Crisis: Interactions Between Disaster, Crisis and Risk Regulation*. She is regularly involved in discussions, with international bodies, business organisations and regulatory agencies.

Claudia Ituarte-Lima is researcher on international environmental law at Stockholm Resilience Centre. She holds a PhD (University College

London), MPhil (University of Cambridge), and a Law Degree (Universidad Iberoamericana). She specialises in law and governance for sustainability and environmental justice. Her research examines the transformation of international law, focusing on biodiversity, climate and human rights law, into new governance forms at the national and local scales. She acts as expert advisor to the Convention on Biological Diversity Secretariat and the International Development Law Organization.

Thomas Johnson is Lecturer in Politics and Asia in the Department of Politics at the University of Sheffield. His research focuses on environmental protest and regulation in China. His work has appeared in publications including *Environmental Politics*, *The China Quarterly* and *Regulation & Governance*.

Jan McDonald is Associate Dean (Research) at the University of Tasmania, Faculty of Law, where she specialises in environmental and climate change law. Her research examines the ways in which current approaches to environmental and resource protection must change to adapt to the impacts of climate change, with a particular focus on the potential application of resilience thinking to environmental law reform.

Lindene Patton is a partner at Earth and Water Law, LLC. Previously, she held senior executive and legal roles at global insurance, technology and brokerage firms. She is an attorney licensed in California and the District of Columbia and an American Board of Industrial Hygiene-Certified Industrial Hygienist. She holds a BSc in biochemistry from the University of California, Davis; an MPH from the University of California, Berkeley; and a JD from Santa Clara University School of Law.

Ole W. Pedersen is a Reader in environmental law at Newcastle Law School where he teaches and researches most matters related to environmental law. Having studied at the University of Copenhagen, he taught and studied environmental law at Aberdeen University prior to moving to Newcastle. He is joint author of *Environmental Law*, now in its eighth edition. His current work focuses on the regulation of hydraulic fracturing, and the role played by the courts in shaping modern day environmental law.

David Satterthwaite is a Senior Fellow at the International Institute for Environment and Development (IIED) and editor of the journal *Environment and Urbanization*. He is also a visiting Professor at University College London. Most of his work has been on poverty reduction in urban areas. His books include *Squatter Citizen* (with Jorge E. Hardoy) and two books on urban poverty with Diana Mitlin. He contributed to the

IPCC's Third, Fourth and Fifth Assessments. He was awarded the Volvo Environment Prize in 2004.

Ekaterina Sofronova works as a tutor under the Indigenous Tutorial Assistance Scheme, Macquarie University. She also worked as a research assistant at UNSW's Faculty of Law. She obtained her PhD degree from Macquarie University in 2016, the thesis title is: 'Non-Governmental Organisations and Environmental Governance in Russia'. Her research interests include participation of non-state actors in environmental governance, environmental law and environmental governance in post-Soviet countries.

Hua Wang is Professor of Environmental and Resource Economics at Renmin University of China. He served as Chief Expert in Environmental Economics and Policy at the Policy Research Center of China's Ministry of Environmental Protection and Senior Environmental Economist at the World Bank's Development Research Group. He has conducted extensive research in the areas of environmental economics, management and policy and provided technical training and policy advice in various countries. He holds a PhD in Environmental Management and Policy from UNC-Chapel Hill, USA.

Preface

Environmental changes have generated some of the most pressing and difficult challenges of the 21st century. There has been a growing appreciation of their scale and interconnectedness and the ways in which they are the result of human activities. Environmental law used to represent one of the most important regulatory regimes in modern societies, but there are now questions about its ability to manage transnational risks and about the compatibility of law with major strategies for managing the environment. In this collection we focus on two important approaches: one which considers environmental challenges in terms of risks and another which has arisen as we have become increasingly aware of the levels of uncertainty involved in environmental management, namely resilience.

The relationship between resilience and inequality is central to this collection. Resilience approaches to environmental challenges appear to be more democratic and egalitarian than risk approaches, and this forms part of their attraction for some authors and policy-makers. The collection will subject these claims to some scrutiny. Resilience strategies may offer solutions to inequality but they are not without their difficulties, for example they too have uneven social effects. Moreover, there may be tensions between the law and its expectations of certainty, and resilience with its emphasis upon flexible responses to environmental risks and uncertainties.

This collection will address the role of law within this changing landscape and from a socio-legal perspective. The social, economic and political environments we live in are beset with uncertainties. We have witnessed the Brexit vote in the UK and Donald Trump becoming President of the United States, both of which generate uncertainties of all kinds including environmental uncertainties. The environmental effects of the UK leaving the European Union are unclear but a reduction in regulation was one platform of those leading the campaign to leave, and there are concerns that this and the economic consequences of the decision to leave Europe will have damaging implications for environmental protection. Cutting back environmental regulations was also part of the Trump election campaign including threats to withdraw the USA from the Paris Climate Agreement, an Agreement that many commentators already regard as dangerously inadequate and a weakening of transnational commitments to tackle climate change. This context raises fears about environmental risks and also exacerbates the uncertainties around the role of law in the effort to manage the environment.

The collection includes chapters by established authors and also by upcoming scholars who are undertaking innovative research and pushing the discussion on resilience forward. It includes contributions from different disciplines and parts of the world. The collection considers some of the experiments in governance being tried in different parts of the world to accommodate differences and give voice to more diverse groups. It also considers how scientific developments to understand better the mechanisms and practices responsible for climate change offer possibilities for improving legal and insurance tools to manage environmental risks. The endeavour is to stimulate further debate, research and learning, and to hope that we can enhance well-being.

As always I am indebted to those who have supported me in putting together this edited collection. I am enormously grateful to each of the contributors: their chapters are fascinating and I appreciate the time and effort they gave to the collection. Pauline Khng very patiently and thoroughly copy-edited the manuscript, she was a joy to work with. Paz Concha provided invaluable research assistance at all stages of this project, helping with bibliographic searches and also with preparing the manuscript. She was meticulous and efficient and a great assistant throughout.

Clive Briault and Rebecca Elliot were generous with their time and read through the chapters I drafted and offered valuable comments when they had plenty else to do of their own. Finally the team at Edward Elgar should be thanked. Laura Mann initiated the original thinking when we discussed the possibility of a Handbook on risk and resilience in environmental law. But we quickly agreed to try something more experimental which would bring more social science thinking about inequality into the equation. Ben Booth and Iram Satti picked this up and have been very supportive in seeing the project through to publication.

This book is dedicated to my family, especially those in the next generation who are so dependent on the decisions we make today about the environment.

BMH

PART I

Introduction

1. Risk, resilience and inequality: current dilemmas in environmental regulation

Bridget M. Hutter

As our understandings of environmental risks develop so too do the ways we try to manage them. Over the past few decades there has been a change in our knowledge of the damaging effects we have on our environment. There has been a widening recognition that the environmental problems we face are acute and that they are not just local but national, transnational and global. Local problems can have global effects and the mass accumulation and interaction of individual instances of damage to our environment are, according to the worst case scenarios, threatening the long-term future of the planet. We also appreciate more keenly the deep inequalities attaching to both the exacerbation of environmental risks but also their ill-effects. There has also been a change in the way we see and frame problems in terms of risk. Risk narratives imply that we are able to anticipate and control the risks threatening us. Yet the environmental changes we experience challenge this social project. They suggest a level of uncertainty and even contestation about environmental problems and how to cope with them. Indeed, there is growing recognition that some of the ways we manage environmental risks have perverse and regressive effects on different populations.

These changes raise questions about how suited the law is to manage the environment in the 21st century. In the 20th century environmental law represented one of the most important regulatory regimes in modern societies but it now faces a number of significant challenges. There are issues about the compatibility of law with notions of risk and the complex conceptual apparatus of terminology and strategies that has emerged in response to our contemporary understandings of the environmental risks we face. These include questions about the ability of the law to manage transnational risks and to embrace uncertainty and change.

This chapter will first outline some of the most prominent environmental issues we face, including changes in our understandings of environmental risks, uncertainties and damage, and the inequalities attaching to them. It will then discuss the various strategies for managing these risks that have gained traction, focusing in particular on risk and resilience perspectives and the ways in which they may relate to environmental law and its ability to act as a governance device for the environmental challenges we now encounter. The overall collection aims to develop our theoretical understanding of risk, resilience and inequality as it relates to environmental regulation. This demands that we also interrogate the conceptual murkiness surrounding some of the approaches that are emerging before we are able to theorise about how best the law can play a role in promoting environmental concerns and facilitating greater equality.

ENVIRONMENTAL RISKS[1]

Very broadly, environmental risks are threats of actual or potential harm to the environment and consideration of the probability of these adverse consequences occurring. Of key importance in understanding these risks is appreciating the interdependence of the physical and social environments, in particular that risks to the physical environment have impacts on social environments and even more importantly, that risks to the physical environment are the result of human activity. It is for this reason that some commentators differentiate the Holocene, where environmental change was seen to occur naturally, from a new era, the Anthropocene, where human activity has emerged as a major force for environmental change.[2] It is also why existing critical social theory positions challenging the distinctions between the social and the natural have been revitalised (Chakrabarty, 2009). The focus of this collection is on the role that law can play in limiting the environmental damage we are causing.

The environmental risks we face are multiple, complex and interconnected. They affect the climate, ecology, biosphere and oceans.[3] Their causes are manifold and compound. Industrial activity has resulted in atmospheric, aquatic and ecological pollution arising from the use

---

[1] This section is intended as a basic introduction to some of the main issues under discussion so as to give some perspective on the challenges involved in the environmental area. It is not intended to be an exhaustive or high-level discussion.

[2] See Crutzen and Stoermer, 2000 who introduced the term, derived from geology. Note it is still a contested term. See eg. Malm and Hornborg, 2014; Monastersky, 2015.

[3] Rockström et al, 2009, Steffen et al 2015 set out some of the major risks as part of their planetary boundaries research.

of chemicals, pesticides and various kinds of industrial, radioactive and human waste. Industrial and household burning of fuel and cars are major sources of air pollution. Industrial waste is also a major contaminant of water sources and soil, as are pesticides. The depletion of the natural resources generates and exacerbates environmental risk, for example, deforestation, overgrazing, poor agricultural and water management and overfishing which are in part a result of overpopulation (eg. Royal Society, 2012). Related to this is growing urbanisation which can generate significant environmental risks: in wealthy countries where consumption of natural resources and the generation of emissions may be high and in poorer countries where there are health risks and concerns about the ability of infrastructure to keep pace with the rise in population and to do so in sustainable ways which do not add to emissions (United Nations University and Institute for Environment and Human Security, 2014). Moreover, there are complex interrelationships between different sources of risk. Rapid urbanisation for example, may result from rural migration because of droughts and land degradation, in turn this movement may increase sedimentation and place high demands on the local ecology which can lead to further resource depletion. It may also generate high levels of waste which, in turn, can affect the availability of resources and harm biodiversity and threaten to add to emissions and so on (World Economic Forum, 2015).[4]

The consequences of these risks becoming realities are stark. Water and soil contamination seriously affects biodiversity and, in turn, contaminates the food chain and renders land and water infertile. At its most extreme the risks are the extinction of species of plants and animals, and habitat destruction for plants, animals and human beings (Department for Environment, Food and Rural Affairs, 2015; Global Biodiversity Outlook 4, 2011; 2.; International Union for Conservation of Nature Annual Report, 2015: 4; World Wide Fund for Nature (WWF) Living Planet Report, 2014).

Deforestation is a particular concern, especially of the rainforests which are thought to house more than 50 per cent of the world's biodiversity. Deforestation is also a concern as forests play an important role in mitigating climate change.[5] Indeed, the most dramatic environmental risks have been most discussed with respect to climate change which refers to

---

4 These publications emphasise the word 'risks' as they believe that with careful planning the worst effects can be averted (see below). See also Newman, 2006 who argues that the impact of cities on climate change can look very different according to how it is framed.

5 http://www.worldwildlife.org/threats/deforestation

changes in the weather, including temperatures and precipitation, of a city, region or the planet.[6] The Intergovernmental Panel on Climate Change (IPCC) (2007: 1.1) refers to climate change as:

> . . . a change in the state of the climate that can be identified (e.g. using statistical tests) by changes in the mean and/or the variability of its properties, and that persists for an extended period, typically decades or longer. It refers to any change in climate over time, whether due to natural variability or as a result of human activity.[7]

The Stockholm Centre's Resilience Group identify climate change and biosphere integrity as two core planetary boundaries through which other boundaries operate (Steffen et al, 2015). Climate change is core because it refers to 'the amount, distribution, and net balance of energy at Earth's surface' which 'sets the overall conditions for life'. Biosphere integrity refers to the totality of all ecosystems and their biota and 'play a critical role in determining the state of the Earth system, regulating its material and energy flows and its responses to abrupt and gradual change . . . Diversity in the biosphere provides resilience to terrestrial and marine ecosystems.' This high-level framework is intended to facilitate an understanding of environmental risks at a scientific level. Nevertheless, it does help us gain some perspective on the nature, scale and complexity of environmental risks.[8] Other documents help us to appreciate more the relationship with human activities.

The IPCC Fifth Assessment Report 2014 (2015) concluded that warming of the climate systems because of human activities was 'unequivocal' and 'unprecedented' – 'The atmosphere and ocean have warmed, the amounts of snow and ice have diminished, and sea level has risen' (1.1). In addition, there has been an increased incidence of extreme events. The Report warns that: 'Continued emission of greenhouse gases will cause further warming and long-lasting, some irreversible, changes in

---

[6] http://www.nasa.gov/audience/forstudents/5-8/features/nasa-knows/what-is-climate-change-58.html

[7] The IPCC differentiates its definition from that of the UN 'where climate change refers to a change of climate that is attributed directly or indirectly to human activity that alters the composition of the global atmosphere and that is in addition to natural climate variability observed over comparable time periods' (UN 1992: 7).

[8] The Stockholm approach is not without its critics. See for example, http://dotearth.blogs.nytimes.com/2015/01/15/can-humanitys-great-acceleration-be-managed-and-if-so-how/?_r=0 and http://www.stockholmresilience.org/21/research/research-news/7-2-2012-addressing-some-key-misconceptions.html

all components of the climate system, increasing the likelihood of severe, pervasive and irreversible impacts for people and ecosystems. Limiting climate change would require substantial and sustained reductions in greenhouse gas emissions which, together with adaptation, can limit climate change risks' (2). Moreover, the Report predicts that in addition to exacerbating the existing risks, new risks will be generated for the physical and human environments. In particular, they identify high levels of species extinction during and beyond the 21st century, risks to coastal and low-level areas because of sea-level rises and a serious threat to food security.

We should not convey the impression that the risks we are discussing are universally agreed. There is contestation of the evidence of environmental risks. The debates about environmental risks are multidisciplinary and complex. Different disciplines and authors use similar terms in slightly different ways, there are debates about definitions and methodologies, and of course interpretation of the results.[9] Put another way, there are debates about the definitions of risk, the probabilities and overall risk assessments.

The contestation of the evidence partly relates to debates about whether we are referring to environmental risks or discussing environmental uncertainties, where the risks are not calculable (Knight, 1921). Part of the reason for the uncertainty is that the past is no longer such a good predictor of the future. For example, climate change is altering the patterns and the incidence of environmental damage and disasters. It is resulting in new environmental uncertainties which raise basic questions about the status of historical data and whether or not it is a sound basis on which to identify risks and plan for the future (Cox, 2012; Morgan and Stallworth, 2013). This centralises the relationship between learning from past events and being open to the unexpected questions crystallised in the juxtaposition between resilience and anticipation. It also poses particular challenges for law and its ability to cope with uncertainty and play a meaningful role in managing the complex environmental risks and uncertainties that confront us (see below).

Overriding the 'fine print' and detail of the precise parameters of the environmental risks we encounter, there is more general agreement that the implications of these changes are potentially drastic and catastrophic. We have already seen the potential risks to food security, habitation and the availability of water, there are also serious health and energy effects and these are unequal in their effects.

---

[9] The footnotes above have noted some of these points of contention.

INEQUALITY AND ENVIRONMENTAL RISKS

Cutting across all of these issues are deep inequalities between nations, different social groups and between individuals in their contributions to climate change and the extent to which they become victims of the environmental risks it generates.

Environmental inequalities intersect with social inequalities (Blowers and Leroy, 1994; Pellow et al, 2005). Much work has been generated arguing that the poor, ethnic minority groups and women are disproportionately exposed and vulnerable to environmental risks (Downey, 2005; David and Enarson, 2012; Leichenko and Silva, 2014). Health and social impacts have been related to social inequalities both in terms of experiencing the harms associated with environmental hazards and not having access to the benefits of the production and consumption processes generating the harms (see Downey, 2005). Inequalities have been related for example to industrial and noise pollution, access to transport, housing and access to green spaces and biodiversity (Sustainable Development Research Network, 2004). Moreover, these inequalities are reproduced within[10] and also between nations. A recent report by the IPCC (2015: 13) explains that while climate change is affecting the globe 'Risks are unevenly distributed and are generally greater for disadvantaged people and communities in countries at all levels of development' (2.3).

The health effects generated by environmental risks are discussed in a report by the World Health Organization (WHO, 2014) which identified air pollution as the world's biggest environmental health risk, linked to nearly one in eight deaths in 2012. It reported differential effects, with the Western Pacific and South East Asia experiencing the highest number of deaths followed by Africa and the Western Mediterranean areas of Europe. High-income countries were less affected although the report stresses that air pollution is still a major problem in these countries. Household pollution was identified as a greater problem for rural areas and ambient pollution a greater problem for urban areas.

Social inequalities are also significant in disasters when the most marginalised have been found in repeated studies to be the most vulnerable to harm and the least able to recover in the aftermath of disasters (Elliot and

---

[10] Downey 2005 summarises some of this work; other research identifies environmental inequalities within different regional areas, for example, in the USA eg. Clark et al, 2014; Downey and Hawkins, 2008. Asia eg. Bardsley and Hugo, 2013; Lung et al, 2014; Rubin, 2014. Latin America eg. Carruthers, 2008; Collins, 1986; Painter and Durham, 1995. Africa eg. McDonald, 2002; Heerink et al, 2001. Europe eg. Bolte et al, 2010; Chalmers, 2005; Pedersen, 2011.

Pais, 2010; Neumayer and Plümper, 2007; Reid, 2013). It is at these times that the burdens on women are seen to be especially acute as they take on a primary responsibility in supporting roles (Peek and Fothergill, 2008; Reid, 2013).

Exposure to risks and harms is differentially experienced, so too is the contribution to these risks. There has been a shift over the past decade with regard to the highest polluting countries to include the major emerging economies of China and India (McEldowney and McEldowney, 2014).[11] So the developing world is starting to pose a major challenge in this respect. It is also the case that overpopulation is particularly marked in less developed countries and among the poorest in these societies. This has implications for the consumption of natural resources, for urbanisation and for migration (Royal Society Science Policy Centre, 2012).

Newman (2006: 277ff) discusses the differential environmental impact of cities in developed and developing countries explaining that cities in the USA and Australia have far greater impact than similarly sized cities in India. Moreover, he argues that in some respects this can have positive environmental impacts, the key is careful planning. As Satterthwaite and Dodman (2013) argue cities need to build resilience to the effects of climate change into infrastructure investments, development plans and disaster risk management but most city governments lack the capacity to do so.

Transnational inequalities relating to the effects of deforestation reveal that there is not a one-way traffic from rural areas to cities. The effects are of course contingent upon the dependence on forests for hunting, gathering, resources such as rubber and small-scale agriculture (eg. Koop and Tole, 2001; Sant'Anna, 2016) and they are linked not just to rural migration to urban setting but rural migration to forest frontiers, moves that contribute to the overall environmental risks to ecology and biodiversity (Carr, 2009). An important aspect of understanding these effects is more interrogation of the social relations that incentivise greater land use (Painter and Durham, 1995). The World Wildlife Organization details one example, namely deforestation in the Greater Mekong in South East Asia, where land tenure systems are weak and deforestation has contributed to social conflict and migration (http://www.worldwildlife.org/threats/deforestation).

Predictions are that climate change will exacerbate inequities between rich and poor. Indeed, a report in the UK medical journal *The Lancet*

---

[11] Data from the US Department of Energy ranked countries according to their carbon dioxide emissions in 2011. The top four polluters were: 1. China; 2. USA; 3. Russia; 4. India. http://www.ucsusa.org/global_warming/science_and_impacts/science/each-countrys-share-of-co2.html#.VperKV9FDGg

pronounced climate change as much a health issue as an environmental issue. It detailed the effects of climate change on insect-borne infection; malnutrition because of growing food shortages; rising heat-related respiratory and cardiovascular illnesses; and changing patterns of disease, for example related to decreasing supplies of clean water and access to sanitary conditions (Costello et al 2009: 1694). The IPCC (2015) report similarly identified increased levels of poor health among those in developing countries, particularly severe impacts of increasing temperatures and extreme weather events on those 'lacking essential infrastructure and services or living in exposed areas' (2015: 16) and greater poverty, especially in urban areas and areas already suffering hunger. Eventually the report anticipates the displacement of people especially affected, for example by drought or infertile areas where the ecosystem has collapsed and, in turn, this could contribute to conflict and violence.

There are strong links between the notions of environmental inequality and environmental justice.[12] Indeed, the concept of environmental inequality arose in the late 1980s and 1990s around environmental activists challenging the notion that environmental risks affect everyone equally and arguing for environmental justice (Downey, 2005; see also the aims of the charity the London Sustainability Exchange).[13] A blurring of the concepts of inequality and injustice has been criticised in discussions of life chance and class (Abbott, 2015). The difficulties in the environmental case in part centre on a focus on outcomes rather than processes and mechanisms of inequality (Downey, 2005; Pellow et al, 2005). For example, Walker et al (2005: 372) evidenced a socially unequal distribution of industrial pollution sites in the UK but they explain that these patterns of proximity do not always demonstrate patterns of pollution impact and nor do they explain why these patterns exist. There is a need here to consider the political and ethical decisions made about the location of industrial plants (Walker et al, 2005: 373), and the processes, histories and mechanisms by which these decisions are made (Pellow et al, 2005). Some commentators have noted that the ability to defend one's locality may be related to socio-economic status with some groups rendered peripheral to the processes involved and thus central to the environmental risks incurred (Blowers and Leroy, 1994). Moreover, there are concerns that some of the strategies in place to counter environmental risks may further exacerbate

---

12 See Schlosberg, D. and Collins, L. B. 2014 for an overview of the discourse of environmental justice from its development, through the range of principles and demands of grassroots climate justice movements, to more recent articulations of ideas for just adaptation to climate change.

13 http://lsx.org.uk/aboutus/default.aspx

human inequalities through strategies which unevenly burden those in the poorest and most vulnerable positions. For example, these groups may be excluded from political processes that shape the political economy (see for example, Adger, 2006; Marino and Ribot, 2012). It is therefore important to evidence the risks and harms caused by environmental inequalities but also to research the mechanisms by which this happens: the role of economic and political decision-making (Tierney, 2014) and the influence of this on the framing of risk decisions (Clarke, 1989) and at local, national and transnational levels of analysis (Newell, 2005). Of particular importance to this collection are the ways in which the law may reinforce these inequalities and the potential it may have to alleviate them. The whole area of the inequalities attaching to environmental risks underlines the importance of researching the social, political and economic contexts which give rise to these risks, frame their definition and the prioritisation they are given.

WHAT NEEDS DOING?

As we can see the scale, volume and complexity of the environmental challenges we face are considerable. Anticipating the risks and managing them is bedevilled by a lack of reliable data, contestation about this and how to interpret the data and forecasts that do exist. There are multiple areas which need managing and because the vulnerabilities are multi-level they need action at multiple levels from the individual through to community, organisational, societal, transnational and, ultimately, global levels (Adger, 2006).

The broad areas demanding attention fall into a number of broad categories. These include, first an urgent need to lower carbon dioxide emissions. For example, to decrease the use of fossil fuels and cut back transport emissions. Second, a focus on the protection of natural resources, for example, the protection of fish stocks and improved water management. A related third category centres on measures to control population growth, although some authors caution that this is a long-term solution and that it is vital that we also find innovative ways of conserving biodiversity and ecosystems through less consumption (Bradshaw and Brook, 2014). The fourth category is again related to the previous ones as it focuses on urban planning and the need to find positive ways of planning without depleting resources (Newman, 2006). Reducing the inequalities generated by environmental risks is a fifth broad category while a sixth overarching task is to find ways to effect the above, for example, through education, accountability mechanisms and governance systems.

Discussions of environmental equity emphasise the point that issues of intergenerational and intragenerational equity are at stake. The environmental risks we encounter have implications for present but, most importantly, future generations (Boyce, 2007; Gaba, 1999; Weiss, 1992). The balancing of present against future risks presents ethical dilemmas as does the need to balance decreasing emissions and decreasing consumption while improving standards for the poorest and not decreasing environmental standards for the richest. Achieving this without unacceptable coercion also poses challenges. For example, attempts to curtail population growth in the poorest nations needs to be consensual rather than coercive (Royal Society Science Policy Centre, 2012).

Managing these issues is an intensely political process and it is also one in which economics can play a significant role. The economic costs of adaptation and mitigation have not yet been established (see below) but the ethical costs are clear – preventing tens of millions of deaths and misery (Costello et al, 2009: 1,700). The rest of this chapter will set out some of the tensions besetting environmental control with a particular focus on the role of law. We will next consider the role of law in more detail and then map out some of the broader strategies which contemporary environmental approaches have adopted, paying particular attention to risk and resilience strategies.

ENVIRONMENTAL LAW

Environmental law has changed significantly since the early environmental statutes appearing in Western societies first in the 19th century and then in the 1960s and 1970s. Initially the focus was on state-centred statutes to, for example, regulate emissions, the disposal of waste and water quality. The focus was on the source of the pollution and its effects which were thought to be local. Over the past four decades, notions of environmental law have expanded to include broader regulatory approaches many of which were unwritten by, or have taken place in, the shadow of the law. Over time this expanded to include much broader notions of regulatory governance embracing a range of state and beyond the state organisations and actors (Gunningham, 2009). This accompanied, as we have seen above, changing conceptions and understandings of environmental risks in the 20th century. Environmental law became more joined up, holistic and it was also recognised that the law was dealing with greater uncertainty (Hutter, 1999; Fisher, 2013a). There has been a growing recognition that environmental risks are global risks requiring global co-operation and the focus of environmental law broadened further to include transnational laws, treaties and conventions. Alongside these changing concepts has been an expanding institutional regime for environmental regulation.

At a national level in developed countries we have also witnessed a growing portfolio of tools and approaches to environmental regulation. Traditional approaches aimed to prevent or limit emissions through command and control techniques but during the 1980s and 1990s there was a move to incorporate different tools and methods to environmental regulation. These included approaches that targeted different organisational motivations to comply with the law. For example, there has been the use of various market-based instruments, trying to incentivise compliance through economic motivations. For example, tradeable permits, subsidies, taxes and emission caps (see eg. Stavins, 2003). These approaches have been tried in various parts of the developed and developing world (Arsel and Büscher, 2012; MacKenzie, 2009; Stavins, 2003; Swingland, 2003). Likewise, informational strategies have also been tried (André et al, 2011).

Regulation has also moved beyond the state. In some forms this has retained state involvement in the form of state co-option of other sources, for example, forms of co-regulation, enforced self-regulation and meta regulation. The intention here is often to encourage voluntary rather than coercive compliance. There has also been the greater incorporation of beyond the state organisations and actors into state decision-making processes. Beyond this there has been a move from government to governance with other actors increasingly playing and being seen to play a regulatory role, for example, environmental NGOs and financial institutions such as insurance and also consumers through the creation of so-called 'green markets' (Grabosky, 1994; 2013; Hutter, 2011; Prakash, 2001).

The use of additional strategies was in part a response to what some perceived to be a failure of the command and control approach of regulation. The effectiveness of this and of the law is disputed – some believe it has made no difference (Ebbesson, 2010), others believe there has been limited success (Gunningham, 2009). There has been growing agreement that regulation across all sectors demands a combination of different strategies and tools and also the involvement of multiple sources of governance (Gunningham et al, 1998). As McEldowney and McEldowney (2014) observe with regard to the UK:

> Regulating the environment is conceptually complex, involves a diverse range of institutions, techniques and methodologies, and crosses geographical and national boundaries.

The changes we have witnessed have been labelled the 'new environmental governance' by Holley (Holley, 2008; Holley et al, 2012). This denotes an approach marked by greater collaboration between different stakeholders, greater participation and deliberation in decision-making, decentralised and flexible approaches to environmental regulation and ones which incorporate learning (Holley et al, 2012: 4).[14] These changes have taken place across much of the developed world and there are signs that the changes identified in developed countries are emerging in parts of the developing world, especially the major emerging economies of China and India. Work here has underlined a key finding of socio-legal research on regulation in developed countries, namely that a proliferation of laws is not enough, it is effective enforcement that really matters (Agrawal et al, 2014; Stern, 2010; Stuligross, 1999; Van Rooij, 2010; Van Rooij et al, 2013). It has also identified greater participation in regulation, albeit embryonic (Johnson, 2014b; Lee, 2010; Li et al, 2012) and the use of informational disclosure strategies (Zhang et al, 2015). The research evidence that exists suggests that forms and styles of regulatory governance differ between countries (Vogel, 1986; Weale et al, 1996). Moreover, there may be cultural differences, for example with respect to the rule of law, that influence the availability of different regulatory strategies and regimes to the developing world. These may include, for example, differences in political regimes, for instance between authoritarian regimes and democratic ones; cultures where corruption and bribery are more the norm than others thus with the potential to undermine the rule of law; or differing values placed upon environmental management. The important questions for environmental law and regulation are where is law most useful and where does it not help (Gunningham 2009: 20ff)

INTERNATIONAL ENVIRONMENTAL LAW

The growing recognition that environmental risks are global has resulted in increased effort to manage these risks at a transnational level. This has included environmental laws, international treaties and transnational agreements (Coleman, 2012). It has also embraced a variety of players, for example, nation states, multinational businesses, industry associations, standards organisations, social movements and individuals (Braithwaite and Drahos, 2000; Falkner, 2003).

A number of key reports, protocols and transnational institutions have emerged over the past four decades, many of them under the auspices of the United Nations which has emerged as a major facilitator of transnational

---

[14] As we will see below this definition is remarkably similar to some definitions of resilience.

discussions and activities. This role really crystallised with the founding of the United Nations Environment Programme (UNEP) in 1972 to undertake a coordinating and promotional role in the UN for environmental initiatives and activities.[15] A detailed history of transnational environmental developments and the UN is neither possible nor desirable here but a number of key developments are of relevance to our focus on environmental law. Of key importance is the establishment in 1984 of the World Commission on Environment and Development (WCED) under the auspices of the UN and the chair of Gro Harlem Brundtland, then Prime Minister of Norway. The WCED is now popularly known as the Brundtland Commission and its product the Brundtland Report *Our Common Future* (1987), is important in the context of this book as it explicitly addresses issues of global inequalities in environmental development and the need to acknowledge economic and social well-being. The notion of sustainable development refers to 'development which meets the needs of current generations without compromising the ability of future generations to meet their own needs'. The Report not only places the recognition of inequalities and the poor at its heart it also sets out a case that sees the world as a whole, connecting the ecological, social and economic. Moreover it is premised on the idea that it is possible to act in order to protect the environment for future generations.

Sustainable development is an approach that has underpinned much environmental policy ever since but this does not mean that it is without its critics.[16] The concept is regarded as vague and the most obvious difficulty is one running through environmental debates, how to translate the high ideals of the Report into action, especially action that can deal with the underlying tensions between economic development, environmental protection and reducing social inequality (Lee, 2005; Magraw et al, 2015). Notwithstanding these difficulties the Report has had enduring influence. Subsequent meetings and protocols developed the concept and addressed the implementation of a sustainable development approach. For example, the 1992 Rio Earth Summit, involving governments and NGOs, produced among other things, a plan for achieving sustainable development (Agenda 21) and also conventions on climate change and biodiversity. The climate

---

[15] It currently describes its mission as:

- Assessing global, regional and national environmental conditions and trends.
- Developing international and national environmental instruments.
- Strengthening institutions for the wise management of the environment.

http://www.unep.org/About/

[16] See for example, http://www.unece.org/oes/nutshell/2004-2005/focus_sustainable_development.html

change convention eventually led to the Kyoto Protocol 1997 which set internationally binding emission reduction targets for signatories. Since 1992 there have been regular Earth Summits (New York, 1997; Johannesburg, 2002; Rio 2012) all with the intent of progressing international efforts towards addressing sustainable development. Each of these has maintained a focus on inequalities and a desire to address these. For example, the Kyoto Protocol was based on the principle of common but differentiated responsibilities in order to try and avoid placing unfair burdens on developing nations in contrast to developed nations that had already caused much environmental damage. The ambitions of these transnational efforts are not really in dispute but their implementation is, as several major players have refused to ratify treaties or agreements or failed to comply with their conditions (Koehn, 2010).

Alongside these developments there has been a dramatic growth in international environmental law as a distinct field (Bodansky et al, 2015). The history of this expanding field in many respects reflects our general discussion of greater awareness of the holistic effects of environmental risks and the need for collective action but simultaneously a specialisation and fragmentation around different risks and regions of the world (ibid). There has been a marked growth in transnational organisations such as the UN-led institutions, sometimes in co-operation with other organisations. For example, in 1988 The World Meteorological Organization and UNEP established the Intergovernmental Panel on Climate Change (IPCC), essentially to provide scientific evidence on climate change and its social and economic effects. Yet these institutions have limited powers of implementation, the nation state is still central here and many of the protocols and laws are essentially voluntary to the extent that they rely on state-level enforcement and compliance. There are also concerns that these transnational laws and institutions do little to alleviate inequalities and may indeed reflect them along a North–South dimension and also with respect to future generations (Bodansky et al, 2015). Just as much as beyond state regulation at a national level takes place in the shadow of the law so does much transnational environmental governance take place in the shadow of the state (Falkner, 2003).

One approach which has been more recently advocated to try and clarify the principles and obligations of states to their citizens and also to other states, has been a human rights approach to environmental risks, the argument being that climate change, for example, is a violation of human rights (Bodansky, 2010; Knox, 2009; Rajamani, 2010). It is seen as a way of stressing the rights of disadvantaged individuals, communities and states who so often suffer a coincidence of human rights inequalities and poor resourcing with respect to the environment (Humphreys, 2009).

This is a difficult and emerging territory as emission rights (which it is argued have traditionally been privileged) are juxtaposed against human rights. This raises issues around questions such as is there a human right to emissions in order to secure subsistence (Hayward, 2007). It also generates familiar difficulties attaching to other areas of international efforts to manage environmental risks, namely the lack of strong national and international enforcement institutions (Humphreys, 2009).

Beyond this it is also important to consider what the law tries to exclude. As Fleur Johns (2013) argues what the law excludes is as important as what it includes. Some areas of transnational environmental activity are deemed extralegal, some supra legal or infra legal. Johns discusses the IPCC as an example of an organisation which is treated as supra legal, as dealing with science rather than law, science rather than politics. But as science and technology studies demonstrate these apparently different areas are mutually constitutive and in order to understand better the role of law in managing environmental risks we need to take a broader social science view (see eg. Jasanoff, 2004; Mackenzie, 2009).

The environmental domain exemplifies many of the core tensions of regulation writ large across a global stage. Let us now turn to consider how risk and resilience strategies fit into this picture and how they might further our understanding of key questions about the role law can play in managing the global risks associated with the environment.

RISK AND RISK MANAGEMENT

We have already conceptualised the environmental threats we face as risks but an important governance approach has been to use technical risk management approaches to structure governance. Thus we witness risk-based approaches coming to dominate scientific and economic assessments of climate change (Pidgeon and Butler, 2009). This is in line with more general increases in the growth of risk discourses in regulation (Power, 2004; Rothstein et al, 2006). The approach does have many attractions in the regulatory field not least because it is seen as a way of helping to set priorities and also resolve some of the tensions inherent in regulation through apparently objective and scientific methods. As Everson and Vos (2008) observe with respect to Europe, a strengthening of risk management approaches gives science a central role in the framing of problems and the separation of risk assessment from risk management acknowledges the role of values in acting on these assessments.

The precautionary principle was an early precursor to the more widespread popularity of risk-based approaches in the environmental area.

Its focus is on how to act in situations of uncertainty. The approach subjects uncertainty to the apparently rational technical approaches of science for one important subset of uncertainties, namely those where harms could result in irreversible damage (Everson and Vos, 2008). The importance of the precautionary principle is therefore to facilitate action to prevent possible extreme harms in the face of uncertain scientific evidence. It appears in national and regional legislation and also transnational agreements.[17] Its use has led to much debate, with claims that it is incoherent and subject to multiple interpretations (Sunstein, 2005 cf Harremoes et al, 2013). The main difficulties lie with its implementation in particular determining the levels of proof needed in the face of uncertainty and establishing fair processes for making such determinations.[18] Implementing risk-based approaches can also be highly problematic. As we have seen, environmental law is dealing with contested territories and problems where knowledge is unstable and socio-political conflicts and interests are central. Framing environmental law can thus be especially problematic (Fisher, 2013) particularly in terms of determining the costs, benefits and risks involved. Moreover, the templates of law may not fit with those of science (Smith and Wynne 1989). The distinctions between risk and uncertainty pose challenges for law especially when the distinctions are blurred and contested. This has caused some to call for a new dialogue between science and law to meet the challenge (Fisher, 2010; McEldowney and McEldowney, 2011).

Risk-based approaches are wide ranging, there is no single approach. They may be all-encompassing frameworks which orient resources and practices or a more narrowly defined focus on risk techniques (Black, 2005; Hutter, 2004). The notion of risk and associated risk techniques vary between disciplines, for example, economics favour cost-benefit approaches and engineers risk assessment. The ambiguities they embrace may be simplified and glossed over (Wynne, 2002). Moreover, they may be differentially interpreted between different cultures. In practice the difference between risk and uncertainty may be blurred. For example, the necessary data to input to the technical risk assessments may not be available and the skill sets to analyse the information that is available may be lacking (Hutter, 2004).When this happens there is a danger that there may be a move to frame environmental uncertainties as risks so as to render them governable. Governmentality theorists maintain that such

---

[17] For example, at a national level the precautionary principle is generally seen to have its origin in West Germany, it has been widely adopted in EU legislation and also appears in transnational agreements such as the Rio Declaration.

[18] See Fisher et al, 2006 for an excellent discussion of the problems associated with implementation.

processes render risk a technology of governance. O'Malley (2001: 467–8), for example, argues that when combined with notions of 'reasonable foreseeability' risk approaches facilitate the regulation of foreseeable expectations as compared to calculable predictions of the future (see also Joseph, 2013). These approaches arguably help to constitute inequalities as they follow a market logic embedded in their cost-benefit foundations (Adler, 2012). Moreover, they may have a legitimating effect which is partly why Beck (1992) criticised the use of risk approaches in relation to environmental issues. Indeed, the Stern Review on the economics of climate change (2007) gained the subject serious political attention precisely because it was couched in economic language and working within existing rationalities. Pidgeon and Butler (2009) explain that language was essentially the language of risk-based approaches, based in cost-benefit analysis but adapted to try and take into account intergenerational equity. But working within economic rationalities, rather than suggesting radical reform is also regarded as one of the Review's weaknesses.[19]

It is partly for these reasons that some commentators call for the explicit regulation of uncertainty to improve strategy and policy options (Ragas et al, 2008; see below). Others commend much more radical solutions. Heyvaert (2011), for example, argues that notwithstanding the difficulties attaching to conventional risk regulation it is unsuitable for regulating the risks associated with climate change. With reference to the EU she argues that the concept of risk has been narrowly construed to refer to the risks to the environment balanced against the risks to economic considerations. But such an approach has not been applied to climate change, rather the EU has seen climate change as posing risks that are so serious as to render trade-offs inappropriate. This is demanding much more radical and innovative regulation, one which Heyvaert sees as signalling a new radical paradigm for risk regulation. In part this is about facing the harsh political and ethical risks climate change presents. It also relates to humanising the apparent cold dictates of bureaucratic and scientific approaches to decision-making. A popular route here has been to greater openness and participation in the decision-making processes surrounding risk-based approaches (Everson and Vos, 2008). Again these are not without serious difficulties in terms of implementation, nevertheless we have witnessed a growth of attempts to increase democracy in decision-making (Sexton,

---

19 The Stern Review had a mixed reception. Its critics contested the costs and science used in the Review and it was criticised by both those pro-climate change action for being too modest and those who were sceptical for being alarmist. See for example Ackerman, 2007; Nordhaus, 2007.

2013; see below). And it is partly in relation to this that some have turned to alternative strategies that focus around the notion of resilience.

RESILIENCE

The concept of resilience emerged in the late 1960s/early 1970s in relation to the resilience of ecosystems (Batabyal, 1998; Folke, 2006; Holling, 1973) where the focus was upon the ability of systems to cope with change and still persist (Petak, 2002). From the mid-1980s resilience referred increasingly to human environmental interactions, exemplified in discussions of sustainability (Lélé, 1998) and in the late 1970s/early 1980s it appeared in behavioural studies where it referred to an individual's ability to withstand and rebound from crisis (Rutter, 2000; Walsh, 1996). The concept was first used with respect to organisations by Wildavsky in 1988 but it was not until the late 1990s that the application of resilience to organisations gained in popularity (Weick and Sutcliffe, 2001).

Resilience has become increasingly prominent in the 21st century as a strategy for disaster risk reduction (Tierney, 2014: 160). For example, resilience in the face of earthquakes (Petak, 2002) and specific case studies, for instance, relating to Hurricane Katrina (Campanella, 2006), and 9/11 (Gittel et al, 2006; Kendra and Wachtendorf, 2003; O'Brien and Read, 2005). A related development has been an emphasis on urban resilience and the capacity of cities to recover from disasters (Vale and Campanella, 2005) and also social resilience which focuses much more on the capacity of communities to stay together in the face of disaster (Kendra and Wachtendorf, 2003; Manyena, 2006). Urban resilience and disaster resilience relate to organisational resilience in so far as they look at risk and adversity to complex systems, and the ability of these systems to face challenge. Likewise, social and ecological approaches have been combined to develop our understanding of complex social-ecological systems (Berkes et al, 2002; Folke, 2006), the emphasis being upon the importance of understanding the interactions of social and ecological systems and how the former may affect the resilience of the latter (Janssen and Ostrom, 2006). There has also been broader discussion of resilience in relation to health-care systems (Mallak, 1998), business supply chains (Christopher and Peck, 2004), information systems (Comfort et al, 2001) and resilience engineering (Hollnagel et al, 2006; Woods and Wreathall, 2003).[20]

[20] This section is partly based on Hutter, 2010 Chapter 12.

Defining Resilience

There are multiple definitions of resilience and of course difficulties in transferring the concept between different disciplines and domains (Adger, 2000). This has become a multi-disciplinary area with varying genealogies and meanings attaching to the concept of resilience. It has also become a fast moving and highly topical area. At the core of most definitions relating to the environment is the ability of ecosystems, societies, cities, communities, organisations and individuals to survive disturbances, shocks and surprises to reorganise and reassemble so as to persist and maintain core systems, function and identity. Folke (2006: 259) also observes that resilience is also about opportunities and renewal and thus related to adaptive capacity which copes with change and develops with it. His suggestion that 'resilience is an approach, a way of thinking for guiding and organizing thought' (2006: 260) is helpful given the definitional quagmire surrounding the concept of resilience. Nelson (2011) similarly presents resilience as a perspective which helps us to think about the longer term and enhances our understanding of how changes take place. The emphasis is very much upon 'humans in the environment' (Folke, 2006: 263) and enhancing the ability to survive and bounce back rather than aim to try and control nature (Ebbesson, 2010).

Tierney (2014: 169ff) identifies four common characteristics of definitions of resilience, namely: notions of robustness, resistance and strength; redundancy so there is provision of alternatives, options and diversity; resourcefulness; and rapidity, that is how quickly a system can restore. She usefully differentiates two types of resilience: inherent resilience which the law can contribute to, for example, through engineered structures with building codes; and adaptive resilience which is a mix of pre-planned and novel activities including responsiveness to surprise and decentralisation.

An important perspective on resilience is offered by Nelson (2011: 116) who stresses that resilience is about explaining persistence and change, it is essentially about adaptation (see below). It provides a way of thinking about many contemporary environmental challenges and their implications.

RESILIENCE AND RISK REGULATION[21]

The relationship between risk regulation and resilience is much debated. Classic approaches discuss the relationship with respect to policy choices

[21] This section draws on Hutter, 2010 Chapters 1 and 12.

depending on levels of certainty. Risk strategies are advocated where the risks are known and calculable and resilience where there is uncertainty. Wildavsky's classic work (1988) juxtaposes anticipation and resilience. He urges caution in the use of anticipatory strategies, arguing that anticipation can lead to unnecessarily wasted effort and wasted resources because of the high volume of hypothesised risks, many of which are exaggerated or are false predictions. Anticipatory strategies, argues Wildavsky, reduce the ability of organisations and societies to cope with the unexpected. Indeed, many preventive programmes have their own unexpected risks attached to them. He argues that more attention should be paid to enhancing resilience and warns against focusing too much on the dangers of risk and not benefiting from the opportunities.

Other authors caution against drawing too sharp a distinction between risk regulation and resilience. Macrae (2010) for example, argues that regulation and resilience may in practice have much in common especially at the level of what he terms 'regulatory work', that is, the micro-level of practical, everyday risk management. Here regulatory resilience is continuous and formalised and both regulatory and resilience regimes penetrate deep into organisations and try to become constitutive of them: both are to some degree future-oriented; and both are precautionary. The similarities between a decentred (rather than narrow state-based) definition of regulation and resilience strategies are especially close. Of particular relevance here is that they are democratised, encouraging participation throughout an organisation, thus highlighting the need for coordination, and learning from risk occurrences. But some normative debates around resilience caution that while there is a tendency to regard resilience as 'a good thing' this may not necessarily be so. Rogers (2013) advises that there are positive and negative articulations of resilience: the positive emphasising participation and empowerment and the negative stressing experts, technology and individual responsibility. This negative view is prominent among governmentality commentators who warn that resilience is also a form of governmentality as it shifts responsibilities from the state to society and to individuals (Chandler, 2014; Rogers, 2013; O'Malley, 2010).

Another theme in the literature is that the relationship between risk, regulation and resilience is a dynamic processual one. Park et al (2013) for example see resilience as 'the outcome of a recursive process that includes: sensing, anticipation, learning, and adaptation' and they see this as complementary to, but distinct from, risk analysis. Comfort et al, (2010: 273) similarly emphasise that resilience is a long process – 'it needs to be institutionalized, involves social collaboration and involves a balancing act between risk and resources, between vulnerabilities and escalating or unmanageable catastrophe'. It is partly for these reasons that some commentators are not convinced by claims the resilience is transformative or a radical democratic alternative. Nelson (2011) argues that resilience works within the current system and needs to be considered in light of social goals and how benefits and risks are distributed (see also Tierney, 2014). Nelson (2011: 117) argues that the promotion of resilience is just as rife with issues of power, access and political decisions, as other strategies such as adaptation (see below). Leach (2010) similarly argues that resilience is inherently a matter of social framing by actors with different preferences and resources (see also Duit et al, 2010). These accounts challenge the notion that resilience is more democratic, egalitarian and bottom-up than other strategies. The relationships between risk, resilience and inequality demand greater empirical interrogation so that the circumstances which might facilitate their effectiveness in relation to their environmental goals and achieving greater social justice and equality might be better understood. Moreover, these need to be examined in relationship to the ways in which the law can facilitate change.

RISK AND RESILIENCE: RELATIONSHIP TO EACH OTHER AND ALSO OTHER STRATEGIES

Risk and resilience approaches have emerged as two popular approaches in the environmental field, with resilience emerging as especially popular in recent years. But it is important to appreciate that they are two recent arrivals in a fairly overcrowded space and while we are not able to discuss in any detail the full array of strategies it is important to map out/introduce some of the other main approaches and their relationships to risk and resilience-based strategies. There are definitional issues: relational ones, a lack of empirical data in addition to the normative and ethical issues that beset the area. Smit and Wandel (2006: 286) suggest that notwithstanding the variable usage of terminology in the literature there is a basic model. This model considers the vulnerability of systems (whether they be global, local, physical or social) as being reflective of: the exposure of the system to risks; and the sensitivity of the system to hazards in addition to the ability/capacity/resilience of the system to cope/adapt/recover from the effects of the hazards. Risk management and resilience strategies aim to enhance the ability of the system to cope with the risks and hazards with which it is confronted, their differences, as we have seen, are their differing relationships to notions of uncertainty: risk management approaches are deemed most suitable where there is some certainty about the risks and resilience approaches being more suitable where there is uncertainty.

Notions of risk and risk management imply that risks can be anticipated and managed (Hutter, 2010). There are dangers to this, for example, the incentives for governments, policy-makers and organisations to give the illusion that they have transformed uncertainties into risks through the preparation of, for example, contingency plans (Clarke, 1999). The area of environmental risk is however one where there has been a relatively early step back from the expectation that all risks can be managed. This is signalled in two complementary strategies related to the basic model underlying the vulnerability of systems, namely mitigation and adaptation strategies. Both strategies refer to the ability of a system to respond to new challenges and typically they are discussed in relation to climate change.

Mitigation strategies attempt to slow down or reduce the system's exposure to change but it is generally accepted that this is not fully possible (Nelson et al, 2009: 397) hence the need for complementary adaptation strategies. Like many of the other strategies and concepts in this area, adaptation has its roots in the social and physical sciences and is a concept open to multiple interpretations (Gallopin, 2006: 293; Janssen and Ostrom, 2006: 237). At the core of most definitions is the notion of a system's ability to cope and respond to change. While some authors discuss this adaptation as something that may be inevitable and naturally occurring, it is most useful in the context of this discussion to stay with those authors who regard adaptation as a process of deliberate change (Nelson et al, 2007). The decision then rests on whether the adaption strategies that are adopted adapt to maintain the status quo or to manage change to a new system. Some authors see the attraction of resilience being that whereas adaptation works to maintain the current system, resilience opens up the possibility of adapting to new systems: where adaptation is aimed at preserving the status quo is where it can be seen to be undermining resilience for these authors (Nelson, 2011: 116). But again authors divide on this issue; some discuss resilience as being about the 'preservation of the behavior of the system as expressed by its state remaining within the considered domain of attraction' (Gallopin, 2006: 301).

The important point here is that in discussing these different strategies it is important to be clear about what it is assumed their objectives are. The higher level aim is to proactively reduce the vulnerabilities of people to environmental risks (Smit and Wandel, 2006: 289). Adaptation and resilience are both about the capacity of a system to respond, about how the system reacts when exposed to risks. But there can be tensions between the two strategies. Nelson et al (2007: 407ff) argue that adaptation research tends to focus on specific risks whereas resilience research focuses on complex systems. There can be trade-offs between the two, for example adaptation in one location may reduce resilience elsewhere (see also Adger et al, 2011). Resilience perspectives offer, claim Nelson et al, a perspective on evaluating the implications of adaption strategies on the system and into the future. Moreover, resilience approaches stress the need to conceptualise social and ecological systems as related coupled systems.

It is a matter of social decision-making and value priorities whether adaptation and resilience strategies seek to maintain or change the system. As several authors indicate, there may be real vested interests in maintaining the current system and hence its existing inequalities and power relations (Nelson, 2011: 116). Adaptation is not just about decision-making but also about the power to implement those decisions (Adger, 2006: 268). What is also clear is that governance plays an important role. For example, governance can play an important role in influencing the adaptive capacity of a system alongside economic development, technology and human capital (Nelson et al, 2007: 399). For some commentators the law and the legal system have an important role to play in this. McDonald (2011) for example, argues that the legal system can provide a 'principled foundation' for change and also the protection of the socially disadvantaged. This may be through regulating for anticipatory adaptation, facilitating fair liability and compensation schemes for when harms are caused and also for ensuring accountability for actions taken in emergency situations.

As we have seen there is a plethora of different concepts occupying environmental discussions. In part these are a response to changes in our understandings of environmental risks, uncertainties and damage. This collection focuses on risk and resilience strategies and their relationship with law and the promotion of greater equality. In particular, it considers if there are ways that environmental law can facilitate improvements to the environment without exacerbating existing inequalities and preferably improving them. Part II of the book considers the changing environmental landscape with reference to environmental law. It offers two contrasting views of the existing legal systems and the potential of the law to build resilience to climate change impacts and to effect transformations in environmental control. Chapter 2 draws on the Australian experience to discuss the role that the law might play in rethinking legal rights and responsibilities towards the natural world. Chapter 3 considers environmental law in the UK and the limitations attaching to calls for resilience both with respect to the uncertainties about the risks we face and also the extent to which public participation, as an important dimension of resilience, is facilitated by law.

Part III focuses on inequality and the social and economic consequences of environmental law. Chapter 4 analyses how inequalities relating to climate change impact on the life chances of individuals. It does this through the prism of resilience, arguing that this is especially revealing of key inequalities and the transformations necessary to improve the conditions of the least advantaged. Chapter 5 discusses the extent to which collective environment-related property law contributes to equity and how human rights approaches might be helpful in facilitating this. It uses data from Latin America to explore these questions. Chapter 6 focuses on inequalities in urban settings with a focus on transnational data and also the ways in which local governance issues, some involving the law, can contribute to these inequalities.

Issues of governance are taken up more directly in Part IV. Chapter 7 considers experiments in the new environmental governance and how able environmental law is to contribute to adaptive governance. Chapter 8 turns to what some commentators have hailed as a new governance structure, namely insurance, and it discusses how the tensions around science and law impact on insurance contracts. Chapters 9 and 10 consider different aspects of risk, resilience and environmental law in China. Chapter 9 discusses government strategies to enhance resilience through wider governance tools such as information disclosure and public participation. Chapter 10 offers a different perspective on these issues, arguing that environmental risks are inextricably linked to political risks as environmental risks pose a significant political threat to the authorities. It discusses how government suspicion of beyond the state actors may be an obstacle to efforts of greater inclusion of the public in environmental regulation.

In Part V, Chapter 11 pulls together what we have learned from the collection. It draws out the main theoretical and analytical themes identified in the volume and discusses what we can learn and take away from the collection. It considers which themes demand greater examination and which help us to expand our theoretical understanding of risk resilience and inequality as it relates to environmental regulation. The chapter also reflects on what we can say about more pragmatic policy concerns on the basis of these chapters, in particular the experiments discussed in different chapters and their applicability to different social and economic contexts of environmental regulation.

PART II

A changing environmental landscape

2. Risk, resilience and environmental regulation: using law to build resilience to climate change impacts

Jan McDonald

INTRODUCTION

The impacts of climate change are likely to affect virtually every ecosystem on earth and aspect of human endeavour (Field et al, 2014). The level of committed climate change means that some impacts will continue to occur long after mitigation efforts have reduced or reversed current rates of greenhouse gas concentrations. The slower and weaker those efforts, the more enduring and emphatic the impacts are likely to be. While the outcomes of the Paris Agreement of the UNFCCC suggest a more ambitious target for climate mitigation (Cornwall, 2015), it will still be some time before success can be judged and then for the effects of emissions reductions to be realised.

Species and ecosystems (Burrows et al, 2011), and food and crop production (Challinor et al, 2014) will be affected by warming of the land and sea as well as by changing precipitation patterns and extreme events (Coumou and Rahmstorf, 2012). These include more frequent and intense bushfires and storm events on land (Field et al, 2014), and marine heatwaves (Hobday et al, 2016). Urban populations and infrastructure will be affected by extreme events, especially heatwaves, flooding and severe storms. Coastal communities face threats of inundation and erosion. The likely human health impacts of climate change range from expansion of vector-borne diseases, to heat-related food-borne diseases, heat-related mortality or morbidity, to more indirect mental health issues.

The impacts of climate change will be felt differently in different countries, regions and localities, and the social and economic implications of impacts will also vary based on the adaptive capacity of the individuals, business sector, community and nation state (Allison et al, 2009). Interactions between impacts at different scales are impossible to predict, as are the interactions between the various biophysical, technological and policy responses. Climate change therefore portends uncertainty and heightened variability at multiple scales, and across multiple sectors, exacerbated by feedbacks and step-wise changes (Nelson et al, 2009; Craig, 2010; Ruhl, 2010). For many impacts, it will mean the crossing of thresholds and irreversible change. This uncertainty and interconnectedness create immense and complex governance challenges (Nelson et al, 2009). This chapter considers the ways in which law and governance reform can embed resilience approaches in order to promote climate change adaptation. Rather than examine a specific regime, such as biodiversity conservation, land use planning, water or coastal management, it seeks to draw out broad lessons from the burgeoning literature on 'resilience thinking', and its implications for future governance for adaption.

THE LIMITATIONS OF CURRENT APPROACHES

The enormity of the adaptation task ahead is matched only by the inadequacy of existing legal and governance arrangements to meet that task (Ruhl and Salzman, 2007; McDonald, 2010, 2011; Ruhl, 2010; Craig, 2010; Craig and Benson, 2013; Garmestani and Allen, 2014; McCormack and McDonald, 2014; Odom Green et al, 2015). The goals of our current legal regimes, as well as decision-making structures, methods and processes are ill-equipped to cope with the complexity and interconnections of linked social and ecological systems, let alone the additional challenges that climate change presents (Arnold and Gunderson, 2013).

The goals of legal systems focus too narrowly on single issues or regimes and place a strong emphasis on political and economic goals. Even countries like Australia that embraced the principles of ecologically sustainable development (ESD) (COAG, 1992) and largely redesigned their environmental laws in the post-Rio era to reflect those principles, have tended to apply those laws with a stronger focus on 'development' than ecological sustainability (Peel, 2008; Hobday and McDonald, 2014) or planetary boundaries (Rockström et al, 2009).

While sustainable development or ESD remains the stated objective of most environmental and resource management laws, national and international indicators of ecosystem health have declined over recent decades: many have done so catastrophically (Millennium Ecosystem Assessment, 2005; Steffen et al, 2009; Australian State of Environment Committee, 2011; Hobday and McDonald, 2014; Steffen et al, 2015). Despite the integration of economic, social and ecological imperatives being at the heart of ESD, the segmented approach to regulation of natural resource exploitation has persisted. Separate regimes for forestry, fisheries and mining are often excised from fundamental environmental obligations and typically do not even refer to ESD goals or underpinning principles (Godden and Peel, 2010; Craig, 2010; Craig and Benson, 2013; Garmenstani and Allen, 2014). This critique is arguably more a matter of flawed or inadequate implementation, rather than a criticism of ESD itself.

The deeper critique of ESD as a regulatory goal is that the notion of sustainability rests on a 'conservative assumption of ecological stationarity' (Craig, 2010; Craig and Benson, 2013; Benson and Craig, 2014) and linear change – 'that natural systems fluctuate within an unchanging envelope of variability' (Milly et al, 2008, p. 573). This approach has assumed that there may be seasonal or other fluctuations, but systems will otherwise remain relatively static: the possibility of regime shift is rarely countenanced. Implementation of ESD in law typically assumes that continuing development – understood to mean exploitation of the natural world for private economic gain – is compatible with maintaining or returning 'natural environments' (species, ecosystems and landscapes) to some historical baseline or with striving for, then maintaining, some optimal balance between exploitation and conservation (Benson and Craig, 2014; Garmenstani and Allen, 2014). Under this paradigm, management of human uses of the natural world lies largely within human control and assumes we can know what kinds and levels of impact can take place without serious adverse consequences (Craig and Benson, 2013). The impacts of climate change call into question the capacity for human intervention to control future ecosystem function. Recent experience of recurring and sometimes concurrent drought, bushfire and flooding in the USA, Europe and Australia bear this out. In a practical sense, legislatures have struggled to articulate ESD principles in a way that offers real guidance to decision-makers and courts about how they should be implemented. Instead, statutory language either affords decision-makers no discretion or lists multiple principles or factors that the decision-maker must weigh up. In practice this has meant they are typically applied in favour of private property and development rights (Fisher, 2010; Godden and Peel, 2011).

In addition to problems with the goals of our environmental and natural resources laws, decision-making processes and structures are generally unresponsive to change (Doremus, 2010). Environmental decision-making in most developed countries is centralised (at either the national or sub-national level), but fragmented for each resource or environmental value, with uniform processes for decision-making (Ruhl, 2011). Current approaches to environmental law are premised on the law being able to provide certainty and stability, through a complex arrangement of prescriptive regulation, judicial precedent and procedural requirements

(Craig, 2010; Ruhl, 2011; Odom Green et al, 2015). Yet the failure of environmental laws to deal with change may actually create more uncertainty in the long term (Craig, 2010; Arnold and Gunderson, 2013).

The decision-making processes in most environmental, resource and planning laws are linear (Ruhl, 2011; Arnold and Gunderson, 2013, p. 10,428), involving a front-ended system of spatial planning and development approval, with environmental impact assessment as its centrepiece (Glicksman, 2009; Craig, 2010; Ruhl, 2010; Ruhl, 2011). These approaches emphasise certainty, the conferral of development 'rights', and finality of decision-making; they make little allowance for adjustment and responsiveness. Environmental assessment processes assume that future impacts are predictable with fairly high levels of certainty, and make projections about impacts based upon a stationary baseline. Cost-benefit analysis techniques tend to overstate economic gains and frequently understate environmental or social impacts, especially indirect and cumulative impacts or future impacts that are dismissed by discounting methods.

The poor response of modern environmental law to existing stressors such as habitat modification, resource exploitation, pollution and invasive species, combined with the prospect of these stressors being exacerbated in unpredictable ways by climate change, highlights the inadequacies of current approaches. The challenge, therefore, is to identify approaches and goals that move beyond preservation or restoration of the status quo, since maintenance of the status quo is simply unfeasible (McDonald et al, 2016). Governance arrangements will have to be premised on dynamism, rather than a stable set of baseline conditions, and must recognise the existence of ecological thresholds. Working out how to provide this kind of flexibility and responsiveness (Craig, 2010; Ruhl, 2010; Ruhl, 2011; Craig and Benson, 2013), while offering appropriate certainty in the delivery of multiple objectives across complex, linked socio-ecological systems (SES) is where resilience thinking may assist.

RESILIENCE THINKING

Since the term 'ecological resilience' was first coined in 1973 (Holling, 1973), there has been an explosion of theoretical and applied work on the concept of resilience (Olsson et al, 2015). Resilience has numerous meanings, both in popular discourse and specific disciplinary contexts (Olsson et al, 2015; Ruhl, 2011, Davidson et al, 2016). Resilience concepts are found in engineering, psychology, sociology, business systems and organisational theory (Davidson et al, 2016). Many of those definitions presume a 'normal' or baseline state to which an individual or system returns following stress or disturbance. The concept of socio-ecological resilience advanced by the work of scholars and practitioners forming the 'Resilience Alliance' rejects the idea of system stability. SES resilience may broadly be defined as the capacity of a system to absorb disturbance while still retaining its basic function and structure (Folke, 2006; Walker and Salt, 2006). The definition itself is not terribly helpful, and it is the broad approach to resilience 'thinking' that holds greater value for law.

Key to SES resilience is the idea that social and natural systems do not operate independently, but form complex linked socioecological systems (Berkes and Folke, 1998; Ostrom, 2009) with interactions across sectors and scales. Such systems are complex, highly dynamic and adaptive. In managing for one part, influences from, and impacts on, other systems must be considered (Gunderson and Holling, 2002; Berkes et al, 2003). These interactions are reflected in the concepts of adaptive cycles and panarchy, discussed below.

Whereas traditional approaches to environmental management implicitly assume that conditions are stable, or that change is slow and linear, resilience thinking assumes that change and disturbance are integral parts of every system, that change occurs at different rates and that some systems or sub-systems are more resilient to destructive change than others. In SES-resilience terms, systems are considered resilient if they are capable of self-organisation, learning and adaptation (Holling, 1973; Gunderson and Holling, 2002; Walker et al, 2004) in response to disturbance.

Change processes occur in 'adaptive cycles' operating in respect of different sub-systems, at varying spatial, geopolitical and temporal scales. Each adaptive cycle consists of four phases. Rapid growth (exploitation) and conservation together constitute the 'fore loop' and account for the majority of a system's state. Release and reorganisation – the cycle's 'back loop' typically occur faster (Gunderson and Holling, 2009). The importance of the adaptive cycle concept for complex systems thinking rests in the idea that the ability to effect change is greater in some phases than in others. Modes of reforming the system may differ depending on which phase of the adaptive cycle the system is in and the intervention point may vary depending on the phases of the cycles elsewhere in the hierarchy. Resilience scholars suggest that most policy development and legal innovation occurs incrementally during the fore loop phases (Walker and Salt, 2006), yet the processes of release and reorganisation open windows of opportunity for management, policy or regulatory intervention and innovation, particularly following natural disasters or extreme events. Indeed, one might argue that in climate adaptation terms, there is a need for shock or crisis at least in parts of the system, to create the social and political mandate for law reform. Understanding the relationship between nested hierarchies of adaptive cycles – what Gunderson and Holling (2002) call 'panarchy' – helps understand how processes of adaptation at one time, place or context, both influence and are influenced by, those occurring above and below.

SESs are capable of existing in a range of alternate states, with different functions, feedbacks and structures (Nelson et al, 2009). Resilient SESs are those that can undergo change without crossing a threshold into an undesirable state. Resilience approaches therefore emphasise the need to identify thresholds which, if crossed, will bring about undesirable regime shift (Gunderson and Holling, 2002; Folke et al, 2004; Nelson et al, 2009; Thrush et al, 2009). If thresholds are crossed, it may be impossible or unfeasible to shift the system, in which case transformation of the system is the only remaining option.

The growth in literature on resilience thinking has been studied and synthesised from a range of perspectives (Nelson et al, 2009; Olsson et al, 2015; Davidson et al, 2016). While it gains popularity in both academic and political discourses, resilience thinking has been criticised for ignoring or underplaying the problems of agency, conflicts of interest, and unequal distributions of wealth and power (Olsson et al, 2015). The strong emphasis on system function and the principle of self-organisation also tend to oversimplify and depoliticise social change processes (Phelan et al, 2012; Olsson et al, 2015, p. 4, quoting Jerneck and Olsson, 2008) and underplay the difficulty of identifying the boundaries of each system or even levels within a nested system. This is borne out by the literature on successful resilience experiments, which tend to be limited to regional case studies with more defined geographical and ecological boundaries, economic connections and stakeholder representation. There are no examples of resilience approaches being trialled successfully to address problems of national or international dimensions where the governance arrangements are complex, and there are high levels of political conflict, uneven power relations and conflicting economic interests (Phelan et al, 2013).

Another criticism of resilience thinking is its lack of normative content. Contexts such as psychology, engineering, urban, community and disaster resilience almost always imply that resilience is a good thing that should be promoted (Olsson et al, 2015, p. 2). SES resilience scholarship, however, merely supplies the operating principles for delivering the normative outcomes that are agreed through other processes – it does not seek to identify what states are desirable or undesirable. SES resilience scholars suggest that societal values determine which system states we want to support or make resilient (Walker and Salt, 2006) but resilience thinking does not itself offer guidance on how to progress these fundamental decisions.

Indeed, there are many examples of 'perverse resilience' – systems that are highly resilient, but which are ecologically unsustainable or socially unjust (Phelan et al, 2013). In those cases, enhancing the persistence of the system states will entrench existing patterns of social disadvantage or environmental degradation (Bene et al. 2012). In this respect, promoting the resilience of legal and governance arrangements without first ensuring that those arrangements facilitate desirable system attributes can undermine social and ecosystem well-being.

This underscores the importance of making decisions about what state is most desirable and attempting to stay away from thresholds that would move us to undesirable states. If ESD were implemented with appropriate attention to the 'ecological' bottom line, emphasising fundamental goals such as the conservation of biodiversity and intergenerational equity, it might usefully provide the broad normative content that resilience thinking lacks. The impacts of climate change are likely to demand a more nuanced interpretation of ESD, however, because some impacts and trade-offs are inevitable. This will be an uncomfortable conversation for some, because once we decide what kind of future we want, rates of change may dictate that the only way to get there is by wholesale modification of current practices (McDonald et al, 2016). Conversations about future goals in relation to preservation of species versus ecosystem function, places of economic versus recreational, cultural and spiritual value, may well result in a prescription for radical reform, but this is not a task for resilience thinking per se, other than to acknowledge that pursuit of current goals is likely to result in the crossing of thresholds in the future.

A more pragmatic criticism of resilience thinking – perhaps more a risk that should be guarded against – is that it has become increasingly vague and malleable (Brand and Jax, 2007) as its use is popularised in a range of contexts such as terrorism, homeland security, financial markets and natural disasters. With wider use, resilience risks becoming empty rhetoric or simply another intellectual fashion with little to offer decision-makers facing the challenges of climate change.

The concern of the remainder of this chapter is not to resolve these criticisms, but to consider how the core features of resilience thinking, and prescriptions for its implementation, can enhance and help operationalise the legal regime for climate change adaptation. This obviates the need to choose between resilience, ESD or some other policy objectives, especially since they share many elements in common. Resilience principles could then focus on how best to build responsiveness to change into decision-making structures and processes, identify when thresholds are approaching, and deal with regime shifts (Odom Green et al, 2015). If we design our institutions and governance arrangements to promote the resilience of desired states, we are more likely to avoid crossing these thresholds, or at least be better equipped to reorganise and transform in ways that still meet social and ecological needs. The ways in which this should occur are considered further below.

APPLYING RESILIENCE PRINCIPLES TO PROMOTE CLIMATE-ADAPTIVE LAW

The Resilience Alliance identifies seven prescriptions for promoting SES resilience: maintaining diversity and redundancy; managing connectivity; managing slow variables and feedbacks; fostering complex adaptive systems thinking; encouraging learning; broadening participation; and promoting polycentric governance systems (Simonson et al, 2012; Biggs et al, 2015). The discussion in this section considers how each of these elements translates to, and can be reflected in, legal provisions or arrangements. In some cases, legal architecture is required to give effect to these prescriptions as regulatory goals, while others may require a more fundamental reconfiguration of the legal and institutional architecture designed to achieve substantive goals (Arnold and Gunderson, 2013, 2014).

Maintaining Diversity and Redundancy

Ecosystems with many different components (e.g. species, actors or sources of knowledge) are generally more resilient than systems with few components. Redundancy provides 'insurance' within a system by allowing some components to compensate for the loss or failure of others. Redundancy is more valuable if the components providing the redundancy also react differently to change and disturbance (response diversity). In a socio-ecological context, this means maintaining both biological and institutional diversity and redundancy, with a focus on important functions or services that have low redundancy.

The example of biodiversity conservation is most apposite. Climate change poses unprecedented challenges to biodiversity on a global scale, by inducing range shifts and exacerbating existing stressors (Dunlop and Brown, 2008; Steffen et al, 2009). The conservation of biological diversity is already the subject of regulatory regimes in most countries, though their responsiveness to climate stressors is limited. In general terms, the regimes consist of two strands: mechanisms for the identification and establishment of a system of protected areas that are managed primarily for the conservation of their natural values; and mechanisms aimed at protecting individual species of threatened or endangered plants and animals. This second strand consists of two components. The first is reactive measures that require decision-makers to consider, and avoid or mitigate, the impacts of development on listed species. The second component is proactive measures such as developing and implementing species recovery plans.

A key challenge for such frameworks is how to promote their responsiveness to climate change impacts without undermining conservation objectives (Dunlop et al, 2013; McDonald et al, 2016). The climatic suitability of many protected areas to safeguard the species for which they were originally established is a key issue. More dynamic approaches to protected area management, including enhanced conservation management of private land surrounding existing protected areas, including land held by indigenous groups, will be necessary, but existing legal models tend to draw sharp distinctions between the public domain, which is 'available' for conservation, and private property, which may be exploited as the owner sees fit (McCormack and McDonald, 2014). Complementary legal mechanisms that involve partnership with private landowners, such as conservation agreements, stewardship payments and some minimum form of ecological duty of care may be required to enhance the climate-adaptiveness of our conservation estate.

The legal architecture for protecting specific listed species also requires legal reform if diversity and redundancy are to be enhanced. It is rare for environmental impact assessment processes to result in the refusal of a project. At best, impacts are mitigated through changes to the design or operation of proposed activities. Biodiversity offsetting enables development to proceed despite predicted impacts on species and their habitats. Offsetting allows the destruction of one site in exchange for securing protection (through purchase or other means) of another 'ecologically equivalent' site (Bull et al, 2013; McKenney and Kiesecker, 2010; Fallding, 2014). At present, the practice of offsetting makes virtually no allowance for the impacts of climate change, so potential offset sites are identified based on current climate suitability even where modelling shows that they will lose their climatic 'equivalence' within the life of the project.

Recovery planning is expensive and cannot be undertaken for all species, so while the requirement to develop such plans is often enshrined in law, it may be formulated as a permissive power rather than a mandatory obligation. Even where plans exist, their implementation is dependent on funding. Plans may include activities such as invasive species management, revegetation or habitat restoration, conservation introductions or, in extreme cases, *ex situ* conservation measures, all of which are resource-intensive. While the law can lay the foundations for such measures, political commitment is required for their effective delivery.

Beyond the conservation sector, introducing diversity and redundancy into governance arrangements themselves can enhance the system's overall capacity to respond to shocks. This includes diversity across tiers of government, from local to national; across agencies within government (e.g. overlapping regulatory requirements across environment, water, agriculture, fisheries etc.); and across state and non-state actors, including both non-government organisations (NGOs) and private sector groups (Ruhl, 2011; Arnold and Gunderson, 2014).

In Australia's current approaches to environmental, natural resource and land use planning regulation, redundancy is emphatically eschewed. So-called 'one-stop shops' are proliferating across the country, typically conferring on one level of government – often local government – the power and responsibility to make decisions on behalf of higher tiers of government (Hobday and McDonald, 2014). Within a level of government, composite processes are used to override separate approvals requirements under multiple statutes, vesting a single entity with an overarching approvals power. While most governments offer assurances that this will not reduce the level of regulatory oversight, removal of 'unnecessary' overlapping approvals is a key (*if not the key*) goal of this efficiency drive. Duplicating or overlapping functions or 'institutional redundancy' may run counter to traditional goals of (usually economic) efficiency. But it better equips the system to cope with change by enabling a diversity of approaches to achieving the same resource management or environmental goals, and by ensuring that there are elements of the governance framework that can compensate for the failures or limitation of others. Building redundancy into regulatory design reduces the possibility of system failure. The challenge, therefore, is in designing arrangements that do not unnecessarily duplicate functions, but that provide for a series of 'safety nets' when one mechanism or tier of decision-making alters.

Redundancy can also be nurtured in ways that support other resilience requirements. For example, creating opportunities for greater or more meaningful governance by NGOs and the private sector spreads roles across diverse groups and benefits from diverse sources of knowledge. The value of polycentric governance to resilience is explored in more detail below. It refers to the 'patterns of interorganisational arrangements' between governmental units, public agencies, and private businesses, including the promotion of self-regulating tendencies (Ostrom and Ostrom, 1965, pp. 135–6, quoted in Aligica and Tarko, 2012, p. 242). Polycentric governance reduces the risk of failure in one element of the system at the same time as promoting wide participation and multi-scalar governance approaches.

Managing Connectivity

Resilience thinking requires close attention to both the nature and strength of interactions between components in a linked system. This can be understood in the context of an ecosystem or landscape, as well as in an institutional sense. In many cases – especially when considering landscape scale management and the range-shifting effects of climate change, this means promoting connectivity to facilitate migration and range shifts, to enhance recolonisation after disturbance and compensating for local extinctions with inflow from neighbouring areas. Specific connectivity projects that focus on 'landscapes and processes' rather than 'sites and species' (Wyborn, 2011) are an excellent example of this kind of initiative. These include the Joint United States–Canadian Yellowstone to Yukon Conservation Initiative and Europe's Natura 2000 network. These projects or programmes are typically the product of policies and funding arrangements, rather than enshrined in formal legal requirements. While connectivity is referred to in a range of protected area and conservation management plans and documents, the dominant approach to conservation around the world is to parcel up our protected areas (Lausche et al, 2013).

In many instances, the objectives of natural resources and conservation laws require revision to make the promotion of connectivity a more explicit goal. Indeed, even the Convention on Biological Diversity, the international agreement that lays the foundation for domestic conservation efforts lacks a reference to ecological connectivity, though it is an important emphasis in the 2005 Programme of Work on Protected Areas. New legal tools may also be required to deliver those objectives, with guidance to be drawn from measures relating to migratory species (Kettunen et al, 2007). These are likely to include agency mandates to identify important areas for wildlife corridors, stepping stones or refugia, undertake bioregional planning to better coordinate reserve management across the landscape and deeper engagement with private landholders. Again, while new or revised laws can play a critical role, a broader view of the governance of connectivity is called for, engaging a range of actors with a variety of information and market instruments, as well as more formal legal tools.

At the same time as landscape-scale connectivity is enhanced, decision structures and actors themselves need to be better connected. Enhancing the connectivity of decision-makers across and within networks will typically enhance the flow of information and trust between actors, as well as build points of common ground. Law's general emphasis on linear decision-making and the difficulty of accounting for cumulative impacts in traditional environmental impact assessment processes show how current approaches do a poor job of connecting and integrating decisions and actors.

It is important to note, however, that 'managing' connectivity also acknowledges that connectivity may sometimes be bad. In some cases, modularisation may be preferable, in order to build in redundancy and insulate the wider system against shocks. Examples of the benefits of a modularised approach to systems management include electricity grids, firebreaks and quarantine protections. In some cases, modularity of governance arrangements may enable the system to continue to function when components fail. In decision-making terms, requiring that decisions be made by agencies at multiple tiers of government can provide this form of modularity and safety net. The same can occur when, for example, project approvals are required from multiple agencies, such as infrastructure, energy, conservation and planning.

Manage Slow Variables and Feedbacks

The third core feature of resilience approaches is the importance of managing slow variables and feedbacks (Simonson et al, 2012; Biggs et al, 2015; Walker and Salt, 2006). Slow variables are the major influences that shape a system and maintain its ability to function. Managing slow variables requires first that we monitor them – to detect slow changes that might bring us closer to an undesirable threshold – then respond to signals that demonstrate shifts in critical slow variables. Few countries do a particularly good job of monitoring, even though it may be a highly cost-effective investment to prevent undesirable regime shifts, be they economic or ecological. Most monitoring is privately conducted and relates to compliance with specific project approval conditions, rather than large-scale processes that are underpinned by any legal mandate. Seldom is the monitoring itself monitored for accuracy or collated to present a more holistic picture of system health.

The cost of comprehensive monitoring is high, but so too is the risk of failing to detect and respond to slow variables, so it must be a critical part of reformed governance arrangements. State of the Environment Reporting is an ideal vehicle and should be legislatively required, with defined parameters and criteria and associated programmes for data collection. Polycentric approaches, of the kind outlined below, may assist in garnering citizen science in this endeavour (Chambers et al, 2016). For example, the Australian RedMap initiative allows members of the public – usually recreational fishers and divers – to catalogue sightings of marine species found outside their traditional ranges. With thousands of entries across Australia, Redmap is providing an evidence base for demonstrating the impact of warming oceans on a range of species (Robinson et al, 2015). It also provides an opportunity for public engagement and education which may in time create new opportunities for participatory governance in the managing of marine areas for climate adaptation.

Of course, monitoring alone is only the initial step towards managing slow variables and strengthening feedbacks. As Cumming et al (2013, p. 1,143) observe:

> . . . The crux of the problem of fostering sustainable, resilient landscapes is thus the problem of designing or developing appropriate institutions that will act flexibly, proactively, and at appropriate scales to strengthen feedbacks that modify and moderate demand for ecosystem services and incorporate the trade-offs between human well-being, profit and exploitation of ecosystems.

A key challenge in promoting responsiveness to change is the path dependency created by existing institutional structures, including the primacy of property rights in Western legal traditions, that make it hard to alter priorities, roles and responsibilities in the face of subtle or slow changes (Macintosh et al, 2014). Experience suggests that shocks are often needed to prompt radical changes. For example, coastal erosion or flooding caused by severe storms may trigger the introduction of planning and development controls that gradual sea level rise does not. Similarly, spikes in mortality and morbidity among vulnerable populations of humans or species associated with extreme heatwaves may prompt changes to early warning systems, urban design or conservation management, that would not have occurred in response to small rises in average temperature. There is therefore a clear role for legal mechanisms that ensure an appropriate response to new information about these slower system shifts, to tighten feedbacks so that changes can be implemented before (or better still, without) the dramatic and potentially irreversible consequences of extreme events. This requires agreed criteria in law for further monitoring and review, the predetermination of 'thresholds of critical concern' and agreement on pre-defined interventions when system variables reach these thresholds (Arnold and Gunderson, 2013, 2014).

It will not be possible to anticipate all possible changes and identify all potential critical thresholds; it will still be necessary for decision-makers to adjust current activities or introduce new measures as important changes to slow variables are identified. This is primarily a political problem, as adjustments may require the modification or discontinuation of current productive land uses. The sooner our legal regime redefines the balance between private rights and public duties in the conferral of development approval and regulating land uses, and private actors adjust their expectations and actions accordingly, the easier it will be to manage slow variables in a way that minimises the risk of dramatic system shocks.

Foster Complex Systems Thinking

The fourth prescription for promoting resilience thinking is the need to foster more complex adaptive systems (CAS) thinking (Simonson et al, 2012; Folke et al, 2005). Management approaches that optimise specific resources or services that have particular value(s) may increase system vulnerability to shocks because they ignore cross-scale inter-relationships (Garmestani and Allen, 2014; Odom Green et al, 2015). Yet modern bureaucracies generally, and those established to manage natural resources in particular, tend to be structured into discrete units that are more manageable or are focused on one resource, sector or attribute (Craig, 2010; Ruhl, 2010; Craig and Benson, 2013). Whole-of-system approaches would acknowledge the likelihood of multiple connections occurring on different levels, and accept unpredictability and uncertainty (Craig, 2010). Early efforts at the challenging task of promoting CAS can be seen in the climate change adaptation and disaster management scenario planning attempted at local and regional levels, albeit outside formal legal mandates or requirements. The most sophisticated examples of these identify thresholds and formulate contingency plans for when thresholds are crossed.

The calls for better integration and less fragmented approaches to resource management are not new, but they are very hard to achieve. In Australia, efforts at integrated catchment management and many regional and strategic plans show promise at embedding complex systems approaches, but these have typically failed to account for temporal/intergenerational variables, and have often excluded one or more critical system elements. Highly integrative frameworks and processes are also very expensive to undertake and maintain. As a general rule, they tend to arise outside formal legal arrangements, with outputs serving as aspirational statements, rather than binding obligations.

Strategic bio-regional planning mechanisms hold most promise as the first step towards proactively incorporating and acknowledging complexity and interactions between system elements (APEEL, 2017). Strategic planning is multi-sectoral and explicitly recognises and addresses trade-offs between potentially conflicting end uses. Its forward-looking focus provides the temporal dimension that is critical if the impacts of future climate change are to be addressed. Strategic planning at the bio-regional scale captures the interactions between activities in connected landscapes, and is more likely to involve the full range of public and private stakeholders. While each planning process will be different, the scope, purpose, processes and participants for undertaking such strategic planning exercises should ideally be reflected in, and enforceable through, legislation.

The costs of background research and stakeholder participation make such processes expensive as well time consuming. It is unlikely, therefore, that governance arrangements will become better integrated in one rapid reform – change is more likely to be gradual. Like the complexity of the systems themselves, they are also likely to emerge from multiple sources such as pilot projects, funding or education programmes, before becoming embedded in law (Cosens, 2013, 2014).

While one should not underestimate the difficulty of reflecting complex adaptive systems thinking through law, efforts should be made in the meantime to dismantle structures that explicitly perpetuate sectoral divisions. The exclusion of many resources regimes – such as forestry, mining and fisheries – from general environmental protection, nature conservation or public participation obligations, is the most obvious example of where sectoral governance arrangements fail to take a complex systems approach (Craig, 2010). Distinctions in the treatment of land under public and private tenure is another. To the extent that such laws operate as a barrier to complex systems thinking, they should be revisited.

Encourage Learning

Resilient governance arrangements are those that encourage learning, and by implication, modify activities in response to lessons learned (Simonson et al, 2012). Adaptive management mechanisms are the principal vehicles for encouraging learning (Craig, 2010; Ruhl, 2005; McDonald and Styles, 2014). Adaptive management is defined in many different ways. Strong adaptive management is understood as a structured approach to formulating and testing hypotheses, whereas weaker versions equate to 'informed trial-and-error' or 'learning-by-doing' management strategies that simply involve changing management approach when new information requires (Ruhl and Fischman, 2010). Whichever version is adopted, it requires flexibility of both institutions and legal instruments, and formal processes for collecting, assessing and acting on new information (McDonald and Styles, 2014; Craig and Ruhl, 2014).

As noted earlier, our current legal frameworks are poorly designed for adaptive management. The strong preference for front-end decision-making processes and the conferral of development rights following environmental impact assessment processes establishes a path dependence that makes it hard to 'learn by doing'. Enhanced monitoring and inbuilt review mechanisms are the best ways of formalising an adaptive management approach (Ruhl, 2005; Arnold and Gunderson, 2013, 2014; Craig and Ruhl, 2014). Yet examples abound of cases where we have failed or refused to learn or respond to documented system failures. If front-end approval processes are to persist, these failures should be addressed. Incorporating triggers into approval requirements and operating conditions that require action where desired outcomes are not being achieved would address these kinds of failures.

Learning and adaptive decision-making can be encouraged in other ways (McDonald and Styles, 2014). Explicit statutory objectives and management mandates can require decision-makers to take future change and uncertainty into account, so that their decisions are more precautionary and leave more room for adjustment. Decision frameworks can be reconfigured to allow for contingencies and statutory stipulation of the time frames over which such change may occur can enhance the certainty of such measures (Odom Green et al, 2015; Cosens, 2013). The capacity to vary water allocation rights in response to water availability is an example of such approaches (Hill Clarvis et al, 2014). Harvest decision rules in fisheries management that commence automatically when monitoring indicates stock rates have reached pre-defined levels can also contribute to management informed by learning. In a climate adaptation context, perhaps the most high-profile attempts to enable learning to take place are so-called 'rolling easements' – triggers that limit the life of a development approval on hazard-prone coastal land (Macintosh et al, 2014). Such triggers have included the passage of a specific time period (say 20 years) or the occurrence of a specified event, such as the encroachment of an erosion escarpment, to be closer to buildings or infrastructure. Both approaches have encountered considerable resistance in Australia, including legal challenges and, in some cases, statutory repeal (McDonald, 2015).

As well as decision structures that encourage learning, institutions can contribute to this resilience feature by creating a 'safe to fail' organisational culture. Most modern government agencies do not reward experimentation, and contracting budgets provide little room for what may be seen to be resources wasted on failed pilot projects or processes. A shift in this organisational mindset that encourages staff to take a more structured approach to learning by doing is a critical complement to legislative mandates for adaptive management (Cvitanovic et al, 2015).

Broaden Participation

From the need to acknowledge systems complexity flows the importance of facilitating broad participation. It is hard to imagine governance arrangements that account for system complexity and dynamism without engaging meaningfully with a wide range of stakeholders. Participation builds trust and support, introduces new perspectives and ways of doing, and creates shared understanding (Simonson et al, 2012). It is the primary mechanism by which to ensure considerations of inter- and intragenerational fairness can be introduced. Of course, broad participation is not a unique feature of resilience approaches – it is widely recognised as a fundamental element of good governance and ESD. The mandate for public participation in environmental decision-making is a fundamental element of environmental justice, reflected in the ECE's Aarhus Convention and the provisions for access to information, notice and comment, and third-party appeal rights in many statutes. These treatments have tended to be focused on traditional modes of formal participation, resting on outmoded centralist models of governance. Resilience thinking contemplates a more fundamental shift in participation that serves as a precondition to, or element of, polycentric governance. Consistent with the mandate to design for redundancy, broadening participation in this sense entails a reimagining of the governance 'compact', to expand the actors involved in new governance arrangements to include both private sector and NGOs.

Localisation of decisions is often cited as a way to enhance participation (Craig and Ruhl, 2014), but this must be balanced against the need to ensure that smaller decisions contribute to enhanced management of the larger system (Nelson et al, 2009 p. 409). While some argue that it is more appropriate to make decisions involving trade-offs at the local level (Odom Green et al, 2015), where those directly affected have an opportunity to participate, the local scale carries greater risk of vested interests bearing too much influence, and compromising the national or international environmental interest (Nelson et al, 2009 citing Adger, Brown and Tomkins, 2005 and Plummer and Armitage, 2007). To address this, Odom Green et al (2015) point to the value of bridging organisations that are formally recognised by government but which serve an information dissemination and coordination function across multiple stakeholders and governance levels.

Promote Polycentric Governance Systems

Finally, as an extension of the complex systems approach and the inclusion of broad stakeholder participation, resilience approaches emphasise the importance of polycentric governance systems. Polycentric governance involves systematic collaborative processes with institutions across scales, and with groups holding different knowledge and perspectives. It typically involves 'nested' institutions interacting across hierarchies and structures, and a mix of public, private and community actors. Polycentric governance approaches enhance redundancy, connectivity and learning across scales and cultures, in theory enabling them to deal swiftly with change and disturbance (Simonson et al, 2012, p. 17). Done well, new forms of polycentric governance hold the best potential to acknowledge and ameliorate the risks of climate impacts falling disproportionately on the most vulnerable groups within local communities, and at national and international scales. Designing systems to promote the representation and participation of vulnerable groups in decision-making processes increases procedural equity, which, in turn, expands the prospect that more substantively equitable decisions will be made where trade-offs are required (Nelson et al, 2009, p. 410).

Polycentric governance aims to match decisions to biophysical scales, with better coordination and integration, recognising that lower levels can be more responsive to changing conditions. Again, it may take some time before polycentric models become the rule rather than the exception. The role for formal legal interventions is likely to be limited as, by definition, polycentric governance contemplates a mix of voluntary, market-based, information and regulatory approaches. Inclusive legal arrangements and the establishment through law of new coordinating or boundary organisations can improve the conditions for polycentric approaches to flourish, but it is more likely that current legal arrangements act as a barrier. An important first step, then, is to scrutinise the formal legal frameworks for natural resource and biodiversity management to ensure that they do not dictate a centralised, linear decision-making model that precludes such approaches.

Polycentric governance also contemplates that the arrangements relevant to particular climate impacts may require guidance from different levels and actors, and that arrangement should be nuanced and responsive to address particular challenges. This means that the response to some impacts may be highly localised, while others may be guided by multilateral or regional instruments. So, for example, it may be possible and appropriate to devise guiding principles in relation to how nations should modify conservation laws to enhance their climate adaptiveness, regardless of how those laws are currently designed. Similarly, groups of nations are already taking more coordinated approaches to disaster resilience and emergency management, though in general these are yet to be underpinned by formal legal instruments. Even where it is not possible to develop international norms for climate change adaptation, there may be valuable national or sub-national exemplars that can be shared across borders.

CONCLUSIONS

There is mounting evidence that a business-as-usual model of biodiversity conservation, fisheries, marine, water and land management will see the loss of species and ecological communities, and reduced ecosystem complexity and function under climate change. More intense and frequent weather extremes and natural disasters will impose their own ecological, social and economic losses. Responding to climate change is therefore imperative for intra- and intergenerational justice. In the face of these pressures, there is growing acceptance of the need for a new environmental governance paradigm. Current legal and governance approaches are premised on linear change that references historical baselines and practices. These approaches will struggle as we face a future for which there are no historical analogues.

The stability afforded by the Rule of Law in most countries and in international law may provide the foundation for reform but may also serve as a barrier to the kind of transformation that dangerous climate will force upon us. Governance regimes that incorporate the processes advocated by resilience thinking are better able to manage ongoing and unpredictable change. Building resilience features into legal systems can promote self-organisation when shocks occur. The emphasis of resilience thinking on the links between social and ecological 'systems', the complexity and dynamism of such systems and the risk (or possibility) of crossing a threshold into an alternate regime lay a foundation for the design of laws for climate change adaptation.

Whether we like it or not, climate change will demand that trade-offs be made and neither ESD nor resilience really confront the politically uncomfortable distributive justice implications of climate change. Some versions of ESD contain references to both intra- and inter-generational justice, although the choices between competing societal values are mostly implicit in our current laws. The core elements of resilience thinking, such as polycentric governance and broad participation, are more likely to expose and test these values. The engagement of a more diverse array of voices and perspectives in climate adaptation decision-making does not guarantee more equitable outcomes, but those objectives will at least be on the table. Operationalising resilience thinking through law at all levels – from the global to the local – gives us a better chance of ameliorating the social and ecological injustices of climate change.

Implementing resilience principles requires a nuanced understanding of how, where and when to apply them, and how the different principles interact and depend on one another. Much of the literature and case studies on resilience approaches deal with specific river basins, watersheds, local communities or regions. There are not yet examples of success stories where resilience has been deliberately or explicitly embedded in legal frameworks. Australia's freshwater management frameworks seek to reflect some of the elements outlined here, as does national fisheries management, though none of these could be said to demonstrate all of the attributes outlined in this chapter. Many of these principles also find some expression in other natural resource management laws, but it is fair to say that the dominant approach remains one that is reactionary – either seeking to remediate and restore damage done or avert disaster when crisis looms. A key challenge will be in 'upscaling' resilience thinking in practical governance terms, translating the early scholarship to wider and different geopolitical and legal contexts.

Resilience thinking still demands that we agree on our normative object – what does 'good resilience' look like under climate change? Ecologically sustainable development may endure as a meaningful policy and regulatory goal, but it will need to be refined and elucidated, to embed the core features of resilience thinking aimed at avoiding thresholds and managing inevitable transformation. This is both an unavoidable and promising opportunity to strive for higher levels of resource and ecological stewardship as we confront the task of climate change adaptation.

3. Resilience in environmental law: epistemic limitations and the role of participation

Ole W. Pedersen

RESILIENCE AND ENVIRONMENTAL LAW

When surveying the debates and literature on resilience, one is left with an acute sense that 'resilience' is to today's scholars and commentators what 'risk' was just a few years ago. Presently, debates have seemingly moved on from discussions on how best to manage and communicate risks to how best to develop resilient systems of management and governance. In this substitution of terminology, resilience is most commonly defined as a 'measure of persistence of systems and of their ability to absorb change and disturbance and still maintain the same relationship between populations or state variables' (Holling, 1973) and/or the 'reduced vulnerability to environmental risk experiences, the overcoming of a stress or adversity, or a relatively good outcome despite risk experiences' (Rutter, 2012). Unsurprisingly, up to this point, most of the resilience literature has focused on the extent to which law and regulation reflect resilient practices, and implicitly, also whether the law thereby manages to facilitate resilience in the natural environment.

One thus encounters a significant amount of scholarly interest surrounding the perceived lack of resilience in environmental legal systems designed to facilitate environmental protection (Arnold and Gunderson, 2014; McDonald and Styles, 2014; Benson, 2015). Central to much of this literature, which admittedly focuses mainly on US law, is the implicit assumption that humans and the natural environment are faced with unprecedented and, to some extent, unforeseeable risks (though we will see that this argument inevitably poses some problems), which demand a redesign of existing methods and means of regulation. These risks include, most prominently, climate change impacts, biodiversity loss and species extinction (Ruhl, 2011; Craig, 2016). In this conceptualisation of certain serious risks, the concepts of tipping points and the emergence of the concept of the Anthropocene feature prominently, signalling a sense of urgency (Kim and Bosselmann, 2013). In addition, a central theme running through much of this work is the appreciation that the subjects of much of environmental law (the natural environment, ecosystems, new technologies, and economies and markets in general), are highly complex yet adaptive systems which must be managed by an adaptive and flexible system of regulation. In other words, the law ought to reflect the subject which it regulates, taking the form of reverse mirror thesis (Tamanaha, 2001).

Taken together, this serves as a platform upon which an argument for transforming the law is based. Thus, the most commonly advanced argument is typically that existing environmental law is inherently ill-suited to dealing with these types of unprecedented risks: the law is seen as inflexible, maladaptive and as lacking responsiveness (Arnold and Gunderson, 2014). In response, the proponents of resilience thinking identify a series of characteristics which environmental law ought to possess. These include:

- Built-in review and monitoring mechanisms;
- Multiplicity of statutory objectives;
- The reconsideration of environmental decisions on an ongoing basis;
- Staged, tiered and/or conditional approvals of projects impacting on the environment;
- Sunset clauses in statutes, allowing for re-assessment of objectives (resulting in statutory provision being regularly and periodically reviewed); and
- Enhanced public participation throughout the decision-making process.

These properties would ideally go some way towards remedying the critique levied against the present system of environmental law, primary among which is 'the expectation of administrative law that a decision-maker can make fully informed decisions up-front [which] is antithetical to adaptive management's underlying premise' (McDonald and Styles, 2014; Ruhl, 1997).

As noted above, much of the literature on resilience and environmental law has thus far focused on environmental law in the USA. In light of this, it seems relevant to ponder how well UK environmental law fares against the listed characteristics of resilience. The first point to make is that in so far as resilience is fostered by way of adaptability and flexibility there is reason to believe that today's environmental law fares rather well.

One reason for this is the fact that present day environmental law in the UK represents a plethora of different statutory and administrative instruments, measures and approaches, covering a wide spectrum of regulatory methods (Macrory, 2014). Thus, while environmental law is often considered a paradigm embodiment of the regulatory command and control approach (which is per definition considered to be inflexible and rigid), the reality is that environmental law today is made up of a combination (admittedly, often a bewildering combination) of statutory and non-statutory policy-based instruments. These include traditional instruments alongside a whole host of additional systems and means, providing for flexible implementation through incentive-based arrangements together with methods which allow the regulatory decisions to reflect local and present contexts.[1] As a result, UK environmental law may well be deemed to embody features of resilience thinking.

Consider for example the system of regulation set up to regulate heavy industrial pollution in the UK found in the Environmental Permitting Regulations (England and Wales) 2016 and its underlying European Union rules which the UK government is obliged to implement as a matter of EU law (for the time being).[2] On the face of it, this is a paradigm example of command and control regulation. A violation of the Regulations' central requirement of a permit for those carrying out a regulated activity constitutes a criminal offence and thereby entails the risk of the imposition of a sanction. This impression of a linear command and control system quickly fades, however, once the actual workings of the regulations are considered. Most importantly, the background against which specific standards are set by the Environment Agency for particular activities and facilities is through the so-called best available technique (BAT) norm which, as the name suggests, is not a one-size-fits-all standard applied across the board.[3] Instead the BAT standard provides for a differentiated system of regulation, whereby different sectors and operators are subject to standards which are specifically drawn up with that sector in mind. Moreover, the manner in which specific BAT standards are developed further serves to highlight inherent flexibility in the system. BAT is not a static norm but is developed by reference to so-called background BAT Reference (BREF) documents which are drawn up through a technocratic yet participatory process (at EU level) where regulators, industry

---

1 Scotford and Robinson (2013), argue that parts of the environmental law are indistinguishable from politics.

2 The Environmental Permitting (England and Wales) Regulations 2016.

3 This is the primary statutory agency in England, created in 1996, responsible for pollution and waste control.

representatives, scientists and NGOs take part (Lange, 2008). A significant downside of this flexible and technocratic process is, however, that it potentially affords a privileged position to certain interests and actors over others (Abbot and Lee, 2015). In this process, existing asymmetries in respect of inequality of involvement and participation are likely to be intensified. Nevertheless, this importantly results in a situation where the 'front-end' standard-setting of the regulatory process does not necessarily reflect the ideas typically associated with command and control systems. When turning to the 'back-end' of the regulatory process, it becomes equally evident that we are dealing with a system which exhibits significant amounts of flexibility and adaptiveness. This is particularly so when considering the fact that one underlying EU directive (Industrial Emissions Directive, 2010) allows for local derogation from BAT standards both on account of the setting of stricter as well as less strict emission standards.

A further factor is the extension of the recently introduced civil sanctions' regime to the permitting regulations in the context of enforcement. This is most notable in the use of enforcement undertakings, whereby the Environment Agency, instead of commencing criminal proceedings, may enter into a civil agreement with an operator who has committed an offence. One of the main reasons behind introducing this regime in general, and the enforcement undertakings in particular, was that these would allow for added flexibility and appreciation of individual circumstances in the regulatory process (Pedersen, 2013a). This latter point partly serves to highlight the increased extent to which environmental regulators in the UK enjoy a great deal of discretion in the administration of the law (Fisher, Lange and Scotford, 2013, pp. 89–92). While there are of course downsides to this increase in discretion, from a resilience point of view, it serves to highlight how present day UK environmental law is not necessarily (if it ever was) a system of simple rigid statutory commands which are implemented and enforced in an unyielding fashion by the regulators (Hawkins, 1984). In other words, UK environmental law may well in fact already exhibit some of the flexibility and adaptability which the resilience critics of the law seek to implant in it. Importantly, however, in order to come to this conclusion one has to look beyond the statutory framework and examine the manner in which the system works on the ground.

Linked to the issue of flexibility is the fact that further potential for adaptability in the statutory framework is secured through the high frequency with which environmental law-makers make use of secondary legislation (Scotford and Robinson, 2013). While this is not unique to environmental law, environmental law is particularly rich on secondary legislation to the extent that many of the main statutory regimes forming the backbone of UK environmental law are promulgated through secondary rather than primary legislation in the form of Acts of Parliament. Though this naturally makes for a bewildering assortment of different regulations it has, from the point of view of the rule-maker, the significant advantage of allowing for flexibility as a result of the relative ease with which such secondary instruments are amended when the need arises.

The properties of resilience associated with undertaking monitoring and reviewing of the law in light of factual developments is not just implicitly facilitated through the workings of a system based on secondary legislation, but is also found explicitly in parts of the law. This is most prominent in the Climate Change Act 2008 and its central emphasis on parliamentary oversight as a mechanism for its enforcement. Whereas this emphasis is significantly different from the move towards less formal systems of sanctioning found in the environmental permitting regulations, it nevertheless represents an example of the law's adaptability. The main reason for this is found in the obligations on the Secretary of the State to lay before Parliament yearly reports detailing the amount of UK emissions thereby allowing parliamentary oversight of the progress towards meeting the Act's overall obligations (s.16, Climate Change Act 2008).[4] While Parliament would no doubt have been able to request such information anyway, the explicit obligation on the Secretary of State, signals the important emphasis which the Act attaches to continuous review and potential adaption in light of this.

In addition to these factors all approximating some form of flexibility and adaptability in environmental law, a feature worth recalling is the extent to which environmental law and regulation as a sub-discipline within parts of administrative law is singled out for special treatment when it comes to the way in which environmental cases find their way to the courts. Though it is often (and rightly) pointed out that access to justice in environmental law is prohibitively expensive for many people, it does not disguise the fact that environmental cases before the courts benefit from favourable treatment (in terms of process not necessarily substance) when it comes to legal standing and the extent to which applicants are able to seek protection from high costs. Much of this is owed to the 1998 Aarhus Convention[5] and its emphasis in its 'third pillar' on access to justice. These obligations have slowly found their way into UK law to the

---

4 HM Government <http://www.legislation.gov.uk/ukpga/2008/27/section/16>

5 An international treaty adopted under the auspices of the United Nations and the first of its kind to explicitly provide for individual environmental rights.

extent that applicants in so-called Aarhus judicial review cases ultimately are exposed to a much lower cost level (and thereby risk) when it comes to bringing environmental cases to the courts. This potentially gives rise to a more robust and resilient body of law as it is less onerous for NGOs and members of the public to challenge decision-making procedures in the courts compared to other areas of law. It also means that decisions made by public authorities, like the Environment Agency, are perhaps subject to a higher degree of scrutiny by NGOs and members of the public when these relate to the environment (e.g. *R (on the application of ClientEarth) (Appellant)* v. *Secretary of State for the Environment, Food and Rural Affairs (Respondent)*).

In sum, what emerges from this brief overview of some of the central parts of, and recent changes made to, environmental law in the UK is a picture of a system which is not necessarily one lacking in characteristics of resilience. On the contrary, it seems that across a spectrum of environmental law (not necessarily in every instrument within the law), one encounters a high proportion of adaptable and potentially flexible instruments, reflecting features called for by those pursuing the argument of resilience. As a consequence, what emerges is perhaps a body of law which is in fact resilient in certain aspects though perhaps not in every single one.

THE *EX-ANTE* PROBLEM WITH 'DESIGNING' RESILIENCE

In light of the analysis above one central question emerges. Notwithstanding that current environmental law shows some sign of being resilient, there is a strong emphasis within the literature on the need for an even more resilient body of law. Thus, it is worth pondering whether it is at all possible to deliberately instil resilience in the law as advocated in much of the literature (Arnold and Gunderson, 2014; McDonald and Styles, 2014). Much of the resilience and adaptation literature answers this in the affirmative. In this, however, one encounters an acute sense of the proponents of resilience thinking having their cake and eating it. For example, many of the features which are identified as providing resilient features are not necessarily found in systems, be it natural or non-natural, as a result of design. The resilient features are instead a result of long-term development and evolution and/or randomness: efforts to try to reproduce these in a regulatory system may not be feasible (Macrory, 2014). In other words, it is doubtful whether it is at all possible to simply 'transplant' features and characteristics from, for example, an ecosystem or a marketplace into the anthropogenic system of environmental law. As highlighted in much of the literature on resilience and adaptiveness, the systems which serve as a background for the calls for a more adaptive and resilient law are highly complex and multifaceted. From this, however, it does not necessarily follow that the transplanting of specific properties deemed worthwhile from these systems into a regulatory regime will entail the desired resilience and adaptiveness. It may well be that once a feature or characteristic from one system is transplanted into another system it dispels the properties of the system from which it came and instead takes the form of the regime into which it is appropriated (Fish, 1994, p. 239).

A perhaps more pressing problem with the attempt to deliberately design resilience features into the law relates to the epistemological limitations implicit in the emphasis on resilience. The argument for a more adaptive and resilient environmental law often rests on a two-pronged line of reasoning. The first assumption is that environmental law will face a series of unprecedented and in part unforeseen risks (foremost among which is climate change). That is, the regulatory system has little experience of the environmental risks with which the system is likely to come into contact in the future, resulting in a situation where the system itself and those charged with designing and administering the regulatory system lack full knowledge about the potential risks. The second assumption evokes what Hayek (1998) termed the 'hubris of reason', in assuming is that these unpresented risks can be tackled by way of in-built flexibility in the regulatory system. Notwithstanding that the premise of the first assumption is that many of the risks which the regulatory system is likely to encounter will be unprecedented (i.e. it is not known what form, magnitude or extent they may have), the second assumption supposes that we can plan for and adapt to them. The argument goes: 'We do not yet know the shape, form and content of the risks we will encounter but we are nevertheless confident that a system designed with these specified properties in mind is superior in dealing with those risks.'

The inherent self-contradiction in this line of reasoning is perhaps best underlined by Marglin who argued that where 'the only certainty about the future is that the future is uncertain, if the only sure thing is that we are in for surprises, then no amount of planning, no amount of prescription can deal with the contingencies that the future will reveal' (cited in Scott, 1998, p. 344). That is, instead of using the manifestation of the unprecedented as a reminder of our 'epistemic deficit', the response of those advocating a more adaptive and resilient body of law is to argue that our epistemic deficit can be countered by instilling flexibility in the law. In some respect, this is perfectly understandable. For inherent in the call for a more adaptive and resilient regulatory system is the presupposition that the present is necessarily significantly advanced in terms of progress, knowledge and rationality, compared to any comparable point in the past. In such situations, there is, of course, nothing wrong with rejecting existing structures from past, less enlightened positions (Hirschman, 1991; Pedersen, 2015).

Recalling the point made above that many of the features often considered to represent resilience and adaptiveness are not necessarily designed with such properties in mind, it is reasonable to question whether it is at all possible to explicitly design features into the law which are able to 'copy' the organic resilient system. Once again Hayek's work serves as a useful reminder of the limitations associated with the attempt to construe responses to the unknown when he warns against what he saw as the 'constructivist fallacy' under which institutions will serve our 'purposes only if they have been deliberately designed for these purposes' (Hayek, 1998, p. 8). Instead it cannot be ruled out, and therefore at least consideration ought to be given to the fact that a resilient and adaptive body of law is not necessarily achieved through explicit design but through happenstance and serendipity.

In addition to the epistemological limitations encountered when seeking to explicitly design and facilitate properties of resilience in the law, there may well be reason to think that other limitations play a potential role. Thus, other factors include: legal limitations (e.g. in the form of constitutional and legislative requirements which seek to facilitate certain qualities in the law such as legal certainty and the rule of law which may well run counter to the flexibility inherent in the call for resilience and adaptiveness); and practical limitations (where resilience is facilitated by way of administrative fiat and by affording regulatory agencies discretion this may well be hampered by the often significant financial restraints under which some of the agencies find themselves). One telling example is the impact which the funding cuts to the Environment Agency's budget has had on its ability to enforce central parts of the environmental law, relating in particular to waste crime.

Notwithstanding this critique of the reasoning pursued in much of the literature on resilience and environmental law, there is nevertheless some merit in the drive towards resilience. The argument that environmental issues and risks are multifaceted and varied seems entirely reasonable and incontestable. To some extent, that is why environmental regulation looks the way it does today, representing a varied framework of, as highlighted above, different regulatory and statutory mechanisms and tools (Scotford and Robinson, 2013, p. 388). The main issue, however, relates to the rather modest appreciation of the argument that for these exact same reasons it is inherently difficult to draw up a comprehensive regulatory system which allows us to sufficiently address these risks (Pedersen, 2013b). The drive for resilience, however, is entirely understandable but the main thrust of the critique put forward here rests on the assumption that 'we must be suspicious of paradigms that pretend to give a clear-cut answer' (Hirschman, 1970, p. 339). For, as Hirschman points out: often the 'initial effort to understand reality will almost inevitably make it appear more solidly entrenched than before' (ibid.). Thus, in an attempt to respond to this conundrum, it is worth considering if indeed there are other avenues through which we can at least achieve some resemblance of resilience in the law. Seeing as the critique advanced above is in part anchored in the work by Hayek whose work has strong connotations of fundamental liberal democratic ideas, it is worth considering if such principles may instead serve to develop forms of resilience. One such avenue may well be that of public participation.

PARTICIPATION AS A MEANS TOWARDS FURTHER RESILIENCE

One perhaps slightly overlooked factor in the resilience literature to date has been the role played by the wider public. That is, so far most of the environmental law resilience scholarship has focused on the manners in which resilience can be instilled in the legal system itself. As intimated above, there is reason to believe that certain parts of the law already exhibit a certain degree of resilience. This section, however, will focus on the role played by the public in an attempt to consider whether mechanisms of public participation can be seen as successful means for allowing the public to shape specific environmental decisions which impose risk upon the public. To the extent that the public is seen as being able to shape such decisions, this may be seen as facilitating resilience. Not necessarily in the regulatory system itself but in the parts of the public subjected to particular environmental risks.

The emphasis on whether the law is able to reflect 'local' concerns and perceptions relating to particular environmental risks is important in light of the wealth of evidence indicating that for many environmental risks perceptions vary significantly between the public and 'experts', as well as between certain population groups. Thus, differences in risk perceptions by reference to sex, race and socio-economic background have been evidenced across environmental risks, indicating that women are more concerned with risks associated with hazardous waste than men (Bord and O'Connor, 1997); risks associated with soil pollution (Gutteling and Wiegman, 1993); and less supportive of nuclear power (Brody, 1984). Likewise, differences have been identified in perceptions of risks associated with air pollution across race (Johnson, 2002). And, there is reason to believe that white males perceive environmental risks to be lower, compared to white women, black men and black women (Flynn et al, 1984; Finucane et al, 2000). In addition, research suggests that black and other non-white minorities are more concerned with risks associated with nuclear power, solid and toxic wastes, whereas white people are more concerned with 'global' risks associated with ozone depletion and climate change (Jones, 1998). In this light, it becomes relevant to consider the extent to which environmental law is able to strike a balance between these competing perceptions of risks and whether the law succeeds in incorporating these variations. The main prism through which to do so is the mechanism of public participation.

In general terms, public participation has played a prominent role in environmental law and governance for decades. From domestic to international environmental law, the ability of the 'public' to take part in deliberating on environmental decisions is seen as central, deferring legitimacy on outcomes. Typically, this takes place through a three-pronged approach, or pillared in the Aarhus Convention terminology, emphasising access to environmental information, public participation in decision-making and access to justice in the form of independent review mechanisms. The focus of this chapter will be primarily on the second element of participation. The justifications for public involvement in environmental decision-making are several and include: that such involvement is good in its own right; the claim that participation succeeds in delivering substantively 'better' decisions (i.e. an instrumental purpose); and, linked to this, that certain members of the public are in a position to offer so-called 'situated knowledge', thereby contributing valuable and otherwise overlooked expertise to a decision (Holder and Lee, 2007; Steele, 2001). On the international level, this emphasis has enjoyed a particularly prominent position as the need to involve certain social groups, such as women, indigenous communities and the young is justified on grounds of it aiding in facilitating sustainable development. Implicit in these justifications – though perhaps not explicitly recognised – is the argument that allowing the public to take part in deliberations on the regulation of environmental risks serves to instill in those participants a certain degree of resilience, an ability to shape the regulatory responses to environmental risks and the ways in which societies adapt to these.

From the non-binding declarations of international law, obligations on public participation have over the years undergone a certain degree of firming-up to the extent that international environmental law today confers specific rights of public involvement on individuals. This is most notable in the much heralded Aarhus Convention (1998) which obliges contracting parties to facilitate public participation in a series of environmental decisions. The significance of the Aarhus Convention is perhaps best appreciated by highlighting the readiness with which other international institutions and courts have come to rely on it, as well as the way in which it has rapidly forced changes to domestic rules and practices of the contracting parties. Thus, the European Court of Human Rights has, on several occasions, come to rely on the Aarhus Convention when hearing environmental cases in the context of the European Convention on Human Rights and the Aarhus Convention has significantly shaped UK as well as EU law on the matter.

On the domestic level, public participation has been central to environmental law even before today's extensive system of regulatory controls aimed at prevention and pollution control was introduced. This is most notable from the strong emphasis on public participation found in the system of development control in the planning regime. Notwithstanding the early obligations of public participation in UK planning law have been described as 'vague [and] open-ended', and the claim that public participation took place in an environment of 'official ambivalence', statutory obligations to consult with the public are today part and parcel of the law (MacAuslan, 1980). This is principally as a result of the implementation of EU obligations flowing from, primarily, the Environmental Impact Assessment (EIA) Directive (dating back to 1985), which gives rise to more specific and tangible rights of participation for the 'public concerned' where any projects fall within the directive's reach. In its current form, the EIA Directive expands public participation beyond the initial directive by noting that public participation ought not to be compromised on account of the need for a speedy decision-making process and by introducing a new obligation on the decision-maker. Upon making the decision to either refuse or permit a development, the public authority must inform the public about the ways in which the authority has responded to comments received as part of the development process and to explain how these have been incorporated or otherwise addressed (EU Directive, 2014).

The primary message to emerge from this brief overview is that, at least in principle, public participation forms an integral part of environmental law and the law thereby, seemingly, offers plenty of opportunity for affected individuals to make their representations known to public decision-makers. This is particularly so where such decisions fall within reach of the modified EIA directive. The next natural step in order to ascertain the degree to which the law succeeds in implanting resilience in individuals impacted by decisions is then to see how this works on the ground as it were. When scrutinising how the courts have interpreted the above mentioned rules and regulations, and the way these are applied in practice, there is, however, cause for concern. The subsequent part of the chapter examines these matters in turn.

PARTICIPATION IN PRACTICE

If, in the attempt to ascertain the extent to which the above discussed rules on public participation are interpreted and implemented in practice, one turns to the manner in which the courts have dealt with public participation in practice, one encounters an increasingly mixed picture of highs and lows. In the context of EIA, the initial approach taken by the UK courts in the early cases was famously one of reticence. Thus in *R* v. *Swale Borough Council, ex parte RSPB*, in which the RSBP sought to challenge the decision not to conduct an EIA as part of a planning application for a storage area in connection with a port facility, and thereby also the failure to carry out a consultation, Justice Simon Brown (as he then was) famously held that the decision as to whether a development fell within the reach of the EIA Regulations on account of having a 'significant' environmental impact was entirely a matter for the planning authority's discretion. This overly deferential approach has not, however, entirely withstood the test of time and in its landmark decision in *Berkeley* v. *Secretary of State for the Environment*, the House of Lords famously took steps to underline the importance of the EIA regime and its emphasis on public involvement in environmental decision-making. In a very purpose driven decision, Lord Hoffmann thus highlighted how:

> The directly enforceable right of the citizen which is accorded by the Directive is not merely a right to a fully informed decision on the substantive issue. It must have been adopted on an appropriate basis and that requires the inclusive and democratic procedure prescribed by the Directive in which the public, however misguided or wrongheaded its views may be, is given an opportunity to express its opinion on the environmental issues. (*Berkeley*, 38 per Lord Hoffmann)

Not surprisingly, *Berkeley* has been highlighted as the high-water mark in the courts' approach to, and development of, public participation in the UK (alongside the decision of the High Court in *R (on the application of Greenpeace)* v. *Secretary of State for Trade and Industry*, which famously held that the government's consultation on nuclear energy was fatally flawed). More recently, however, the courts have seemingly reverted to a less purposive stance and fallen back on the assumption that the courts retain ultimate discretion when it comes to providing remedies (i.e. to quash) where decisions have been made in contravention of underlying EU rules on public participation.

In *Walton* v. *Scottish Ministers*, the Supreme Court, in response to a statutory appeal against the approval by the Scottish government of certain specific routes within an extensive road construction network, thus signalled a slight shift away from *Berkeley* by suggesting that the Court will not as a matter of course quash a decision taken in violation of underlying EU rules. Instead, Lord Carnwath suggested that the real issue is somewhat more pragmatically whether the applicant will have suffered 'substantial prejudice', i.e. whether the applicant in the case 'has been able in practice to enjoy the rights conferred by the European legislation' on public participation (*Walton* v. *Scottish Ministers*, 139). The argument that an illegality does not necessarily result in the underlying decision being quashed was further supported by the Supreme Court in *R (Champion)* v. *North Norfolk District Council*, again relating to the failure to comply with the EIA Directive. Once again stressing the fact that notwithstanding the lack of compliance with the relevant EIA procedures (and thereby the formal public participation requirements) the Court found that the public had been fully involved in the decision-making process and that the contested decision would therefore not have been different had the EIA procedures been followed (*R (Champion)* v. *North Norfolk District Council*, pp. 58–60). That is, substantive though not formal compliance had, in the view of Lord Carnwath, in reality taken place.

In light of this change of, at the least rhetoric, one conclusion to draw is that the UK courts are presently less inclined to afford full protection to the importance of public participation in environmental decision-making. This move does not perhaps bode well for the present analysis and its emphasis on public participation as a means with which to facilitate resilience if in reality individuals affected by environmental risks are not able to enforce the underlying rules of public participation. This is particularly problematic where public participation and involvement of individuals may have the potential to serve as a correction to the problems identified above with the primarily technocratic developments of the law. If this is correct, then the approach taken by the courts leaves a lot to be desired from the point of view of resilience. Perhaps an altogether more reasonable reading would, however, suggest that the courts are simply seeking to strike out a more pragmatic line, attempting to balance the competing pressures of the desire of the public for further participation, and the impact this has on the delay and costs of the decision-making. And naturally, the various cases will have to be appreciated in their specific and concrete contexts. Thus, in *Berkeley*, as Lord Carnwath pointed out in *Walton*, the House of Lords was aided by the fact that by the time the dispute came before their Lordships, the developer had withdrawn the proposal and abandoned the project. The strong purposive statements made in *Berkeley* were therefore, while not empty gestures, perhaps somewhat low cost in the context of the specific case (see also *R (Edwards)* v. *Environment Agency*). Moreover, in *Walton*, the applicant had indeed enjoyed the right to participation at several stages throughout the decision-making process and had had ample opportunity to make his representations to the decision-maker (Lord Carnwath, while not under a legal obligation to do so, took inspiration from the fact that the Compliance Committee of the Aarhus Convention had previously found that the applicant had had several opportunities to make representations throughout the decision-making process). Nevertheless, this apparent retreat in the case law on public participation potentially serves to limit the usefulness of public participation as a mechanism through which to impress strands and ideas of resilience upon the environmental decision-making process. Additional support for this is arguably found in some of the empirical work examining the ways in which public participation is conducted on the ground.

Thus work on public participation in decisions relating to major wind energy projects highlights how, in reality, public participation provisions have little impact on high-level policy decisions (Lee et al, 2012). The work by Lee et al suggests that in situations where a policy commitment has been made to a particular course of action, there is often little scope for the public to influence subsequent specific decisions, notwithstanding the statutory entitlement to do so. Tellingly, Lee et al (2012, p. 59) warn against what they see as a 'hollowness in participatory exercises at the consenting stage for major projects'. Moreover, recent work suggests that where official policy and guidance create a presumption in favour of certain decisions and developments, decision-makers seemingly afford more weight to representations and knowledge offered by experts as opposed to concerns raised by members of the public (Rydin et al, 2015). This is likely to surprise few, and it may well be that the public and others expect too much from the public participation mechanisms but in light of the argument made above that public participation provision may have the potential to serve as a corrective influence and thereby indirectly facilitate resilience in decision-making, this is indeed a shame, highlighting that 'frustrations, misunderstandings, and failures [are] located at more fundamental levels: in conflicting values, expectations, and attitudes about participation, and in the limited incorporation of results in the wider policy-making process' (Wesselink et al, 2011, p. 2,689).

CONCLUSION

This chapter has sought to examine the relationship between the concept of resilience and environmental law in the UK. The main claim to emerge from this investigation is that many of the features which are ordinarily associated with resilience are in fact already found in the law, albeit to varying degrees. Importantly, these features have often made their way into the law by way of happenstance and serendipity. An upshot of this, however, is that some of these features may inherently result in existing inequalities being amplified. This is most notable in the part of the law which, through a flexible mechanism of technocratic participation, runs the risk of exacerbating existing structures of inequality and lack of involvement of certain social groups, often the ones most likely to face certain environmental risks at the end of a regulatory process (e.g. in the form of close contact with industrial processes). There is little to suggest that traditional methods and means of public participation are able to counter this. This is important for several reasons for those seeking to develop resilient features in regulatory systems wherever this may be. Foremost is the fact that lack of knowledge of the actual environmental risks significantly limits the ability of a regulatory system to respond to risks. In response to this, the chapter has thus sought to challenge the claim that the characteristics which are most commonly associated with facilitating resilience in a system are capable of being replicated and created in a regulatory system like that of environmental law. Thus the chapter has highlighted how the attempt to develop and facilitate resilience in the regulatory system of environmental law runs into considerable problems when the premises of this attempt are scrutinised in detail. The analysis proffered in this chapter of the experience from the UK consequently suggests that the creation of a resilient environmental law system is a slow, incremental (and naturally frustrating) endeavour.

PART III

Inequality: the social and economic consequences of environmental law

4. Climate change, resilience and the generation of risk-classes

Dean Curran

Climate change poses not only one of the most significant practical problems facing the world today, but also one of its most important intellectual problems. Since the mid-1980s climate change has been an important public issue, yet unlike earlier environmental issues, such as the widespread use of DDT or other forms of air pollution, in particular, ozone depletion, there has been very little progress on this issue. Giddens (2009) argues that this lack of progress on climate change, in which society continues on such a destructive path, despite widespread awareness of its likely consequences, is akin to a paradox. In this context of sustained and relatively uninterrupted social creation of likely exigent harm, focus has shifted, at least in part, from strategies to directly stop the problem through a massive reduction in the cause – as had previously been pursued with DDT or CFCs – to a series of conceptual understandings and strategies that are in large part directed towards limiting their negative impacts without removing the underlying causes. These climate change-associated policy terms, such as 'adaptation', 'sustainability' and 'resilience' are Janus-faced terms. In one sense, they offer a glimpse of a possible social and economic logic that does not adhere to the priority of economic goals over other social and environmental concerns: on the other hand, these terms are often subsumed within overarching discourses and policy strategies that serve to reinforce the status quo of the continued reproduction of the primary causes of environmental destruction (see Adger et al, 2011). The specific focus of this chapter will be on the concept of resilience. This concept manifests this 'ambivalent' quality associated with many of these climate change concepts in quite stark terms, which is worthy of further analysis.

As has been highlighted previously, unlike some of the other key terms employed in analysing climate change, such as 'vulnerability', which has its origins in the social sciences, 'resilience' is originally derived from the natural sciences, specifically ecology (Miller et al, 2010). The need to integrate natural science concepts, in particular, ecological knowledge, into policy discussions of climate change is centrally important given its social and natural dimensions. Nevertheless, taking a concept, and the theoretical implications underlying the concept, developed in analysing natural ecosystems and directly 'exporting' it into human and social questions poses the threat that the underlying assumptions of the ecological concept will be implicitly applied to human societies in a way that fails to adequately address how humans may differ from other species.[1]

The risks associated with this venture are particularly significant with respect to the concept of 'resilience'. Holling's (1973), original, classic treatment of resilience in the context of ecological science analysed resilience as a property of systems, in which despite significant fluctuations in populations, species were able to persist. In fact, for Holling (1973, p. 15), greater fluctuations in individual populations of a species may be advisable qua resilience because they can, in certain cases, increase the resilience of the overall species. Nevertheless, in moving from an ecological study of non-human populations where overall persistence of the species is the primary concern, to the socio-ecological study of human environment interaction, it is necessary that a primary policy goal, such as 'resilience', adequately address not only the moral value of human *populations* as a whole, but also of human *individuals*.

In moving from the de facto valuation of the persistence of existing groups of species within an ecosystem to the value of the continuation and thriving for each individual within a society, it is necessary to move from 'resilience' as a general property of socio-ecological systems to focusing on inequalities in resilience between individuals. This chapter argues that not only are there considerable inequalities in resilience to the economic, physical, and social impacts of climate change between individuals, but that, in many cases, these inequalities are *relational*, such that the advanced resilience of some are often at the cost of weakened resilience of others. In a context of increasing environmental and financial risks, differentials in risk are becoming a fundamental part of overall inequality (see Curran, 2016). In thinking about how these risk inequalities systemically impact on the life chances of individuals, it may be said that individuals come to occupy different *risk-classes*.

This concept, risk-class, was recently coined by Ulrich Beck (2013, p. 63), to highlight the systemic nature of these relationships in response to my earlier critical engagement with his work: 'One could say that Dean

---

[1] The direct importing of natural science models into social science models has a long and often troubled history, with the extremely problematic rise of 'social Darwinism' based on Darwinian natural selection, among the most notable cases.

Curran introduces the concept of "risk-class" to radicalize the class distribution of risk' and to chart who will be 'able to occupy areas less exposed to risk and who will have little choice but to occupy areas that are exposed to the brunt of the fact of the risk society'.

Building upon risk-class as an analytical tool, this chapter explores how the current legal context of widespread *organised irresponsibility* – where environmental and financial risk producers often escape culpability because the specific damages of these risks are not traceable back to their originators (Beck, 1995) – increases the potential for the intensification of existing inequalities.[2] This chapter proceeds to explore some of the fundamental ways in which the relational inequalities of the impacts of climate change and widespread relations of organised irresponsibility are contributing towards the generation of differential risk-classes.

As this discussion of inequality of resilience shows, analysing climate change through the prism of resilience can aid in understanding the impact of climate change insofar as the concept importantly illuminates certain key inequalities unrecognised by many other social science discussions of inequalities. Nevertheless, as is argued below, there are also important limits to the concept insofar as protecting the resilience of the least advantaged to climate change may require moving from the persistence to the transformation of existing social and economic institutions and practices.

This chapter proceeds in four steps. First, a discussion of 'resilience' as derived from natural science literature is developed and then it is shown how the focus on the persistence of species as a whole within a system needs to be significantly modified to adequately speak to the value and legal rights of individual human lives, thus motivating the importance of addressing inequalities in resilience. Second, it is shown how in many contexts inequalities in resilience are relational, such that advanced resilience of some weakens the resilience of others. Third, how these risk inequalities may be understood as differential risk-classes is outlined and how widespread legal relations of organised irresponsibility in the context of environmental and financial risk production is further intensifying these inequalities is addressed. Last, the chapter concludes by briefly discussing the potential contribution of the concept of 'resilience' in terms of

---

[2] The challenges of prosecuting environmental crimes have long been noted (see Beck, 1992b; Pearce and Tombs, 1998). In terms of the lack of responsibility for the damages from financial risk, it has been recently noted how with respect to the 2008 global financial crisis there has developed 'an exceptional criminogenic environment. There were no criminal referrals from the regulators. No fraud working groups. No national task force. There has been no effective punishment of the elites here' (Black, William K. in Morgenson and Story, 2011).

highlighting key inequalities and in illuminating how larger transformations are needed in society if the resilience of each is to be secured.

RESILIENCE: FROM ECOLOGICAL TO SOCIAL GOAL

Resilience is increasingly becoming an important approach for dealing with climate change from a policy standpoint (see Spears et al, 2015). Climate change poses a series of important problems for contemporary societies and in the face of continually escalating production of carbon beyond the limits of what is considered safe, the technical exigencies of dealing with climate change provides a powerful support for the appeal of pursuing resilience. 'Resilience' is defined as the 'quality or fact of being able to recover quickly or easily from, or resist being affected by, a misfortune, shock, illness, etc' (OED, 2010). As the definition of resilience suggests, these threats are usually conceived of as external, in which one needs to find a way to persevere in the face of the threat, rather than address the underlying causes. While a focus on resilience may be disappointing insofar as it de-emphasises addressing the underlying causes of climate change, but rather focuses on helping us weather its storms, part of its appeal may be in fact its practicality, that it might not require what seems like almost a political and economic impossibility at this point – properly arresting the underlying causes of climate change.

Nevertheless, despite this eminent practicality, even concepts that serve as more 'practical' tools have underlying and important presuppositions. In particular, insofar as this technical concept is becoming a key social and political goal, then it is necessary to interrogate the context in which it was developed, the premises which supported the value of the concept in these contexts and whether the utilisation of the concept in a new context supports or undermines the previous premises that supported the concept.[3] One key worry about the concept 'resilience', given that resilience to an external threat is the paradigmatic case, is that it may tend to reify the threat, treating it as an external, given threat (in the way that invasion by a foreign enemy may be understood), rather than as a product of systemic social action. In this vein, it may be said that to discuss resilience with

---

[3] While this type of critical genealogy may have some affinities to Nietzsche ([1887] 1996) or Foucault ([1971] 1984), it has a closer affinity with Weber's critical interrogation of the continued uncritical acceptance of a concept, such as the 'calling', despite the shift to a very different context in which the premises supporting the concept no longer hold (see Weber [1904–5] 2002).

oneself (as the West's production of climate change may be viewed) verges on either mystifying the causes of the problem or simply being paradoxical.

This is a significant limitation of the concept, which it is important to keep in mind – however, it will not be the central limitation addressed in this chapter for two reasons. First, it may be argued that this problem entails that while the concept of 'resilience' is clearly limited, it can still work effectively by being supplemented by other concepts that emphasise how climate change is not a given, external threat. Moreover, it may be said that being able to better rebound from threats is surely better than not being able to do so. Second, there is an issue that is prior to the question of whether the concept needs to be supplemented, which is that, even in cases of external threats, it is not clear if 'resilience' as it has been developed in the ecological sciences and imported into social policy, is a morally acceptable goal to pursue.

This logically prior problem is shown in a particularly stark manner in the foundational paper on the study of resilience in ecology by Holling (1973), 'Resilience and Stability of Ecological Systems'. As Holling (1973, p. 1) declares in introducing the concept 'resilience':

> . . .Individuals die, populations disappear, and species become extinct. That is one view of the world. But another view of the world concentrates not so much on presence or absence as upon the numbers of organisms and the degree of constancy of their numbers.

Holling (1973, p. 2) argues that this way of perceiving ecological systems shifts attention towards the 'conditions of persistence' of a given species. In fact, from a resilience perspective, it may be advisable to have greater fluctuations in population levels (births and deaths) because it can introduce a greater capacity for the population of the species as a whole to 'persist' (Holling, 1973, pp. 15, 17). The value in 'resilience' is attached to the persistence of populations as a whole, not to individual members, and in fact conditions that cause greater deaths of individual members may be optimal from a resilience perspective, based on increasing the overall species' 'capacity to persist'. It is not simply that the persistence of the whole trumps the value of any single individual, rather from a resilience perspective individual lives are only viewed as a means to the persistence of the species in a given ecological area.

Now, as this analysis of the moral implications of resilience, as developed in ecological science, suggests, shifting 'resilience' from the non-human world to the human world creates particular problems.[4] Specifically,

---

[4] Since Holling's (1973) classic piece there have been two major threads of critique of the importance of the human versus non-human divide. Singer (1993) has sought

the moral value of each individual suggests that it is not acceptable to treat individuals as a means to the persistence of a larger group. In some extremely exigent cases, it *may* be legitimate to sacrifice a few for many human lives. Nevertheless, there is a powerful moral argument that each human being is an independent source of moral value – not just in terms of not being harmed by another and that its suffering matters – but that there is a powerful moral consideration against using human beings' lives as a means to the capacity to persist of the larger species.[5] As Rawls (1999, pp. 26, 167) has highlighted in another context in his discussion of classical utilitarianism and consequentialism, there are significant moral failures in accounts of value that neglect the 'distinctness' of persons and of their individual moral value. In particular, the idea of increasing the 'fluctuations' (births and deaths) of human populations so as to increase the capacity of the group to persist is especially problematic from a moral perspective.

Consequently, resilience as a concept aimed at collective groups and systems (see Carpenter et al, 2001; Miller et al, 2010; Adger et al, 2011) proves particularly problematic because this can lead to policy prescriptions that undermine the lives of specific individuals so as to support the resilience of the system or the group as a whole. In this way, without reconstruction, the concept 'resilience' – which may seem like a neutral, technical concept – embodies an unrecognised, but powerful consequentialism that allows sacrifice of specific individuals for larger groups in a way that is fundamentally contrary to powerful moral intuitions and the legal rights based upon these. Dworkin's insight that rights provide powerful protection against consequentialist neglect of the value of each individual's life highlights well the problems with the consequentialism embodied in 'resilience':

> Individuals have rights when, for some reason, a collective goal is not a sufficient justification for denying them what they wish, as individuals, to have or to

to undermine the significance of this divide by arguing for giving animals similar moral treatment to humans, while posthumanism, especially, Latourian ANT (see Latour, 2005), denies a significant divide between human beings and things. Neither of these positions undermines the two key arguments of this section. The arguments of this section are: that in the context that the concept 'resilience' was articulated, different moral value was attached to animal than human life, and this moral valuation embedded in the concept of resilience is not suitable for understanding the contemporary value of human beings. Consequently, this critique can be developed while remaining agnostic (or deferring until later the question) on whether the moral value of each individual human life is greater than the value of an animal life.

[5] For the most notable discussion of the necessity of treating human beings as ends not as means, see Kant ([1785] 2012).

> do, or not a sufficient justification for imposing some loss or injury upon them. (Dworkin [1977] 2013, p. 6)[6]

The following section explores this question of the value of each individual through the prism of inequalities associated with resilience.

RESILIENCE AND THE PROBLEM OF RELATIONAL INEQUALITIES

This holism and consequentialism, which allows unrestricted sacrifice of individuals for the greater number embedded in the concept 'resilience' were implicitly built into the concept as developed in the ecological sciences. Nevertheless, as discussed above, this assumption becomes a significant problem when applied to human actors and social life. As such, the question must be asked: given these faults, should the concept be rejected? In response it may be stated that it may be over-hasty to shift to this conclusion, instead of exploring how the concept of 'resilience' can be revised. The rest of this chapter pursues this task.

In this vein, while resilience is generally considered as resilience of 'systems', in particular, social-ecological systems (Carpenter et al, 2001; Berkes and Jolly, 2004; Miller et al, 2010),[7] it is possible to shift the focus of resilience to a level which does not implicitly embody an unjustifiable consequentialism. This level is the resilience of the individual human life. Focusing on the moral value of each individual does not deny that other things than human beings can have moral value (such as animals, the environment, works of art or social groupings). Rather what it does do is prevent the implicit inference that it is only at the general level of persistence of human populations or systems as a whole that there is value qua resilience. In fact, the resilience of each individual in the face of anthropocentric climate change must be a fundamental normative and policy orientation, alongside the resilience of ecological and social systems as a whole.

In shifting from a primary focus on resilience of systems to that of individuals an important problem arises that is opaque at the level of systems: the considerable inequalities of resilience to economic, physical and

---

[6] While endorsing Dworkin's critique of consequentialism here as an important support for rights, this is not meant to fully endorse his understanding of rights as 'trumps'. For an important interrogation of this idea, see Raz (1986).

[7] See Adger et al (2011, p. 696): 'Resilience is the ability of a system to absorb change while retaining essential function.'

social risks from climate change between individuals. Adding the moral importance of the resilience of individuals to the aim of achieving the resilience of larger systems and groups of individuals may at first appear as only a supplementary purpose to that of securing collective resilience. This conclusion however is mistaken because of the problem of the relational distribution of many environmental risks (see Curran 2013a, 2016). Insofar as some inequalities in resilience are relational, this entails that the advanced resilience of some will result in the weakened resilience of other individuals. Consequently, insofar as resilience to certain risks associated with global environmental change are relational, or 'positional' as Amartya Sen (1981, 1983), has previously put it, then a focus on the resilience of individuals to climate change, and hence the relational inequalities between individuals, poses a critical challenge to technocratic collectivist accounts of resilience that neglect existing power relations.

This relational or positional nature of resilience to certain types of risks can be illustrated through a key risk associated with climate change, short-run and long-run declines in food supplies and how the impacts of declines in food affect the capacity of individuals to persist in their existing life practices. While a society becoming wealthier as a whole may be viewed as one way of increasing its resilience (see USAID, 2014), being in a society in which the overall stock of wealth is increasing may actually further undermine the resilience of many of its least advantaged insofar as this increasing wealth is distributed unequally. As Sen shows, '*relative* deprivation in terms of *incomes* can yield *absolute* deprivation in terms of *capabilities*' (Sen 1999, p. 89, original emphasis). Following Sen's discussion in *Poverty and famines* (1981), we may say that a relative decline in terms of income can lead to an absolute decline in food security.

This is not, however, merely a hypothetical possibility, but a key factor in previous famines. Sen (1981), provides a powerful example of how relative declines in income can lead to absolute declines in food security for those who did not experience rising incomes. In Bengal, there was a massive famine in the middle of World War II:

> The 1943 famine can indeed be described as a 'boom famine' related to powerful inflationary pressures initiated by public expenditure expansion . . . [A]n important aspect of the famine was its association with *an uneven expansion in incomes and purchasing powers*. Those involved in military and civil defence works, in the army, in industries and commerce stimulated by war activities, and almost the entire normal population of Calcutta covered by distribution arrangements at subsidized prices *could exercise strong demand pressures on food, while others excluded from this expansion or protection simply had to take the consequences of the rise in food prices*. Agricultural labour did not in general

> share in the war-based expansion, except in certain areas . . . where military or civil defence works were in progress. (Sen, 1981, pp. 75, 77–8, emphases added.)

In the case of the Bengal famine, increased wealth of the population as a whole did not increase the resilience of all, but actually undermined the resilience of those who had fallen relatively behind in the space of wealth.

In the context of market-mediated distribution of the means of securing oneself against the impacts of climate change threats, the relational nature of resilience is particularly exigent for certain risks.[8] At this time, there is uncertainty as to the overall effect on food production from moderate increases in global temperatures. However, it is widely believed that if temperatures rise beyond 3°C, relative to pre-industrial levels (1750–1850), there will be significant declines in food production (Stern, 2007, p. 56). The events of the Bangladesh famine of 1974 exemplify well the relational nature of resilience to the types of impacts driven by climate change when the distribution of basic scarce goods is primarily mediated by the market. Flooding led to massive increases in food prices due to the expectation of future food scarcity. These massive price increases, along with the damage caused by the flooding to the purchasing power of those who lost their employment due to the flood led to those with relatively low economic resources being outpurchased for the existing supply of food, and hence experiencing extreme food deprivation (Drèze and Sen, 1989, p. 29).

As climate risks increase food supply volatility levels, it is the relatively greater economic resources of the advantaged that enable them to outbid others to exhibit a monopoly on the private supply of food, while the relatively less advantaged are exposed to the full brunt of supply variations. As Jim Yong Kim, the president of the World Bank, has recently suggested: 'Fights over water and food are going to be the most significant direct impacts of climate change in the next five to 10 years' (Kim in Elliot, 2014). In these 'food battles' in market economies, relative differentials in income and wealth determine whether individuals are able to outbid others to continue to command their previous level of food, thus enabling the relatively wealthy to occupy socially scarce private escape routes from food deprivation (see Drèze and Sen, 1989, p. 12). Consequently, with respect to fundamental necessities of each individual, food (and water), the increased resilience of some through increases in their economic resources can directly undermine the resilience of others.

---

[8] The following discussion builds on Curran (2013a, 2013b; see also Beck, 2013) to speak directly to the issue of inequality and resilience.

INEQUALITIES OF RESILIENCE AND RISK-CLASSES

The relational inequalities associated with climate change have the potential to pose critical problems for existing understandings of risk and justice. Thinking about these inequalities however only in terms of specific individual relations threatens to diminish the full potential of these relations to shift our understandings of risk, power and inequality. The concept of 'risk-class' while sharing the same name as a financial investment category, is, as it has been developed, a socially oriented concept, that can illuminate the systemic and collective dimensions of existing risk inequalities.[9] How systemic differences in benefits from the production of risk and damages from the distribution of these risks generate differential risk-classes has already been pursued with respect to financial risk (Curran, 2015), but has yet to be adequately explored with respect to climate change.

The inequalities of climate change are manifested on all scales, including local, national and transnational. Within local areas, the relegation of the poor to lower land and lower quality housing, while the wealthy occupy higher areas with more secure housing, as was the case with Andhra Pradesh, fundamentally shaped individuals' ability to survive the flood from cyclones in 1977 (see Winchester, 1986, in Blaikie et al, 1994, pp. 154–5). The ability of the wealthy to occupy differential risk-classes based on differential economic resources fundamentally affected their life chances (and, in particular, their 'capacity to persist'). As the discussion above of Bengal suggests, relative inequalities of purchasing power within a nation can generate different risk-classes with respect to food insecurity. Likewise, the fact that the 'richest 11 per cent of the world's population create around half of all carbon emissions, but suffer least from the harmful consequences of climate change' (Oxfam, 2013, p. 4), suggests that transnational risk-class relations have, in turn, become fundamental to global inequalities and power relations.

The ramifications of risk-class relations intersecting and overlapping at local, national and transnational scales may suggest a significant problem for the concept if the intention is to reproduce a primary aim of much class analysis, which is the generation of clear boundaries between different (risk)-classes that sort individuals into only one type of grouping. There are two possible responses that may be made to this objection.

---

[9] Illuminating the systemic and social power relations of risk via concepts that share the same linguistic term with technical financial risk terms, which may be viewed as a type of critical linguistic reclamation project, has been pursued with other terms, such as 'risk arbitrage' (see Curran, 2015).

First, following Erik Wright's (2005) recent discussions of class here, (risk)-class analysis can still make an important contribution to the study of systematic inequalities by studying the relational processes of inequality generation. It is not necessary that clearly defined, universal boundaries be drawn for the different classes to importantly illuminate systemic power relations (Wright, 2005; Curran, 2016, ch. 4). Second, and on a more empirical level, recent transformations in political economy suggest that the most significant developments in inequalities are currently proceeding at the very top, the elite and the very bottom (see Savage et al, 2013; Piketty, 2014; Sayer, 2015), thus suggesting that the problem of drawing boundaries between all of the different 'risk-classes' is less important in tracing key trajectories of contemporary inequalities than analysing the elite and the least advantaged. Distinguishing between elite 'risk-classes' and the most disadvantaged risk-classes and the processes that exacerbate these inequalities is a task that can be pursued without demarcating the boundaries of all possible risk-classes (see Curran, 2015).

RISK-CLASS, ORGANISED IRRESPONSIBILITY AND THE LAW

In the context of a discussion of resilience, inequality and the law, a key relation that is shaping existing risk-class inequalities is that of organised irresponsibility (see Beck, 1992a, 1995, 1999; Giddens, 1999). Organised irresponsibility occurs in contexts where 'there are a diversity of humanly created risks for which people and organisations are certainly "responsible" in a sense that they are its authors but where no one is held specifically accountable' (Giddens, 1999, p. 8). Where the benefits from the production of risk are reversed by the beneficiaries compensating those who have suffered from these risks, then significant differential benefits from risk production tend to only be temporary. It is systemic relations of organised irresponsibility, where risk can be produced without the necessity of later compensating for damages, which permits significant mismatches between the benefits and costs of financial and environmental risks that can generate transformational impacts of risk on inequalities.

Consequently, while organised irresponsibility is a powerful *explanans*, contributing significantly to inequalities emerging from contemporary risks, it is also an important *explanandum*. This condition that needs to be explained is: how can contemporary financial and environmental risks continue to be generated in a context of organised irresponsibility, in which so few of those who are cumulatively contributing to the crises we are currently facing are being held culpable? While detailing the institutional developments that have enabled such widespread organised irresponsibility is well beyond the scope of this chapter, the central development that the evolution of law has played in this development needs to be highlighted.[10] In particular, the systemic impact of organised irresponsibility intersects with a relatively widespread legal interpretation of harm, which tends to be narrow and individualistic, rather than wide and collective. Building upon Beck's discussion of a case in which each factory evaded responsibility for their damage caused because there were many different factories that were polluting and hence no specific damages were able to be traced back to any specific factory (Beck, 1992b, pp. 102–3), we may say, other things being equal, that for any given amount of total harm, the greater the number of contributors and the greater the complexity of connections between action and harm, the less total culpability for harm that tends to be ascribed. So, it may be proposed as a basic tendency in looking at contemporary risk, that the greater the number of the contributors and the greater the complexity of the pathways by which the harm is caused the greater potential for the gap between harm caused and the culpability for the harm. In many ways, the concept 'organised irresponsibility' illuminates how a series of acts, each of which individually may be relatively innocuous, may in systemic combination, cause massive, uncompensated damage.

While there are still important cases of criminal negligence by large corporations (see Pearce and Tombs, 1998), at the intersection of the environment and criminology, many of the current acts that are contributing to the destruction of the world are ordinary acts. These 'ordinary acts' are 'widely and regularly performed by individuals as part of their routine activities; they are generally viewed as acceptable, even desirable', though they collectively produce significant risks (Agnew, 2013, p. 58). While they are harms, they are, at least at an individual level, 'ordinary harms' (Agnew 2013) that would not be considered criminal.[11] As Mill's (1991) defence of a specific interpretation of the 'harm principle' suggests, having the harm of others' interests as a *sufficient* condition (rather than as a *necessary* condition) to prohibit an act would make commercial life and social life more generally almost impossible: minor harms of others' interests

[10] To identify just one, among a vast literature, Djelic and Bothello (2013) provide an insightful discussion of how limited liability has become a 'structural source of moral hazard'. For a more general critique of corporations and irresponsibility, see Tombs and Whyte (2015).

[11] For an insightful discussion in a different context of how a culture of the 'normalisation of deviance' can develop, see Vaughan (1997). Thanks to Bridget Hutter for this reference.

are a fundamental aspect of social action. It is in that space between not affecting one's interests at all and significant and direct harm, that millions of individuals engage in the ordinary harms that cumulatively result in massive environmental problems, such as climate change.

While the description of millions of independent individuals engaging in these ordinary harms does fit an initial attempt to elucidate the power of organised irresponsibility, a purely individualistic interpretation of organised irresponsibility is not adequate. Firstly, the power of contemporary organised irresponsibility is neither a natural nor necessary outcome, but rather a powerful social relation that in many cases is institutionalised through law and the development of existing organisations (see Curran, 2015). In this way, differentials in organisational and political power powerfully shape the scope for the members of different organisations to engage in organised irresponsibility. For example, the opacity of contemporary finance, the wealth associated with it and the continued dependence of states and businesses on finance has markedly contributed to its power to avoid culpability for the massive harms it creates (Engelen et al, 2011).

Second, there are powerful inequalities in the ability to engage in, and benefit from, these social relations of organised irresponsibility. As Beck highlighted in his discussion of contemporary socially produced risk, these risks are the unintended side-effects of the production of *goods* (Beck, 1992a). As such, it may also be concluded that greater economic resources and social power to benefit from the production of consumer goods is likewise the power to create greater unintended and latent negative side-effects through consumption. To provide only one startling case to exemplify the more general point, there are very few people in the West, much less of African peasantry, who can afford to spend £3,000 a month to heat their outdoor swimming pool to bath temperature all-year round, however there are some extremely wealthy people in the Lower Thames Valley who apparently not only can afford to, but actually do use their own 'private resources' in this way (Monbiot, 2009). The privilege to engage in this level of 'ordinary harm' and environmental risk production is clearly conditioned by one's existing resources – it would be extremely difficult for a poor person to engage in that level of 'ordinary harms'. The ability of the 11 per cent wealthiest in the world to create approximately half of the world's carbon emissions (Oxfam, 2013) in a way that is, as of yet, not legally culpable is due in large part, to their greater level of economic resources that enable them to engage to a much greater level in the production of environmental risk through the 'ordinary harms' associated with contemporary consumption.

While the capacity to benefit from contemporary organised

irresponsibility is clearly shaped by existing class inequalities, it is not necessarily reducible to existing class differentials. To provide an example, the 'elite' class (see Savage et al, 2013) is sometimes split with respect to its benefit from contemporary financial risk (Curran, 2015). While financial intermediaries benefitted massively from their ability to 'skim value' from financial transactions and likewise avoid the negative consequences from the downside of these risks, 'elite' asset holders as 'value surfers', have a much more ambivalent relationship to financial risk as they benefit from asset inflation, but also experience significant losses when undisclosed risks manifest themselves in major write-downs (see Erturk et al, 2007). Consequently, the concept of 'risk-class' is necessary to both highlight how socially produced risk is becoming a key source of contemporary inequality and to illuminate how risk differentials are a bona fide source of power in itself which is not necessarily reducible to class resources as in Marxist or Bourdieusian accounts. Elite actors may not necessarily describe themselves in terms of a risk-class. Nevertheless, the major 'risk shift' (Hacker, 2006) and 'privatisation' of many of the risks that the least advantaged face, including pension risks (Blackburn, 2012), employment conditions (Standing, 2011) and welfare retrenchment (Taylor-Gooby, 2012), suggests that there have been shifts in terms of risk that are not easily captured in terms of class as differential relations of production (Wright, 1985) or existing 'capitals' as effective powers to secure goods (Bourdieu, 1984, 2001).

This discussion of organised irresponsibility and risk-class highlights most powerfully the dual nature of 'resilience'. Insofar as the ecological, system-directed conception of resilience is prioritised, these inequalities are elided, and in fact in many cases legitimated in the name of supporting a greater capacity to persist through an uncritical attitude towards whatever type of economic development as long as it includes GDP growth. However, shifting to the resilience of each effectively highlights, in a novel space, how inequalities in risk are a massive source of power differentials which are extremely difficult to legitimate. The concluding section below will briefly discuss how orienting ourselves to the value of each may call into question the legitimacy of the persistence of many of the existing contemporary social and economic systems.

CONCLUSION: TRANSFORMATIONAL RESILIENCE?

The concept 'resilience', often encourages a focus on the persistence of existing social-ecological systems (Adger et al, 2011). Nonetheless, if we value the resilience of each as a *sui generis* goal not reducible to the persistence of larger populations or social and economic systems, then the possibility of persistence of existing institutions and systems becoming a primary goal of policy is called into question. There is a growing climate change crisis that the world has created.[12] Existing social-political systems, have, as of yet, intensified, rather than limited the trajectory of this risk crisis. As such, it has to be contemplated that a focus on the resilience of each individual may actually yield the necessity of the transformation of existing systems of production of wealth and risk (and the political systems that manage these processes). Consequently, rather than resilience serving as an effective technical concept to orient policy, it rather may be interpreted as a thought-provoking theoretical pathway away from the maximising logics of the last two centuries in economics and commercial life and, hence, a partial, but imaginative route to an alternative social rationality.[13]

That the social responsibility of business is to increase its profits (Friedman, 1970) has been embedded in neo-classical economic theory[14] and in business practice. This is particularly the case following the push to a 'shareholder value' system,[15] insofar as failures by management to apparently maximise earnings and share prices are punished by the stakeholders with the greatest control over management, the shareholders.[16] Yet, as Holling (1973) highlights, an approach focused on maximisation is in many ways antithetical to a focus on resilience. Acting to secure resilience prioritises maintaining conditions within an existing 'domain of attraction' that is favourable to the reproduction of the basic needs of the members of the ecological system (Holling, 1973, pp. 9–10). Maximisation, on the other hand, focuses on pushing some existing space

---

[12] This is proceeding alongside the financial crisis and its attendant economic inequality crisis. For recent discussions of the multiple crises we are currently facing (see Gamble, 2014; Walby, 2015).

[13] Weber ([1922] 1978) is the classic text on social 'rationalities' or logics, though Luhmann (1993) and Brown (2015) are recent, important accounts.

[14] As is clear from standard accounts of microeconomic analysis, in which equilibrium is always premised on profit maximisation by each firm, for one example, see Varian (1992).

[15] For one discussion of this transition, see Dobbin and Jung (2010).

[16] To provide one instructive example, a return on equity (ROE) of 15 per cent became an important standard in finance leading up to the 2008 crisis, which exerted significant pressure on the management of financial institutions. While in the mid-1990s, there were significant differences between US, UK and Eurozone banks' ROEs (ranging from above 15 per cent for US banks to around 7 to 8 per cent for Eurozone banks), after 2004 all three converged on 15 per cent (see Engelen et al, 2011, pp. 108–11).

of advantages as far as possible. However, as Beck (1992a) shows, insofar as nature always in some way escapes our control, unintended side-effects will have significant impacts, which create problems for the maximisation approach.

This is not to say that a focus on resilience will not result in unintended negative side-effects. Clearly it will, but maximisation drives existing social and ecological systems as close as possible to the boundaries of their existing *domains of attraction*, so that small, unforeseen side-effects are much more likely to have cascading effects which yield fundamentally different, and often sub-optimal, equilibria. Holling's (1973) discussion of the effects of 'maximum sustained yield' exemplifies this contrast well. In Lake Michigan, the pursuit of 'maximum sustained yield' weakened the resilience of the fish population, pushing them to the boundary of their existing domain of attraction of population levels. This reduced fish population level, then interacted with an unexpected factor (the introduction of a small number of sea lamprey) thus leading to a precipitous drop in fish populations, and a new domain of attraction of very low fish stocks, which could not be reversed (Holling, 1973, pp. 8–9). In this way, as we discover the limits of our knowledge in different areas of life,[17] thinking through the importance of the resilience of each may provide the possibility of perceiving an alternative social rationality to the currently dominant one of maximisation.

Given the dominance of social and economic systems that are oriented to maximisation, which constantly push the bounds of existing domains of attraction and the important social and ecological functions they support, it is likely that the pursuit of the resilience of each may require the *transformation* rather than the *persistence* of existing social and economic systems. The focus on maximisation constantly threatens to push existing ecological systems outside of existing domains of attraction towards *tipping points* (Urry, 2011) that may further intensify the existing inabilities of systems of food production and flood protection to adequately satisfy human needs. While this is a problem for all human beings, attention to massive inequalities in resilience, which are contributing to increasingly important differentials in risk-class, further supports the possibility that the resilience of each actually requires transformation. Many of the ways in which resilience is relational and in which the advantages of some create greater risks for others, is in fact embedded in the world's increasingly dominant

---

[17] There have been important recent innovations in economic theory acknowledging the importance of knowledge imperfections. For one accessible discussion, see Stiglitz (2002).

economic system, 'liberal capitalism'[18] in which the primary means of life are mediated by the market and the distribution of scarce goods is based on the highest willingness to pay. Consequently, the concept of resilience pushes us beyond merely a focus on the persistence of existing social and existing systems to the necessity of contemplating what kind of transformations are necessary to pursue the resilience of each. While this chapter has not been able to speculate on what transformations may be needed, as suggested here, a critical interrogation of the concept of 'resilience' may provide an important analytical tool for contemplating potential pathways to move forward both analytically and practically on these problems.

18 For a further discussion of 'liberal capitalism', see Coates (2000).

5. Transformative biodiversity law and 2030 Agenda: mainstreaming biodiversity and justice through human rights

Claudia Ituarte-Lima[1]

INTRODUCTION: A MOMENTUM FOR TRANSFORMATIVE BIODIVERSITY LAW

A confluence of events provides a momentum for biodiversity law to play a key role in transformations for sustainability. Mainstreaming biodiversity in distinct economic sectors is increasingly recognised as the main strategy to address risks affecting biodiversity and people's livelihoods in the international biodiversity agenda. The Convention on Biological Diversity (CBD) in 1993[2] explicitly recognises the importance of biodiversity integration in sectoral and cross-sectoral plans, programmes and policies (Art. 6d) and national decision-making (Art. 10a). Yet, it is only recently that mainstreaming and integration of biodiversity in other economic development agendas is gaining momentum (see e.g. IDLO, 2016).[3] In the

[1] The author would like to thank Bridget Hutter, Victor Galaz and Per Stromberg for valuable comments on an earlier version of this chapter. Research for this chapter was financially supported by the Swedish Research Council for Environment, Agricultural Sciences and Spatial Planning (Formas) 'Effective and Equitable Institutional Arrangements for Financing and Safeguarding Biodiversity' (254-2013-130) at Stockholm Resilience Centre. All views and possible errors remain my own.

[2] The Convention of Biological Diversity is an international treaty opened for signature during the United Nations Conference on Environment and Development or 'Earth Summit' in Rio in 1992 and it entered into force in 1993. See more information at <https://www.cbd.int/> accessed 1 July 2016.

[3] In June 2016, the International Development Law Organization hosted a workshop in The Hague entitled 'Connecting the dots across the Sustainable Development Goals (SDGs): environment, justice and people' with a framing paper (IDLO, 2016) of the same title. The workshop, in which this author

thirteenth CBD Conference of the Parties[4] (UN Biodiversity Conference) in Cancun, Mexico, in 2016, the parties of this Convention (i.e. the 196 countries which have signed and ratified this international treaty), had as a main topic mainstreaming biodiversity for well-being.[5] Strategic actions to enhance national implementation, in particular through mainstreaming and the integration of biodiversity across relevant sectors is a key element in the multi-year programme of work of the Conference of the Parties up to 2020 (CBD, 2014). Human rights are relevant for mainstreaming biodiversity across sectors because human rights are of a cross-sectoral nature.

In the CBD context, normative advances have also been made on equity, a dimension of justice. In 2010, the Nagoya Protocol on Access to Genetic Resources and the Fair and Equitable Sharing of Benefits Arising from their Utilization (Nagoya Protocol) was agreed in the tenth Conference of the Parties of the CBD in order to advance in the implementation of the CBD's third objective 'the fair and equitable sharing of the benefits arising out of the utilization of genetic resources' (Art. 1).[6] This agreement was a product of intense negotiations following the World Summit on Sustainable Development in 2002 where Heads of State and Government called for negotiating 'within the framework of the Convention on Biological Diversity, bearing in mind the Bonn Guidelines, an international regime to promote and safeguard the fair and equitable sharing of benefits arising out of the utilization of genetic resources' (United Nations, 2002, para. 44 (o)). The Nagoya Protocol refers explicitly to intellectual property rights in relation to benefit sharing, prior informed consent and mutually agreed terms. In its Article 6, it mentions the need to 'establish clear rules and procedures for requiring and establishing mutually agreed terms. Such terms shall be set out in writing and may include, inter alia: . . . (ii) Terms on benefit-sharing, including in relation to intellectual property rights' (Art. 6.3(g)). In the Annex to the Nagoya Protocol, 'Joint ownership of relevant intellectual property rights' is mentioned as

---

participated, brought together experts from UN organisations, research institutions and governmental organisations. For more information see:<http://www.idlo.int/news/events/workshop-environment-justice-and-people?render=overlay> accessed 10 July 2016.

4 The CBD Conference of the Parties (COP) is the governing body of the Convention of Biological Diversity that since 2000 holds a meeting every two years to take decisions on the implementation of this international treaty.

5 This UN Biodiversity Conference was attended by more than 7,000 participants including 4,000 delegates from 170 countries and more than 400 organisations (https://www.cbd.int/conferences/2016).

6 The Nagoya Protocol is available at <http://www.cbd.int/abs/text> (see Ituarte-Lima and Subramanian 2011; Stromberg et al, 2013).

a potential monetary and non-monetary benefit derived from access and benefit-sharing agreements.

In mainstreaming biodiversity and justice in law and policy, property rights play an important role. Property can signify the social organisation of rights and duties over resources, with physical attributes or with intellectual characteristics (see e.g. Hunt, 2000; Bodenhorn, 2000; Smith, 2003; Ituarte-Lima, 2009). For the purpose of this chapter, I distinguish between intangible property and tangible property. Intangible property refers to the rights and duties over resources with predominately intellectual characteristics such as traditional knowledge of biodiversity,[7] and tangible property to those rights and duties concerning resources with predominately physical attributes such as land, forests, oil and minerals. Although the distinction between tangible and intangible resources is often used in property and heritage law at the international and national levels, it is worth noting that there is not a clear boundary between intangible and tangible resources.[8]

Indigenous peoples' organisations have different perspectives about the so-called intangible property rights including intellectual property rights (IPR) and property rights over traditional knowledge (TK). For instance, indigenous people who are sceptical of intellectual property rights agreements consider that turning knowledge into a commodity, by applying IPR, will only spread Euro-American forms of property and legitimate the extraction of their resources and knowledge. They consider that participation in a structure in which the terms of agreement are recognised by both the oppressor and oppressed is insufficient to challenge hegemony. Thus, some indigenous people have called for a refusal of the terms laid out by the Western governments, corporations or academics that seek TK protection through IPR, irrespective of how favourable or lucrative these agreements may seem (Napier, 2002). In this context, some indigenous people and their allies reject IPR as the appropriate rhetorical domain for achieving just agreements.

Yet, one reason why other indigenous peoples and their advocates have linked the property conceptualisation to traditional knowledge

---

[7] The Convention on Biological Diversity defines traditional knowledge as: 'knowledge, innovations and practices of indigenous and local communities, around the world. Developed from experience gained over the centuries, and adapted to the local culture and environment, traditional knowledge is transmitted orally from generation to generation . . .' (Art. 8 (j)).

[8] For a discussion of this distinction in international law, see e.g. Lixinski (2013) and Brown (2005); and in national law, see e.g. Lewis-Lettington and Mwanyiki (2006) and Monteriro-Penteado (2012).

is the political potency of such a conceptualisation in the global struggles for social justice (Coombe, 1998, 2003; Dutfield, 2001). Traditional knowledge under the Convention on Biological Diversity has become the focus of many third-world governments, indigenous people and NGOs' energies, as it appears to represent an international legally binding treaty that has some potential to contest, for example, the imperatives of the Trade Related aspects of Intellectual Property Rights (TRIPS) Agreement[9] which has generally favoured transnational corporations from relatively more industrialised countries (Dutfield, 2001). Likewise, conceptual advances under the CBD and the Nagoya Protocol may offer possibilities of fostering social equity within states in terms of linking the intangible dimensions of the bundles of property rights with tangible dimensions of property rights, specifically through notions such as the recognition of biocultural community protocols and customary norms (see Articles 12.1; 12.3(a); 12.4 and 18.5) (Stromberg et al, 2012). [10]

Like the normative advances in the international biodiversity law, the 2030 Agenda for Sustainable Development[11] offers a momentum for the transformative development of biodiversity law. Connections between Sustainable Development Goals (SDGs) adopted by the UN General Assembly in 2015 in New York and normative developments within the CBD are explicit. For example, Aichi Target 2 is reflected in SDG Target 15.9: 'By 2020, integrate ecosystem and biodiversity values into national and local planning, development processes, poverty reduction strategies and accounts' (United Nations, 2015). In contrast to a stand-alone issue under the Millennium Development Goals (MDGs), environmental sustainability is now integrated in various targets across the SDGs which also offers opportunities for connecting biodiversity law with the SDGs. For instance, SDG 2 on ending hunger includes Target 2.5: 'maintaining the genetic diversity of seeds, cultivated plants and farmed and domesticated animals and their related wild species' (ibid.).

Furthermore, innovations in the 2030 Agenda provide a momentum for mainstreaming both biodiversity and equity across social and development

---

[9] The TRIPS Agreement under the World Trade Organization (WTO) is the most comprehensive multilateral agreement on intellectual property and it came into effect in 1995. A country which is party to WTO has to also be party to TRIPS. See <https://www.wto.org/english/tratop_e/trips_e/intel2_e.htm> accessed 4 August 2016.

[10] For examples of community protocols, see e.g. ASOCASAN et al (2012). Also Bavikatte and Jonas (2010).

[11] See more at: <http://www.un.org/sustainabledevelopment/sustainable-development-goals/>

agendas through human rights. The 2030 Agenda explicitly mentions '10. The new Agenda is guided by the purposes and principles of the Charter of the United Nations, including full respect for international law. It is grounded in the Universal Declaration of Human Rights, international human rights treaties.' SDG 16 on peace, justice and strong institutions and SDG 10 on reducing inequalities as stand-alone goals are significant innovations of the 2030 Agenda. An increasing awareness is emerging across environmental agendas of a link often overlooked, specifically the need to connect scientific and technical solutions with appropriate legal and policy frameworks at multiple levels backed by accountable institutions and empowered people where inequalities are addressed (Jonas et al, 2012; IDLO 2014, 2016). Important challenges emerge for example in the institutions needed for the respect of the environmental rights and land rights defenders especially in developing countries. In a joint statement, the United Nations (UN) Special Rapporteur on human rights and the environment, John Knox, the UN Special Rapporteur on the situation of human rights defenders, Michel Forst and the UN Special Rapporteur on the rights of indigenous people, Victoria Tauli Corpuz frame, as a global crisis, the risky and even deadly undertaking faced by environmental defenders such as Berta Cáceres, the Goldman Prize winner who was assassinated in Honduras in 2016 (OHCHR, 2016). They consider that 'the international community has reached consensus on the new sustainable development goals as a roadmap to a more sustainable, prosperous and equitable future. But those goals cannot be met if those on the front line of protecting sustainable development are not protected' (ibid.).

International guidance on how to implement the socio-ecological dimensions of SGD 16 and SDG 10 at national and local levels is lacking, including how to tackle risks to biodiversity integrity and local peoples by activities with significant impacts on ecosystems and peoples' livelihoods such as the extractive industry. While the above mentioned normative advances in the international biodiversity arena and the 2030 Agenda for Sustainable Development are key for transformations for sustainability, the more challenging phase arises now with their actual implementation at national and local levels.

Considering that one of the pillars of the Convention on Biological Diversity refers to equity and SDG 16 has justice and strong institutions at its core, systematically assessing property rights in national legal frameworks including the way these legal frameworks operate in practice can be a policy support tool for mainstreaming biodiversity and equity. In this chapter, I argue that this assessment should include dimensions of intangible property such as cultural values of ecosystems and traditional knowledge of biodiversity as well as tangible dimensions of property such as land and subsoil ownership. Two main questions will guide the analysis in this chapter. The first question is to what extent environmental-related property law contributes to equity or inequity? The second question is whether a human-rights based approach to property can be useful for synchronising intangible property rights with tangible property rights.

For the purpose of this chapter, the conceptual distinction of tangible and intangible property rights is made for disentangling property rights provisions and assessing the risks and innovations useful for mainstreaming biodiversity and justice approaches. The concept of equity is used because it allows considerations of justice and fairness in the design and operationalisation of law and policy relevant for biodiversity, ecosystems and local people's livelihoods.[12] While recognising the inherent equality in dignity among all members of humanity, the equity concept considers situations of inequality that exist in practice due to, for example, historical processes of discrimination towards indigenous peoples. These discussions are also at the core of international human rights law. The state obligation to provide effective mechanisms for each person or group to exercise their rights, independently of economic, cultural or gender conditions, is one of the discussions that human rights bodies have addressed such as the Inter-American Court of Human Rights.

In this chapter, we refer to a broad range of legal instruments both in terms of their thematic focus and legal status because they can be relevant for addressing socio-ecological risks. Distinct instruments span biodiversity law and property law to human rights and peace treaties, and these thematically distinct instruments can have different legal status. International treaties differ from declarations (e.g. Declaration of Human Rights and Environment, 1994), Recommendations (e.g. the Recommendation on the Safeguarding of Traditional Culture and Folklore UNESCO, 1989) and agendas (e.g. 2030 Agenda). Some environmental and human rights lawyers and scholars call the former 'hard law' and the latter 'soft law' (Kirton and Trebilcock, 2004). Yet, the divide between binding and non-binding in environmental law has become blurred with new types of transnational laws and agreements (Bodansky et al, 2007). The chapter is informed by resilience thinking in, for example, addressing multi-level legal dynamics and complex socio-ecological interactions (see e.g. Ebbesson and Folke, 2014). The focus will be on Latin America because

---

[12] For more discussion on equity under the CBD, see e.g. Ituarte-Lima and Subramanian (2013). For equity as a legal principle in environmental law, see Sands and Peel (2012); and for the relationship between equity and ecosystem services see e.g. McDermott et al (2013).

of the serious risks there to biodiversity integrity and people's livelihoods posed by extractive industries but also because of innovative normative developments that have emerged in this region at the national levels, for example, in Peru, and regional level specifically in the Inter-American System of Human Rights.

ASSESSING PROPERTY RIGHTS AS A LEGAL TOOL FOR MAINSTREAMING BIODIVERSITY AND EQUITY

In this section, I assess specific examples of existing property provisions in selected national laws in Peru related to above and below ground biocultural resources.[13] The choice of Peru is motivated by its legal and policy developments regarding access to, and benefit-sharing of, biological diversity and associated knowledge (ABS). Peru has also ongoing debates on ABS reflecting similar discussions in some other developing countries in Latin America that are rich in biological and cultural diversity as well as subsoil resources such as oil and valuable minerals. In this respect, Peru has representative characteristics that identify with other Latin American countries and can provide lessons learned for other regions of the world.

Intangible Biocultural Property Rights

Certain laws and policies within the Peruvian legal system can be seen as a means to mainstream biodiversity and equity. For example, the state has the duty under the Constitution to promote 'biological diversity conservation'[14] and 'general wellbeing based on justice'.[15] In line with these provisions, the cross-sectoral governmental 'Plan Bicentenario: el Perú hacia el 2021' (Centro Nacional de Planeamiento Estratégico, 2011) has relevant elements for both biodiversity and equity mainstreaming by having as part of its objectives 'the conservation and sustainable use of natural resources with an integrated ecosystem approach' and aiming to promote the 'conservation and sustainable use of the country's natural patrimony

---

[13] In this section, I build on the case study in Peru in Ituarte-Lima et al (2011).

[14] Constitución Política del Perú 1993, Art. 68. In order to ensure accuracy, the quotes and references to the Peruvian Constitution and other Peruvian legal and policy documents are based on the original text in Spanish; the translation from Spanish into English is mine.

[15] Ibid, Art. 44.

with efficiency, *equity* and social wellbeing . . . and revalue traditional knowledge' (emphasis added).

An innovative law relevant for implementing the above mentioned constitutional provisions and the Plan Bicentenario, as well as for discussing both biodiversity and equity mainstreaming in the Peruvian legal system, is the 'Law introducing a protection regime for indigenous peoples' collective knowledge associated with biological resources', called Law 27811 which was adopted on 24 July 2002.[16] For reasons described below the content of this law is also especially suitable for analysing biocultural property of local people of an intangible nature. Law 27811 establishes a regime that includes, on the one hand, licence agreements, and on the other hand, public, confidential and local registers of traditional knowledge related to biodiversity. Peru is the first country with a large indigenous population to create such a regime (Alexander et al, 2004).[17]

Certain provisions of Law 27811 are relevant for mainstreaming equity including the equitable distribution of costs and benefits derived from the use of biodiversity and associated knowledge.[18] The term environmental justice can be useful in mainstreaming biodiversity and equity because it builds on contemporary justice theories which address fair distribution of environmental goods together with other aspects such as participation, representation and recognition (Schlosberg, 2007). Besides justice theories, an advantage of building on social movements' interpretations of environmental justice is that they tend to go beyond the dichotomy between the individual and the collective in addressing concerns regarding a responsible interaction of people with nature. In the use of the term environmental justice, social movements 'apply conceptions of justice not only to individuals, but also to groups and communities as well. Here movements have no problem stepping beyond the almost unanimous consensus of justice theorists that definitions of justice apply to individuals alone' (Schlosberg 2007, p. 5). This is important because Amazonian people often view as collective, their rights associated with their biocultural heritage including biodiversity knowledge.

---

16 See: <http://faolex.fao.org/docs/texts/per35624.doc> accessed 22 July 2016. For more information about the consultation process of Law 27811, see Tobin and Swiderska (2001). There are also other laws under the Peruvian legal system that could also be relevant for biodiversity mainstreaming such as e.g. the Ley de mecanismos de retribución por servicios ecosistémicos (2014), see <http://faolex.fao.org/docs/pdf/per135640.pdf> accessed 20 July 2016.

17 Art. 5.

18 Ibid.

Law 27811 explicitly refers to the above mentioned elements of justice (fair distribution, participation, representation and recognition) and relates them to indigenous peoples' collective knowledge about biological resources. Aspects of distribution and participation are reflected in the objectives of Law 27811, which include the promotion of just and equitable benefits-sharing derived from the use of collective knowledge associated with biological resources, and the guaranteeing that use of this knowledge is made with the prior informed consent of indigenous peoples.[19] The representation dimension is present throughout the legal text specifically with the notion of 'representative organisations of indigenous peoples who possess collective knowledge' and with the role of individual leaders representing these organisations in, for example, the Fund for Indigenous Peoples Development.[20] As regards the recognition dimension, Law 27811 adopts a declarative regime in which the state does not grant but recognises indigenous peoples' rights associated with collective knowledge about biodiversity.[21] It explicitly recognises that indigenous peoples hold 'rights which precede the State formation'.[22]

Operationalising the socio-ecological dimensions of SDG 16 and SDG 10 at the national level requires assessing the way national biodiversity laws such as Law 27811 link with other cross-sectoral legal and policy instruments such as the Constitution and cross-sectoral governmental plans such as the Peruvian Plan Bicentenario. Mainstreaming biodiversity and equity in distinct dimensions of property rights such as land and forest rights mentioned in these cross-sectoral instruments would also contribute to make effective biodiversity-related knowledge rights of Amazonian people. In many cases, effective land and resource tenure rights are a precondition to exercise the rights stated in Law 27811 due to the fact that traditional ecological knowledge is often connected to specific land and ecosystems. In turn, the recognition of rights preceding the state formation in Law 27811 could also be used to interpret provisions referring to land and forests in cross-sectoral legal instruments in a progressive way i.e. in a way that the bundle of property rights of forest people is respected.

Tangible Property Rights: Rights over Land and the Subsoil

Land property rights are particularly relevant to people depending directly on biodiversity and ecosystems for their livelihoods. In the Peruvian

---

19 Law 27811, 2002, Art. 5.
20 Law 27811, 2002, Art. 39.
21 See e.g. Law 27811, 2002, Art. 1.
22 Law 27811, 2002, Art. 2(a).

rainforest, Awajun people are one of the many ethnic groups that inhabit the Peruvian Amazon region. Awajun, together with the Wampis, Achuar and Shuar, belong to the Jivaro ethnic group. The Awajun territory spreads out over 30,000 sq km in the Amazon basin in northern Peru. This rainforest region in Peru has remarkable diverse flora and various endemic species (Croat et al, 2005); the other recognised geopolitical regions in Peru are the coast and mountains. The Jivaro ethnic group has specialised knowledge about the ecosystem, flora and fauna, including familiarity with particular places to hunt animals and gather fruits and medicinal plants in certain areas (Descola, 1996). The biological diversity in Amazonian peoples' land is partly derived from the selection and dissemination of certain plants by local people, which, in turn, contributes to the progressive adaptation and variety of flora (Croat et al, 2005). For an illustration of the ecosystem and housing where an Awajun family live, see Figure 5.1 and Figure 5.2, respectively.

Despite the recognition of the rights of the Awajun and other indigenous people as rural and native communities by the Peruvian legal system, these groups are often discriminated when attempting to exercise their environmental-related property rights. Article 89 of the Peruvian Constitution recognises rural and native communities' legal personality; acknowledges their autonomy in their organisation, communal work, and use and free disposal of their lands within the framework of the law, and mentions that the state respects their cultural identity. Yet, this same Article 89 uses the category of 'land abandonment' (which in reality is often not at all abandoned but provides the livelihood for indigenous peoples and local communities) and refers to Article 88 which explicitly states a preference for agricultural expansion (which often stands in stark contrast to indigenous peoples' land use).[23] Under this Article, the land deemed legally abandoned reverts to state dominium for adjudication and sale.[24] In practice, these lands can also be used by extractive industries as such actions do not fall under the category of 'land abandonment'. Amazonian people's environmental management systems may contribute to the biocultural diversity of rainforests. However, they are often not considered as exercising agrarian property rights (Ludescher, 1997). When land is not used for commercial cultivation, which is the case of many Amazonian communities, it can be easily deemed abandoned (ibid.). This situation has opened the door for forest peoples' dispossession (Barié,

---

23 This Article uses the term 'preferably' (*preferentemente*) but does not mention in relation to which other activities.

24 Constitución Política del Perú 1993, Art. 88.

Figure 5.1 Peruvian Amazon

Photographs: Ituarte-Lima (2006).

Figure 5.2 Interior of an Awajun household

2003) affecting people's rights over forest resources and spaces, including sacred sites or areas of cultural significance.

Constitutional provisons on the conservation and sustainable use of biological diversity and Amazonian people's property rights over the land were especially challenging to implement during the armed conflict between Peru and Ecuador.[25] UNEP (2009, p. 17) reports that conflict 'tends to confuse property rights, undercut positive environmental practices, and compromise dispute resolution mechanisms'. For more than 150 years, the border between Peru and Ecuador – which constitutes a relatively inaccessible rainforest region – has repeatedly been contested between these two countries. Major armed conflict occurred during 1942 and, in the same year, the two countries signed the Rio de Janeiro Protocol aiming to overcome the border dispute (St John, 1996). However, hostilities continued, especially during 1981 and 1995 (ibid.). Finally, in 1998, after peace negotiations and the intervention of other countries (Argentina, Brazil, Chile, and the USA) the Acta Presidencial de Brasilia (1998) was signed, and the international borders between the two countries were specified and agreed (Alcalde et al, 2009).[26]

In overcoming conflicts, it is necessary to 'ensure that there are processes in place within peace agreements for the transparent, equitable and legitimate definition and realisation of property rights and resource revenues and tenure' (UNEP 2009, p. 31). The Acta Presidencial de Brasilia (1998) recognised the need to update bilateral cooperation mechanisms for promoting economic and social development (Alcalde et al, 2009). Likewise, this treaty highlighted that these mechanisms should promote biodiversity conservation and the sustainable use of the ecosystems of the common border and strengthen the cultural identity of native populations (ibid.). After the peace agreement, in the mountainous Cordillera del Condor border region between Ecuador and Peru, a bi-national project implemented by Fundación Natura and Conservation International–Peru, with technical support and monitoring provided by both governments, the International Tropical Timber Organisation (ITTO) culminated in the creation of Condor–Kutuku Conservation Corridor, also labelled as a Peace Park.[27] Subsequent to the signing of the Acta Presidencial de Brasilia, some Amazonian peoples organised several meetings in both

---

[25] For a study of the political negotiations and tensions between Peru and Ecuador, see López Contreras (2004).

[26] The Acta Presidencial de Brasilia is available at: <http://www4.congreso.gob.pe/comisiones/1999/exteriores/libro1/2avolum/02acta.htm>

[27] See <http://www.conservation.org/publications/Documents/CI_Policy-Center_Peace-building-Case-Study_Ecuador-Peru.pdf>

countries and created an umbrella organisation called Consejo de Pueblos Wampis, Awajun and Shuar (COPWASH). This initiative is 'a process of exchange and strengthening of ancestral family ties' (COPWASH, 2003). In a meeting in Santa María de Nieva-Peru in 2002, an Aguaruna leader stated that 'this plan is part of the words, feelings and thoughts of Shuar, Awajun, Wampis; through the interaction of our visions of life, it shall serve to crystallize and consolidate peoples' development with identity' (ibid.).[28] The project is supported by Coordinadora de Organizaciones Indígenas de la Cuenca Amazónica (COICA), which is a regional Amazonian organisation with its national affiliates Asociación Interétnica de Desarrollo de la Selva Peruana (AIDESEP) in Peru and Confederación de Nacionalidades Indígenas del Ecuador (CONAIE) in Ecuador. The members and representatives in the project proposal are Consejo Aguaruna y Huambisa (CAH) in Peru and Federación Interprovincial de Centros Shuar (FICSH) in Ecuador. Hence, the Wampis, Awajun and Shuar have asserted the transnational dimension of their relations by forming the COPWASH organisation – which unites Amazonian people located in both countries – and by prompting alliances between national organisations such as AIDESEP in Peru and CONAIE in Ecuador, and COICA with a regional scope (Ituarte-Lima, 2011).

Beyond land property rights, there are also other relevant property rights provisions in the Peruvian Constitution 1993 which have, in practice, adversely affected biodiversity and exacerbated forest people's historical dispossession and contributed to inequity. Although forest-dependent communities may have recognised property rights over land under the Peruvian legal system, that does not mean they have also acquired property rights over subsoil resources. Articles 54 and 66 of the 1993 Peruvian Constitution mention that the state has sovereign control over renewable and non-renewable natural resources and is entitled to give extractive concessions.[29] Concessions over mining resources are an example of subsoil resources which have generated risks to biodiversity and the livelihoods of the Amazonian people such as to the Awajun, Shuar and Wampis indigenous peoples mentioned earlier. The Cordillera del Condor, on the border of Peru and Ecuador, is a topographical and geological singular place which has ecological niches with rich biodiversity with even species yet to be described (Özkaynak et al, 2012) and plays a key role in the great hydrological cycle connecting the Andes

---

[28] The Aguaruna are also called Awajun.

[29] For more information about forest concessions in Peru, see Salo and Toivonen (2009).

with the Amazon (Alcalde et al, 2009). Özkaynak et al (2012) consider that mining activities put at risk biodiversity in both countries including those located in protected areas in the Cordillera del Condor.[30] They also consider that resistance to mining and demands from Amazonian peoples in the Cordillera del Condor have not found the right channels and certain conflicts have involved high levels of violence such as the repression in Bagua in 2009 in Peru, which came to be known as the 'Bagua massacre' (Özkaynak et al 2012; Chicaiza 2010). In June 2009, Awajun and Wampis protesters demanded the repeal of 11 legislative decrees that they considered created the conditions for the dispossession of their lands and natural resources by large extractive corporations (Santos-Granero and Barclay, 2011). The Peruvian government, using an elite police force with armoured vehicles, helicopters and tear gas removed the Awajun and Wampis protesters who were equipped with spears and rocks, and were blocking a road near the town of Bagua. Thirty-three people died in the confrontations, including nine policemen and it is estimated that around two hundred civilians were wounded by police shots (Santos-Granero and Barclay, 2011).

As in the case of concessions over mining, conflicts about the appropriate allocation of rights and duties on natural resources have also arisen as a result of the state's concessions for oil exploration and extraction in the Peruvian Amazon (Orta-Martínez and Matt Finer, 2010). In the mid-1990s, the Peruvian government conceded concessions to transnational oil corporations for the exploration and exploitation of hydrocarbons in indigenous territories (see Finer et al, 2008; Urteaga-Crovetto, 2000). For example, the oil exploitation by different companies including Occidental Peruana Inc., Petroperú and PetroPeru and associated environmental effects including biodiversity impacts in the Corrientes river for more than four decades has been a source of conflict (FECONACO, 2006). Since 1997, the Federación de Comunidades Nativas del Río Corrientes (FECONACO), a federation of Amazonian communities living by this river, has denounced the effects of such oil exploitation and associated water pollution in the livelihoods and health of indigenous people (Chirif 2006; see also FECONACO, 2006).

In the development of a toolkit for mainstreaming biodiversity and equity in effective ways, it is important to consider tools and indicators for assessing not only the text of the laws and policies but also how laws

---

[30] The Cordillera del Condor includes, among others, the Podocarpus–El Cóndor Biosphere Reserve and the Tabaconas Namballe National Sanctuary in Peru.

and policies operate in practice. Property rights over land and subsoil resources are challenging contexts for reaching SDG 16 in peace and justice and building strong institutions in a way that biodiversity and equity are mainstreamed in practice. In some cases, national property laws relating to forest and subsoil ownership have had adverse effects on biodiversity and have exacerbated local people's historical dispossession while contributing to inequity. The actual impact of a broad range of law and policies from property law to peace agreements as well as the role of a wide range of actors from governments, to local communities and transnational non-governmental actors such as Conservation International and the case of COICA mentioned earlier are important considerations.

A HUMAN-RIGHTS BASED APPROACH TO PROPERTY RIGHTS AND JUSTICE

As mentioned earlier, SDG 16 includes justice and strong institutions as key elements. Property provisions in national legal frameworks offer a space for legal innovation for environmental justice but can also pose significant risks to biodiversity and generate environmental injustice, as shown in the above section. Hence, how to understand the conceptual connections between property and justice becomes relevant in further understanding the socio-ecological dimensions of this SDG 10 and its focus on ending inequality. In this section, I examine whether the Inter-American Court's specification of property rights with a human-rights based approach is suitable for understanding the relationships between tangible and intangible property rights and mainstreaming equity and justice approaches in socio-ecological dimensions of property rights. I focus on the *Community Mayagna (Sumo) Awas Tingni* v. *Nicaragua* case (thereafter Mayagna case) which involves extractive industry concessions by the state specifically for large-scale logging in Nicaragua in the land inhabited by the Community Mayagna (Sumo) Awas Tingni (thereafter Mayagna community). What is of interest here is examining if this case which discusses socio-ecological dimensions of property rights can be useful for deepening the understanding of the connections between tangible and intangible property rights, and the relationships between property rights and justice.[31]

[31] For case details of *Community Mayagna (Sumo) Awas Tingni* v. *Nicaragua*, see Ituarte-Lima (2004).

Property Rights

When examining the Mayagna case, the Court acknowledged distinct dimensions of property rights as well as various forms of exercising these rights. In its final judgment,[32] the Court considered the scope of Article 21 and the *travaux préparatoires* (preparatory works) of the American Convention on Human Rights (thereafter American Convention). The American Convention, in its Article 21 under the title 'Right to Property', provides that 'Everyone has the right to the use and enjoyment of his property'. According to Judge Garcia Ramirez (2001, para. 11, p. 3), in the preparatory works of the American Convention one can trace the evolution of the language of Article 21 to its present-day wording and considered that:

> The language in which this right is framed was meant to accommodate all subjects protected by the Convention. Obviously, there is no single model for the use and enjoyment of property. Every people, according to its culture, interests, aspirations, customs, characteristics and beliefs, can institute its own distinctive formula for the use and enjoyment of property. . .

The Court, given the characteristics of the Mayagna case, considers that some specifications are required on the concept of property in indigenous communities. The Mayagna are an example of a community with direct dependence on their ecosystems in their daily life and who make their living from agriculture, hunting and fishing, among other activities. The Court defines property recognising both tangible and intangible dimensions of property:

> 'Property' can be defined as those material things which can be possessed, as well as any right which may be part of a person's patrimony; that concept includes . . . corporeal and incorporeal elements and any other intangible object capable of having value. . . (Inter-American Court of Human Rights (2001) para. 144).[33]

---

[32] Inter-American Court of Human Rights (2001) I/A Court H.R., Case of the *Mayagna (Sumo) Awas Tingni Community* v. *Nicaragua*. Merits, Reparations and Costs. Judgment of 31 August 2001. Series C No. 79. The Court's judgment was made in 2001 and the case was closed in 2008. All documents referring to the Court's judgment including the opinion of the judges are available at <http://www.corteidh.or.cr/cf/Jurisprudencia2/index.cfm?lang=en> accessed 16 July 2016. For the monitoring of compliance with the judgment, see I/A Court H.R., Case of the *Mayagna (Sumo) Awas Tingni Community* v. *Nicaragua*. Monitoring Compliance with Judgment. Order of the Inter-American Court of Human Rights of 3 April 2009 <http://www.corteidh.or.cr/cf/Jurisprudencia2/index.cfm?lang=en>

[33] cf *Ivcher Bronstein* case, *supra* note 9, para. 122.

In considering the Mayagna context, the Court highlights tangible dimensions of property rights such as recognising land rights as the basis of indigenous groups' economic survival. Likewise, the Court recognises intangible dimensions of property by recognising that the close ties of indigenous people with land are a fundamental basis for their 'cultures, their spiritual life, their integrity' and adds: 'For indigenous communities, relations to the land are not merely a matter of possession and production but a material and spiritual element which they must fully enjoy, even to preserve their cultural legacy and transmit it to future generations' (Inter-American Court of Human Rights (2001) para. 149).

Further elaborating the reasons for supporting their argumentation in the Mayagna case judgment, Judges Cançado Trindade, Pacheco Gómez and Abreu Burelli (2001) connect the tangible and intangible dimensions of property rights through identifying the linkages between the Mayagna communities' land property rights with their family, cultural and religious development. These judges recall the public hearing held in the Inter-American Court in November 2000, where two members and representatives of the Mayagna community highlighted 'the vital importance of the relationship of the members of the Community with the lands they occupy, not only for their own subsistence, but also for their family, cultural and religious development. Hence their characterisation of the territory as *sacred*, for encompassing not only the members of the Community who are alive, but also the mortal remains of their ancestors, as well as their divinities' (para. 2).

Property Rights and Intertemporal Dimensions of Justice

Connecting property with the intertemporal dimensions of justice constitutes another entry point for understanding the links between tangible and intangible property rights as well as the dimensions of justice. In interpreting Article 21 of the American Convention, Judges Trindade, Pacheco Gómez and Abreu Burelli (2001) considered that the intertemporal dimension of what seems to characterise the relationship of the indigenous persons of the Community with their lands needs to be acknowledged bearing in mind the facts of the case. They considered that what can be inferred is that 'just as the land they occupy belongs to them, they in turn belong to their land' (para. 8). They referred both to intertemporal rights and responsibilities that arise from this characterisation of the land by the Mayagna community including the 'prevalence that they attribute to the element of *conservation* over the simple exploitation of natural resources'. These judges also refer to the importance of the:

> . . . spiritual and material relationship of the members of the Community with the lands they have occupied, not only to preserve the legacy of past generations, but also to undertake the responsibilities that they have assumed in respect of future generations (para. 9).

As in the above case, Judge Garcia Ramirez (2001), on the Mayagna case, referred to the right of indigenous peoples to 'uphold their responsibilities towards future generations' quoting Article 25 of the Draft Declaration on Discrimination against Indigenous Peoples, prepared by the United Nations Economic and Social Council's Sub-Commission on Prevention of Discrimination and Protection of Minorities (E/CN.4/Sub.2/1994/2/Add.1, 20 April 1994). Citing Article 24, he articulated the relationship between tangible land property rights and intangible dimensions of property of some indigenous peoples, and in particular, their 'distinctive cultural and spiritual relationship with the land, territories, water. . .'. Garcia Ramirez (2001) cited the Geneva Convention No. 169 Concerning Indigenous and Tribal Peoples in Independent Countries, by the International Labour Organisation (Geneva, 1989) including Article 14(1) on tangible dimensions of property, specifically 'ownership and possession of the peoples concerned over the lands which they traditionally occupy' and Article 13(1) on intangible dimensions in particular the duty of the governments to respect 'the special importance for the cultures and spiritual values of the peoples concerned of their relationship with the lands or territories . . . in particular the collective aspects of this relationship' (para. 7).

Property Rights and Access to Justice

When analysing Article 21 on property rights, as applied to the Mayagna case, the Court assessed relevant national legal instruments and referred to Article 5 of the 1995 Constitution of Nicaragua which recognises ethnic pluralism as part of the principles of the Nicaraguan nation. The Court (para. 116) acknowledged that this Constitution also recognises the different forms of ownership, respect for self-determination and autonomy of indigenous peoples, and stipulates that the forms of property, including communitarian property, will be guaranteed and encouraged without discrimination. Likewise, the Court (para. 119) called to articles relevant to property rights under cross-sectoral laws such as Law No. 28 (1987) regulating the Autonomy Statute of the Regions of the Atlantic Coast of Nicaragua including Article 9 that provides that natural resources 'must benefit their inhabitants in a just proportion' and which recognises property rights over collective land. Based on the above, the Court considers that norms recognising and protecting indigenous communal property exist in Nicaragua and hence consider that the right to property under the American Convention was not violated in the Mayagna case.

Yet, in articulating the arguments of their judgment and in concluding that other rights were indeed violated, the Court makes the connection between property and access to justice. The Court concludes that the state violated Article 25 of the American Convention on rights to judicial protection of the members of the Mayagna community, in connection with Article 1(1) on the obligation to respect the rights and freedoms and the right to non-discrimination and Article 2 on the state's obligation to adopt legislative or other measures as may be necessary to give effect to those rights or freedoms.

Recalling that Article 25 on 'Right to Judicial Protection' is a cornerstone of the rule of law in a democratic society (para. 112), the Court considers that for the state to comply with obligations derived from this Article 25, 'it is not enough for the remedies to exist formally, since they must also be effective' (para. 114). The Court (para. 104 (n)) refers to the arguments of the Commission relevant for equity, specifically that:

> . . . for indigenous peoples, access to a simple, rapid, and effective legal remedy is especially important in connection with the enjoyment of their human rights, given the conditions of vulnerability under which they normally find themselves for historical reasons and due to their current social circumstances.

In interpreting Article 25 in connection with Article 2 of the American Convention, the Court interprets the state obligation concerning access to justice not only in reference to judicial protection but also expands the interpretation to encompass the obligations related to legislative and executive measures including adopting, in its domestic law, the necessary legislative, administrative or other measures to create effective mechanisms related to property rights. Furthermore, the Court makes relevant arguments for connecting property rights and justice not just in theory but also in practice. The Court (para. 136) considers that the state has obligations to both 'suppressing practices of any type that carry with them the violation of guarantees set forth in the convention' and 'developing practices which are conducive to effective respect for such guarantees'.[34] In applying these arguments to the Mayagna case, the Court referred to dimensions relevant to both tangible land rights, specifically the delimitation and titling of the property of the members of the Mayagna community in connection with intangible dimensions by raising that this delimitation

[34] cf *Baena Ricardo et al* case, *supra* note 9, para. 180; and *Cantoral Benavides* case, *supra* note 48, para. 178.

ought to be made in 'accordance with the customary law, values, customs and mores of that Community' (para. 139).

Other international instruments resonate with the considerations of the judges which link the intangible with tangible dimensions of property such as the Akwé:Kon voluntary guidelines for the conduct of cultural, environmental and social impact assessments regarding proposed developments on, or which are likely to impact on, sacred sites, lands and waters traditionally occupied or used by indigenous and local communities (CBD, 2004), Recommendation on the Safeguarding of Traditional Culture and Folklore (UNESCO, 1989) and UNDRIP, the United Nations Declaration on the Rights of Indigenous Peoples (UN 2007). For example, UNDRIP refers to the rights of indigenous peoples towards future generations. As for intangible dimensions, Article 13 guarantees indigenous peoples the right to 'revitalize, use, develop and transmit to future generations their histories, languages, oral traditions' and 'distinctive spiritual relationship' with their lands (Art. 25). In terms of tangible dimensions, the UN (2007) recognises indigenous peoples' 'right to the lands, territories and resources which they have traditionally owned, occupied or otherwise used or acquired' (Art. 26).

DISCUSSION AND CONCLUDING REMARKS

A transformative development of biodiversity law would entail mainstreaming biodiversity in laws and policies concerning the extractive industry including oil extraction and large-scale mining because of significant risks posed to biodiversity integrity and equity in biodiverse countries by these sectors. While I have provided Peru as an illustration, other developing countries, for example those in Africa, also face related risks (see Abuodha, 2002). Based on Articles 7(c) and 8(l), the CBD Executive Secretary has stressed the importance of regulating and managing processes and activities that have significant adverse impacts on biodiversity.[35] While the 2016 UN Biodiversity Conference addressed issues affecting particularly agriculture, forests and fisheries, the upcoming 2018 UN Biodiversity Conference will address explicitly the energy, mining, infrastructure and health sectors. Decision XIII/3, adopted by the Conference of the Parties of the Convention, explicitly recognises that

[35] CBD, Note by the Executive Secretary: Mainstreaming and the Integration of Biodiversity within and across Sectors (10 November 2015). https://www.cbd.int/doc/meetings/biodiv/impws-2015-01/other/impws-2015-01-background-en.pdf

'extractive industries as oil and gas and mining . . . have the potential to impact adversely on biodiversity' and '102. Decides that the Conference of the Parties should consider, at its fourteenth meeting, the mainstreaming of biodiversity into the following sectors: energy and mining; infrastructure . . . and health;' (emphasis added).

Another reason for mainstreaming biodiversity in the extractive industry sector responds to the need to overcome inequality especially in many emerging and middle-income countries with significant challenges and with existing strong social inequalities towards certain groups within these countries. For instance, the risks posed by the extractive industry are particularly acute in the case of local people in more vulnerable situations who depend directly on particular ecosystems for their daily subsistence and who hold valuable traditional ecological knowledge such as the Awajun Amazonian people mentioned earlier. Furthermore, defending biodiversity integrity and human rights of local populations have become risky and even deadly endeavours in some places in Latin America and South East Asia (OHCHR, 2016) especially where strong economic interests such as in the case of the extractive industries, co-exist with weak institutions and corruption. These findings including the multi-level legal dynamics and complex socio-ecological interactions are relevant for sustainability science literature on transformations for sustainability. The resilience literature is becoming increasingly interested in the processes that lead to sustainability transformations (Olsson et al, 2014), and reconnecting to the biosphere (see among others, Folke et al, 2001). Further studies are needed that explicitly discuss the interface between distinct dimensions of resilience, biodiversity law and interconnected socio-ecological risks.

Laws relevant for addressing socio-ecological risks and fostering sustainability transformations cover a wide range of different laws which raise specific difficulties and also reveal the limitations of environmental law. While prescriptions in international legal treaties such as the CBD are considered to be binding ('hard law') between the state parties because the respective state 'has consented to be bound by a treaty which is in force' (Art. 2 (g) Vienna Convention on the Law of Treaties 1968), international environmental regimes in general and biodiversity law in particular face significant challenges in addressing socio-ecological risks. Some authors (e.g. Driesen, 2003) consider that most environmental treaties are weak when compared to trade agreements because under the World Trade Organisation (WTO), adjudicative decisions bind parties, with or without their consent, and also these agreements are able to incorporate trade restrictions as enforcement tools. This is not the case under the CBD. Similarly, countries are bound to various international treaties and may have different obligations under international law. For example, the USA, a major economic player including in the extractive industry sector, is not a state party of CBD (it has signed but not ratified this treaty) but is a state party of agreements relevant for the environment under the WTO. An area for further research for mainstreaming biodiversity and justice across laws and policies are the environmental justice concerns that emerge from making transnational extractive industry corporations responsible for their environmental impacts and human rights violations across borders (see e.g. Ebbesson, 2009; Savaresi, 2015).

Considering the wide spectrum of different laws addressing socio-ecological risks, specific legal assessment tools are needed for operationalising biodiversity mainstreaming and the socio-ecological dimensions of SDG 16 and SDG 10. This chapter has revealed the importance of developing legal assessment tools that can bring to light innovations on socio-ecological-related property rights such as provisions under the Peruvian Law 27811 and Plan Bicentenario, but also legal tools that can uncover legal fictions such as 'abandonment of land' that pose risks to biodiversity and people's livelihoods. The progressive recognition of intangible property rights including under the Peruvian Law 27811 will not be completely effective unless there is synchronisation between these biocultural rights provisions and distinct socio-ecological-related property rights specifically in the so-called tangible property including land and subsoil property rights in constitutional law, agrarian law and energy law. This chapter has shown that peace agreements of a bilateral nature such as the Acta Presidencial de Brasilia between Peru and Ecuador and property-related provisions included in them can be part of the legal instruments to mainstream biodiversity and equity with impacts from the binational scale to the community level.

This chapter has also highlighted that human rights normative developments especially in the Inter-American System of Human Rights can be helpful for implementing socio-ecological dimensions of SDG 16, in particular its justice and strong institutions components. Likewise, normative developments on conceptually linking property and justice can be helpful in mainstreaming biodiversity and equity in sectoral and cross-sectoral laws and policies. A human-rights based approach to property is suitable for this purpose and can help synchronise intangible and tangible property rights. The findings of this chapter revealing connections between biodiversity and human rights, and specifically, concrete linkages between property rights, access to justice, cultural rights and rights of environment defenders are relevant for academic and policy discussions on the interdependency and invisibility of civil and political rights, and economic, social and cultural rights.

The Inter-American Court of Human Rights (2001) has recognised that 'human rights treaties are live instruments whose interpretation must adapt to the evolution of the times and, specifically, to current living conditions' (para. 146, p. 74). Current risks to the living conditions of people in more vulnerable situations and to biological and culturally diverse areas demand transformations for sustainability. Time will tell whether the momentum for strategic synergies between biodiversity law, 2030 Agenda, human rights law and legal and policy advances on linking tangible and intangible dimensions of property rights, can translate to more just relations where all human and non-human beings can thrive.

6. Inequalities in environmental risks and resilience within urban populations in low- and middle-income nations

David Satterthwaite

INTRODUCTION

An interest in environmental risks goes from those risks facing an individual (for example, drinking unsafe water) to those facing the whole planet and virtually all life forms (for example, human-induced climate change). For human populations, most environmental risks can be assessed for their health impacts and with clear pathways – from the presence of an environmental hazard to who is exposed to the hazard and who is most impacted – for instance because they are particularly susceptible to the hazard and/or lack the capacity to cope and to adapt. Environmental health risks are present in all the environments where women and men, boys and girls are: housing and living conditions; working conditions; access to services and their quality; and open space. And they include pathogens (disease-causing agents), pollutants and physical hazards.

The importance of understanding environmental risks is because they cause or contribute to a very large proportion of the health burden (years of life lost/premature death, illness and injury) in low-income and most middle-income nations. They have an even larger contribution to health burdens that are easily prevented or cured. Much of the (limited) literature on environmental risks in urban areas in low- and middle-income countries focuses on their impacts on low-income groups or groups facing discrimination. However, in the past few years, there has been a growing interest in understanding inequalities in risks, in part to show who is most at risk and why, in part to show what is possible in the reduction of risk. Equality for health means the absence of unfair and avoidable or remediable difference in health among population groups (WHO definition cited in Solar and Irwin, 2007) so this can also be interpreted as the absence of exposure to the pollutants, pathogens and physical hazards that contribute to unfair and avoidable difference.

This interest in understanding and addressing inequality is also evident in the Sustainable Development Goals (SDGs) to which almost all national governments have committed for 2015–2030. These include universal provision of risk-reducing infrastructure and services, adequate and safe housing, and access to justice. And to leave no one behind. Indeed, a *Lancet* editorial (2015) ended with the comment 'Prioritising and equitably addressing urban health post-2015 is an opportunity to accelerate improvements in health – sustainably and justly.' The Millennium Development Goals that preceded the SDGs had much less interest in equality.

WHY FOCUS ON URBAN POPULATIONS?

By 2016, 55 per cent of the world's population lived in urban areas and this percentage is projected to rise to 66 per cent in 2030 (United Nations, 2015). Virtually all the growth in the world's population in the next few decades is expected to be in urban centres in what are currently low- and middle-income nations (ibid). Whether or not the SDGs are met within an urbanising world or dangerous climate change avoided, depends heavily on the quality and capacity of urban governments.

Within the literature on development and on environmental risks, there is a strong theme that rural populations are larger and face the most serious problems. There is constant reference to 'urban bias' (i.e. that urban populations are favoured in the policies and funding of governments and international agencies) that goes back at least to the 1970s (see, for instance, Lipton, 1977). There was also the dramatic moment when what is perhaps the most influential book on environment and development issues – *Our Common Future* (World Commission on Environment and Development, 1987) – almost had its chapter on urban issues cut (as if urban areas have no importance in discussing environmental issues).[1] There have been many papers insisting that almost all poverty is in rural areas (see in particular Ravallion et al, 2007, and for a review of this literature see Mitlin and

[1] The author of this chapter worked with Jorge Hardoy and the secretariat of the World Commission on Environment and Development to write the chapter on urban areas. Mrs Brundtland who headed this commission asked for the chapter on urban areas to be cut from the Commission's Report and it was only through the opposition of J.W. McNeill, the head of the Commission Secretariat, that this was avoided.

Satterthwaite, 2012). The reports of the Joint Monitoring Programme for Water and Sanitation set up by UNICEF and WHO constantly stress how provision for these is much worse in rural areas than in urban areas (see WHO/UNICEF 2014, 2015). All this suggests a need to focus on risks to rural populations.

But this chapter suggests that the scale of environmental risks in urban areas (and the poverty that often underlies many of these risks) have been under-estimated, especially in low-income and most middle-income nations. In part, this has been masked by that lack of disaggregated data. For many nations, not only is the data available on environmental risks very inadequate – but it come from national sample surveys that present only aggregate statistics 'for urban areas'. What a growing number of studies are highlighting is the large sections of the urban population or those of particular cities that face very serious environmental risks and high levels of premature death and serious illness and injury (see Sverdlik, 2011). It is precisely when attention is given to inequalities within particular cities that the scale and nature of the health burden suffered by their low-income population from environmental hazards becomes evident. Indeed, in some cities or smaller urban centres, not only may there be no urban bias, but there may be an urban penalty with health burdens higher among urban populations than rural populations (Mitlin and Satterthwaite, 2012). A *Lancet* Commission recognised that cities' health advantages compared to rural areas are not guaranteed and that these benefits must be 'actively promoted and maintained' over time (Rydin et al, 2012, p. 2,079). Vlahov et al (2011) note how capturing and addressing such health inequalities will also depend upon gathering health data that can be disaggregated, providing relevant health statistics for each neighbourhood or small area.

Two of the defining characteristics of urban areas are the scale of the population and their spatial concentration (density). Many nations' definition of urban areas is on the basis of a population threshold although this varies a lot – from a few hundred to 20,000 or more inhabitants (see United Nations, 2015). Some include a minimum density. We know that urban areas can have very high health standards – for instance in among the highest life expectancies at birth. We also know that environmental health risks in cities can be kept very low – as evidenced in their very small contribution to premature death. But this depends on the competence, capacity and accountability of their governments and of course on the extent to which higher levels of government support this. Concentrate people, industries and motor vehicles and all their wastes without a local capacity to manage this and cities become among the world's most unhealthy places. This can be seen too in very low life expectancies at birth, the high infant, child and maternal mortality rates and the very large preventable health burdens. Where data on these are available for wards or districts within cities, these show how conditions are much worse in particular wards and districts. This is especially so if the focus is on conditions in informal settlements as described in more detail below.

ENVIRONMENTAL HEALTH RISKS

There are many dramatic comparisons that can be made to show the scale of inequality related to environmental health risks. For instance, when reviewing case studies of provision for water in urban areas for a UN Report on Water and Sanitation in 2003, we found a 500-fold difference in the price of water per litre (UN-Habitat, 2003). There are many studies showing the large differences in levels of indoor air pollution between (mostly low-income) households that rely on dirty fuels and have poor ventilation, and higher income groups that use clean fuels (these are reviewed in Satterthwaite and Sverdlik, 2012).

Available data on health outcomes that are heavily influenced by environmental risks such as under-five mortality rates in urban contexts point to a more than 30-fold difference; these rates should be and often are under 5 per 1,000 live births but they have been found to exceed 150 in some of the very few studies in informal settlements (APHRC, 2002). In addition, there are still many nations that have average under-five mortality rates of more than 100 per 1,000 live births in urban areas and it is likely that among poorer groups it will be much higher than this, and conversely, among richer groups, much lower. What is also revealing is inequalities in health outcomes within particular cities – for instance in infant, under-five and maternal mortality rates. But in trying to assess environmental risks in particular urban contexts and how these differ socially (e.g. by income group) and spatially (e.g. in comparing formal and informal settlements) we are faced with an astonishing lack of detailed studies and a very large number of contributory factors. Figure 6.1 illustrates this as it lists the many economic, social and environmental determinants of health in urban areas.

The World Health Organization (WHO) defines the social determinants of health as the conditions in which people are born, grow, live, work and age.[2] WHO notes how these are shaped by the distribution of money, power and resources at global, national and local levels. Of

---

2 <http://www.who.int/social_determinants/en/>

course for urban areas they are profoundly shaped by the competence, capacity and accountability of their (local) governments. It is worth noting how there is little discussion of the environmental determinants of health, as environmental determinants are subsumed within social determinants. Here we come to the confusion arising from the word 'environmental' being used to denote environmental health issues and environmental issues related to natural resource use and waste generation (including greenhouse gases). But it is difficult to separate many key health determinants into 'social' and 'environmental' – see for instance regular, safe-to-drink water supplies and good quality toilets available in the home are key environmental health determinants (greatly reducing risks from diarrhoeal diseases and other water-borne, food-borne and water-washed diseases) but whether or not these are provided are socially or politically determined.

In Figure 6.1, the interest in this chapter is in the scale and nature of unequal health outcomes and the contribution of environmental health risks. Figure 6.1 does not list environmental health risks but contexts where environmental risks can appear (working and living conditions), factors that can contribute to such risks (including lack of capacity to act within local governments) and factors that can address risks (including health-related knowledge and empowerment).

In looking for factors that contribute to unequal health outcomes, the focus can be on key global and national influences – for instance the success of the city economy within the global system of production and the incomes and livelihoods generated. Or the impacts of the policies and funding allocations of national government – for instance where these do or do not make funding available or support local revenue generation to address environmental health risks. Or the contribution of international funding agencies (or in reality for most agencies the lack of a contribution as they have chosen not to support urban projects or choose not to focus support on risk-reducing infrastructure and services). Or the focus can be on city/municipal government influences on health outcomes – for instance in the extent to which they provide or ensure provision of risk-reducing infrastructure (safe, sufficient, regular easily accessed and affordable water supplies, toilets within the home with safe removal and disposal of faecal matter, all-weather roads, covered drains, electricity among others) and risk-reducing services (health care and emergency services, schools and day-care centres, regular household solid waste collections, effective policing). It is worth emphasising what was noted earlier – how much the diminution of environmental health risks in urban contexts depends on the competence, capacity and accountability of their local governments.

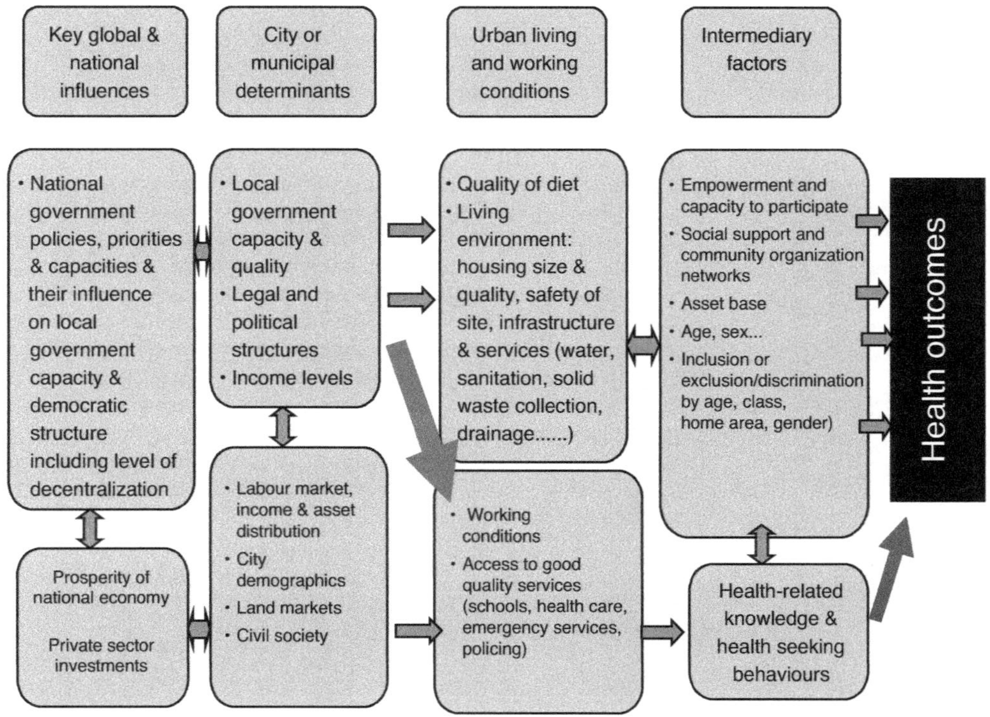

Source: Mitlin and Satterthwaite (2012). An early version of this figure is presented and discussed in Cairncross, Hardoy and Satterthwaite (1990). It has been improved and added to since then – see for example, Kjellstrom and Mercado (2008); Vlahov et al (2007).

Figure 6.1 The many economic, social and environmental determinants of health in urban areas

INEQUALITIES IN ENVIRONMENTAL HEALTH RISKS AND HEALTH OUTCOME

Inequalities in exposure to environmental health risks are well understood – such as in exposure to biological pathogens (e.g. those causing diarrhoeal diseases and acute respiratory infections), chemical pollutants (e.g. high levels of indoor or outdoor air pollution) and physical hazards (e.g. motor traffic or extreme weather). This is also the case for inequalities in health outcomes – for instance inequalities between social groups in premature death (especially for infants, children and mothers). There are also many inequalities in housing and living conditions, working conditions and access to services that fall within the economic, social and environmental determinants of health.

These inequalities (and the inequity that underlies them) can be seen and compared between nations – for instance in average life-expectancy at birth or in the scale of the preventable disease burden. There is an enormous range of indicators available to compare conditions or government performance at national level. These same inequalities can also be seen and compared within nations (e.g. between different population groups as in rural versus urban populations) and within specific localities (e.g. by street or ward within a city). Ironically, there is far less data available on indicators that have relevance for risks at the ward and street level (i.e. where it can actually inform where interventions are needed and with whom) than at the national level.

Any discussion of inequality is interested in comparisons between groups so it is important to be clear about which groups are being considered. Two startling comparisons have been used to highlight the need for action on health inequalities in high-income nations. In 1990, life expectancy at birth for an African-American in Harlem was lower than for a man in Bangladesh (McCord and Freeman, 1990). Glasgow's Calton area had a life expectancy at birth of 54 years in 2011 and this was reported as the lowest life expectancy in the United Kingdom and Europe and of many areas of the world.[3] But if the first of these had compared life expectancy at birth of a man in Bangladesh suffering from discrimination and living in one of the poorest parts of Dhaka, then they would have had a much lower life expectancy than the man in Harlem. Take the poorest area of a city in India or Kenya and life expectancy at birth will be much lower than that in Calton.

---

[3] <http://www.theguardian.com/society/2006/jan/21/health.politics>

INEQUALITY IN RELATION TO THE SOCIAL AND ENVIRONMENTAL DETERMINANTS OF HEALTH

There is little detailed research into the health problems facing women and men, girls and boys in informal settlements in the Global South even as these contain around a billion people (see Sverdlik, 2011). There are studies giving some insights into the health benefits from better quality housing from high-income nations but the differentials in housing quality are so much smaller. There are more data on inequality in some of the key social or environmental determinants of health – for instance on access to water, toilets, health care and emergency services, policing – and housing quality. But the global datasets that are meant to measure and monitor progress are very crude.

It is worth exploring in more detail provision for water and sanitation in urban areas in low- and middle-income countries, partly because of its importance for reducing environmental health risks, and because data are available for most countries over the past 25 years. What is also worth noting is how little this contributes to understanding inequality, as well as greatly under-estimating the scale of the health burden for urban populations.

The data on provision for water and sanitation is produced by the Joint Monitoring Programme of WHO and UNICEF (WHO/UNICEF 2014, 2015). This provides statistics for rural and urban populations' use of drinking water and sanitation facilities from 'improved sources'. It has no capacity to provide more disaggregated statistics – for instance for particular cities – as most of the data sources it draws from are national sample surveys. It also provides very little detail in terms of inequality because 'improved provision' is defined so broadly. So a household with water piped into its premises that is regular and safe and plumbed into kitchens, toilets and bathrooms is treated as the same as a household that only has access to a standpipe that may be distant from their home, with irregular supplies, long queues and unsafe to drink. Similarly, a household with a flush toilet in their home connected to sewers with a regular water supply (for flushing) and a basin for hand washing in the toilet is in the same category of 'improved' provision as a household with a pit latrine with a slab.

There is a need for much more disaggregation and detail in indicators assessing the quality of provision for water and sanitation. Figure 6.2 illustrates this as it shows how environmental health risks associated with water and sanitation diminish as the quality of provision increases. If data were available on provision for water and sanitation within several different categories as in Figure 6.2, it would show the inequalities in provision and in the risks associated with this much more clearly.

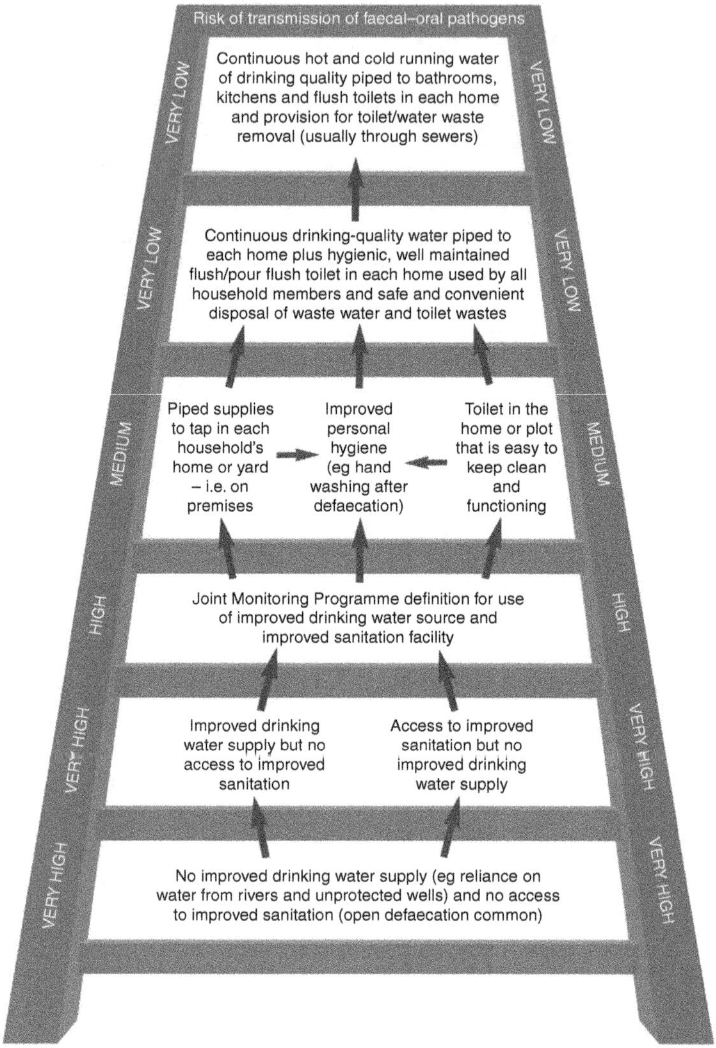

Source: Satterthwaite (2016, p. 113). The idea of constructing a ladder that highlighted improvements as the ladder was climbed can be traced to the classic paper by Arnstein (1969). Work on household energy also developed an energy ladder to show how rising incomes generally mean a shift in fuel use towards cleaner fuels and electricity. The use of a ladder to illustrate different levels of provision for water and sanitation has been discussed in some UN and JMP reports, for example, Figure 1.1 in UN-Habitat (2003), which drew on Prüss et al (2002).

Figure 6.2 Different standards of provision in urban areas mean different risk levels

We get some idea of this through the data collected by the UN Joint Monitoring Programme (JMP) on the proportion of urban and rural populations using drinking water sources that are piped on premises. This is a better measure for water provision that can lower environmental health risks than aggregating the different 'improved' sources noted above although it still lacks attention to whether the water is safe or regular. The JMP also notes how even water piped on premises is often faecally contaminated (WHO/UNICEF 2014, 2015). But if provision for water for urban populations is assessed on this basis, it shows far less progress than if it is assessed based on all kinds of 'improved sources'. Among what the UN terms 'developing countries', only 72 per cent of the urban population has water piped on premises in 2015 compared to 95 per cent who use 'improved' sources. For the least developed countries, only 32 per cent of their urban population has water piped on premises compared to 86 per cent that use 'improved' sources (WHO/UNICEF, 2015). The United Nations claims that between 1990 and 2015, the Millennium Development Goal target of halving the proportion of the population without sustainable access to safe drinking water was met (ibid). But this is only if measured in terms of who has 'improved' sources which is a long way down the ladder from who has sustainable access to safe water. For urban populations, there was no halving of the proportion without access to drinking water sources piped on premises – for the world, for 'developing countries' or for the least developed countries. There were even many nations that went backwards – i.e. they had a lower proportion of their urban population with water piped on premises in 2015 than in 1990 (Satterthwaite, 2016).

Inequalities in key determinants of environmental health risks such as water quality, accessibility, regularity and cost are easily measured, even if current global statistics do not do so. But there are a range of determinants of environmental health risks that are less easily measured – for instance satisfaction with housing and services, and absence of eviction threat – and thus lack of stressors relating to these. There are also the social and political factors that limit government responses to environmental health risks in informal settlements – including pressure from middle- and upper-income groups to evict them (see Bhan, 2009). Richard Wilkinson, in an interview about the book he co-authored with Kate Pickett (Pickett and Wilkinson, 2010) notes how it details the 'pernicious effects that inequality has on societies: eroding trust, increasing anxiety and illness, encouraging excessive consumption'.[4] Green and Hulme (2005) note that:

---

[4] http://www.yesmagazine.org/happiness/want-the-good-life-your-neighbors-need-it-too

'As the gap between the rich and the poor grows, it becomes easier for elites to assert a conceptual distance between themselves and those living in poverty, whose poverty is blamed on their culture, their ignorance, lack of skills or their farming practices' (Green and Hulme, 2005, p. 876).

WHAT CAN WE CHANGE?

Figure 6.1 contains many health determinants that local governments and local civil society organisations cannot address – for instance they cannot influence the international price of key commodities such as oil or food staples even as these can have strong influences on incomes or nutrition. They have little or no influence on the policies of international development assistance agencies. They have little scope to influence directly labour markets or the distribution of incomes. But as noted above, they can influence the provision of risk-reducing infrastructure and services, and thus profoundly influence inequality in exposure to risk. Most cities in upper-middle and high-income nations may have high levels of inequality in incomes and assets yet also have very little inequality in access to risk-reducing infrastructure and services.

Figure 6.1 also lists a range of intermediary factors that influence health outcomes. Some are obvious – for example, knowledge of health risks and how best to act on them both for prevention and for rapid and appropriate treatment where needed. Here there is the key issue of groups who face discrimination that disadvantages them in (for instance) access to risk-reducing infrastructure and services – and this discrimination may be on the basis of age, class, ethnic group, residence (such as stigma for those living in areas considered 'slums') and gender – and so underpins inequality.

The intermediary factors also include those that can reduce inequality in influencing local government policies and practices – especially the empowerment and the capacity to participate and to act, brought by civil society organisations. One of the most interesting developments here is the emergence and growth of federations formed by slum/shack dwellers or homeless people that are now active in more than 30 nations. (For details of what each of these are doing see www.sdinet.org; and Satterthwaite and Mitlin, 2014 for a summary of their work.) The foundations of these federations are community-based savings groups in which most members and managers are women. These savings groups give members safe places to save and immediate access to funds when needed. Savings group members also provide each other with social support and solidarity. One member commented, 'the federation is my sister', another said that, 'we are not collecting money we are collecting people'. As these savings groups federate, they have more influence on local politicians and civil servants. They also demonstrate to local authorities their capacities – to design, build and manage community toilets and washing facilities, to build houses (when they can get land) and to upgrade existing settlements. They also undertake surveys of informal settlements and prepare maps to strengthen their capability to prepare appropriate responses and negotiate support for these from government agencies. These are powerful forces reducing a whole range of inequalities including access to government support and services, social support from their peers, as well as how other groups view them (with their relationships with local politicians and civil servants completely changed), and addressing gender discrimination.

BEYOND LOCAL RISKS

Then there are inequalities in the draw that individuals or households make on finite resources and sinks – the most dramatic being the vast inequalities in historic and current contributions to anthropogenic greenhouse gas emissions through which we are currently heading for dangerous climate change. And there are inequalities between nations and between localities within nations in the capacity to reduce environmental risk arising from disasters and from climate change.

Graham Haughton (1999) noted that there are five environmental equity issues that need addressing. The first two of these are the two components of sustainable development highlighted in *Our Common Future* (World Commission on Environment and Development, 1987): inter-generational equity (development that does not compromise the ability of future generations to meet their own needs); and intra-generational equity (commitment to meeting needs of the present). The third is trans-frontier equity that stops urban consumers and producers transferring their environmental costs to other people or eco-systems (e.g. pollution generated in a city contributing to acid rain and water pollution far beyond its boundaries). The fourth is procedural equity: ensuring that people's legal rights are respected and protected, that they are fairly treated and can engage in democratic decision-making processes. The fifth is inter-species equity, with the rights of other species recognised.

CLIMATE CHANGE

Among the range of global environmental issues that need attention (Steffen et al, 2015), anthropogenic climate change is considered the most pressing. It brings three equity issues to the fore: who contributes to it; who is most at risk from its direct and indirect impacts; and who has responsibility for reducing emissions. The key issue here is the mismatch between those that have contributed to, and are contributing to, greenhouse gases (GHGs) and those that are most at risk from the changes these emissions bring. This can be seen at the level of national governments with the issue being the very large differences in national contributions to historic and current emissions – and generally with the nations and regions with the least capacity to adapt being those that have contributed least to GHG emissions. But if consumption-based accounting is used for GHG emissions, there are even more dramatic differences between at one end of the spectrum low-income, low-consumption households and at the other end, high-income, high-consumption households. Consumption-based accounting more accurately identifies what (or whose lifestyle) underpins global warming but it is also more complicated to measure and more difficult politically as it highlights the need to curb high consumption lifestyles.

Climate change issues might seem far distant from the pressing environmental health risks discussed above that such a large proportion of the world's urban population face – the huge deficits in provision for risk-reducing infrastructure and services. But this is incorrect for three reasons. The first is that effective climate change adaptation depends on this infrastructure and these services too – and on the (mostly local) financial and governance capacities that are needed to underpin them. Cities with well-functioning local governments that meet their responsibilities for such risk-reducing infrastructure and services are the ones with the capacity to adjust their provision in response to the new or heightened risks that climate change is bringing. The second is that emissions reduction is so urgent that it requires the contributions of all localities and countries – even those with low emissions per person and very little historic contribution to GHGs already emitted. The meeting of the Conference of Parties to the UN Framework Convention on Climate Change in Paris in December 2015 achieved more than was expected but still less than what is needed to avoid dangerous climate change. At present, the commitments to mitigation made by governments in their Intended Nationally Determined Contributions do not add up to the emissions reduction needed to avoid dangerous climate change. The third is that even wealthy cities with high adaptation capacities will be overwhelmed by climate change impacts if there is not the needed emissions reduction (Revi et al, 2014).

What has been missing from most of the discussions on the UN Framework Convention on Climate Change (and from the Sustainable Development Goals) is how much of what is achieved in development, adaptation and mitigation depends on city and municipal governments.

This is beginning to be appreciated. The SDGs give some mention of this and among the 17 goals, one refers to cities. The Paris Agreement (Article 7) states the following:

> Parties (i.e. national governments) hereby establish the global goal on adaptation of enhancing adaptive capacity, strengthening resilience and reducing vulnerability to climate change, with a view to contributing to sustainable development and ensuring an adequate adaptation response in the context of the temperature goal referred to in Article 2.

This agreement recognises the importance of what are termed 'Non Party Stakeholders' in adaptation and mitigation, and these include civil society, and city and municipal authorities. These are also encouraged to make and register their commitments to scale-up climate actions in a new Non-State Actor Zone for Climate Action platform.[5] But while city or municipal governments are mentioned, they are still only included in lists of other 'non-party stakeholders' and their importance for transformative adaptation receives little attention. The Paris Agreement promotes *the sharing of information, learning and good practices* but only for national governments, not local governments and local civil society. National governments need to recognise how much the needed ambition in their Intended Nationally Determined Contributions (INDCs), in adaptation and in accurate emissions accounting depend on urban governments. Effective (national) INDCs need Urban and City Intended Determined Contributions) too.

RESILIENCE

The concept of resilience applied to urban areas provides a way of thinking about these as a system within other systems (including regional and global systems) in which the social and ecological dimensions of urban life are intertwined (Fraser et al, 2016). It is about their capacity to cope with stresses or shocks – and it is mostly applied to disaster risk and to climate change risk. But considering resilience for urban areas is complicated by the large range of stresses and shocks that cities encounter – from extreme weather events to constraints in water supplies to changes in the prices or availabilities of key resource-inputs and commodities. Each of these also has differential impacts as different individuals, households and enterprises have varying exposures to risk (e.g. do their homes experience

---

[5] http://carbonn.org/

flooding?). They also have different capacities to cope, to adapt and if needed to 'build back better' (Lyons, 2009) so what is rebuilt does not reconstruct the same risks and social injustices (Fraser et al, 2016). Then there are the risks or increases in risk that cities cannot address alone. A city can build its resilience to the direct and indirect impacts of climate change and even plan for lowering emissions but on its own it cannot influence all other emitters to do so. Without the needed reductions in global emissions, even well-resourced and prepared cities will not be able to protect themselves (Revi et al, 2014).

Resilience thinking for urban areas needs to consider the whole urban system and the many interconnections including connections to rural populations, economies and eco-systems (e.g. watersheds) that are usually outside urban boundaries and so outside the jurisdiction of urban governments. There are the complications of urban centres' dependence on other systems over which they have little control. For instance, it is rare for electricity to be supplied by the local government – yet many systems needed for resilience (water pumping and telecommunications) depend on electricity. Avoiding flooding in a city from local rivers may depend on water management 'up-river' (see the example of Surat in Bhat et al, 2013). Most cities also depend on regional, national and international global supply chains that may be disrupted.

In urban centres, the three aspects of resilience (coping, adapting, bouncing forward) depend heavily on the orientation and capacity of its government, also its revenue base and its capacity to work with those most at risk. Many discussions of resilience have lacked a focus on 'people, politics and power' and the political and economic networks that undergird patterns of resource access (Bahadur and Tanner, 2014). These questions of the distribution of power are inherent to the operation of urban systems, and also to how resilience itself becomes defined within such systems (Friend and Moench, 2013). So key issues here are whose resilience gets enhanced and whose priorities get addressed (Paavola and Adger, 2002; Fraser, 2005; Forsyth, 2014)? Much needed city-wide infrastructure investment has the potential to displace large numbers of people so there are issues on how they are rehoused, and to what extent they approve of, and shape this. Better watershed management for flood protection may be complicated by informal settlements in watersheds.

Urban governments also need to be able to work with neighbouring jurisdictions (with political complications if these are governed by different political parties); they need frameworks, funding and capacities that require collaboration with national and state/provincial ministries or secretariats.

But what can be done in urban centres with weak or unresponsive local governments and large deficits in risk-reducing infrastructure and services? To what extent can households and community organisations contribute to their resilience? In urban centres, it is generally within low-income groups that risks are concentrated – because of locations and sites (the only land available to them is sites at risk from flooding or landslides), housing quality and lack of provision for risk-reducing infrastructure and services. The inhabitants of such settlements generally lack the resources to address this by moving to safer neighbourhoods. There are many case studies showing how the residents of settlements such as these take measures themselves to protect their homes or assets (Jabeen et al, 2010; Odemerho, 2015; Kiunsi, 2016). There are also examples of collective responses (see Baker, 2012; Bosco Isunju et al, 2016).

But grassroots organisations cannot produce the needed city-wide trunk infrastructure such as water treatment plans, water mains, sewers and sewage treatment plants, and storm and surface drains. They do have a capacity to address these within their settlements but they need to be integrated into the larger systems. Community-managed water pipes usually need water mains to draw from and their drains need to feed into city-wide drains to be effective. If low-income groups are living on high-risk land sites, it will need local government support to reduce these risks or offer the inhabitants safer alternatives. The success of community-based adaptation in urban areas is often dependent on the community organisation developing good relations with their local governments and working together.

Fraser et al (2016) suggest that a concern for equity and fairness in adaptation (and resilience) has to look at who benefits from the mobilisation and allocation of resources for adaptation. Who gets opportunities for, or outcomes of, actions that support adaptation to occur (ensuring that adaptation for one group does not jeopardise adaptation for another)? Will the Green Climate Fund support local governments and community organisations in undertaking community-based adaptation? And in the adaptive process, how are risks defined by affected people themselves? As Fraser et al (2016) note, a focus only on mitigation and adaptation actions may not be enough to sustain a just response to climate change. This may need an open dialogue and new action and policy to address underlying development failures.

WHO CAN ACT ON LOCAL AND GLOBAL ENVIRONMENTAL AGENDAS?

An assessment of the capacity to act on climate change adaptation and mitigation covering nine cities (Bartlett and Satterthwaite, 2016) highlighted how this depended on conventional risk-reducing infrastructure and services, and city governments with the capacity to plan and manage city expansion. The city of Rosario (Argentina) is particularly interesting. The assessment of its policies by Hardoy et al (2016) shows that it has no explicit climate change strategy or programme, nor any office coordinating initiatives that contribute to mitigation or adaptation. Its adaptation strategy is simply a set of isolated responses to other city needs. But Rosario has had a strong coherent governance system that includes a commitment to development, decentralisation, transparency, accountability and participation. It has a long tradition of urban planning and land-use management, with a commitment to environmental sustainability and a strategic plan that involves multiple stakeholders and encompasses the whole metropolitan area. Many of the city's development programmes and initiatives contribute to disaster risk reduction and to adaptation – improved provision for infrastructure, upgrading of informal settlements, a much admired municipal health care service with focus on prevention, the expansion of public space and initiatives for energy efficiency, initiatives, in short, that have enhanced the common good in Rosario. All of these contribute to a city that is more resilient to disasters and climate change impacts (Hardoy et al, 2016).

In effect, city governments now need to act on five agendas:

- Economic success in attracting and retaining investment;
- Addressing (and reducing) poverty;
- Building the information base and capacity to act on disaster risk;
- Adaptation to climate change (including building resilience to its direct and indirect impacts); and
- Contribution to GHG emission reduction.

Of course, these do not necessarily complement each other. 'Business as usual' scenarios with city governments seeking new private investments and expanding infrastructure and electricity production regardless of how much these increase GHG emissions are what is driving us to dangerous climate change. But a focus on risk to individuals and households provides many insights into how these different agendas can complement each other. Poverty reduction, disaster risk reduction and climate change adaptation are all about identifying and acting on local risks. As this chapter has sought to emphasise, much of what is needed to reduce poverty is extending to everyone in a city, effective and affordable risk-reducing infrastructure and services – that lower or remove everyday risks. Disaster risk reduction is about understanding in detail local risk of disasters and recognising how much this can and should integrate with the risk-reducing infrastructure and services produced in poverty reduction. Climate change adaptation has to support and reinforce both of these – but also bring a knowledge of how local risks will or may change, and integrate these into the poverty reduction and disaster risk reduction.

GHG emission reduction does not reduce current local environmental risks although there are measures to reduce emissions that have positive co-benefits with the other agendas. So it would seem to be at odds with the three agendas that do reduce local risk. But without climate change mitigation that avoids dangerous climate change (which probably requires keeping global temperature rise to 1.5 degrees above pre-industrial global temperatures), even cities with the best disaster risk reduction and climate change adaptation will be unable to protect their populations and economies.

PART IV

Governance

7. New environmental governance: adaptation, resilience and law[1]

Cameron Holley and Ekaterina Sofronova

INTRODUCTION

The concept of resilience is receiving widespread attention across many fields (Joseph, 2016; McDonald and Styles, 2014). In an 'age of catastrophe', it has become the touchstone for responding to global problems and risks that are complex, difficult to predict and often have uneven social effects (Beck, 1992a; O'Malley, 2011; Hutter, this volume). Formidable environmental challenges, like water scarcity, biodiversity loss and degraded natural resources, exemplify these complex global problems (Rittel and Webber, 1973; WEF, 2016). Climate change and its cascading risks of potentially unpredictable magnitude will only exacerbate the complexity of these challenges (Godden et al, 2013, p. 235). It is not surprising then that resilience mentalities (with their focus on uncertain and dynamic systems) have increasingly influenced the thinking and practice of environmental law and governance (Chaffin et al, 2014).

Law has played an essential role in managing environmental problems (Garmestani et al, 2013). However, there is significant discord between resilience theories and law's 'traditional' ways of thinking about, and creating arrangements for, governing the environment. Conventional forms of environmental law emerged on the domestic and international stage in the 1970s. These laws were underpinned by a very Westphalian view of the world (Shearing and Johnston, 2010). States believed they understood environmental problems clearly, these problems could be defined in advance and that each difficulty afflicted relatively stable ecological systems with a natural equilibrium (Craig, 2009; Garmestani et al, 2008; Hill Clarvis et al, 2014; de Búrca et al, 2013, p. 730; Holley 2017a, p. 743).

[1] This research was supported by an ARC Discovery Early Career Researcher Award (DE140101216). We are grateful for the comments and suggestions from Jan McDonald.

Based on these assumptions, states exercised their exclusive authority, using uniform and mandatory rules, to try and halt degradation and return ecological systems to their prior 'pristine' natural condition (de Búrca et al, 2013, p. 730; Cosens et al, 2014, p. 3; Garmestani et al, 2014, p. 1).

Unfortunately, this way of thinking about the environment and law now stands in stark contrast with the tenets of resilience theory and its understanding of social and ecological systems as contextual, nested, uncertain, dynamic and having many possible stable states (Garmestani et al, 2014, p. 1; Gunderson and Holling. 2001; Humby, 2014). For example, the uniform nature of traditional hierarchical laws arguably lacks contextualised application to the naturally occurring variability of ecosystems and the scales of their critical functions (Garmestani et al, 2008, p. 1039). The law's centralised, expert-based and state-dominated approach also struggles to harness multiple local knowledges and capacities that can better account for marginalised interests, while also bolstering learning, innovation and responses to uncertainty (Begg et al, 2015; Cohen, 2008; Kramarz and Park, 2016). Moreover, because ecosystems are moving targets, with uncertain and unpredictable futures, fixed laws (that can easily ossify) lack the requisite nimbleness and flexibility to cope with the dynamism and transformation of complex systems (Garmestani et al, 2008, p. 1,039). As one of the forefathers of resilience thinking succinctly sums up: as 'persistent and embracing guides for and inhibitions to actions . . . laws are truly of limited help' (Holling, 2012).

For Holling (2012), even if laws cannot contribute much, they might help further flexibility and manage resilience if they fostered extensive monitoring and allowed for 'self-governance . . . deliberative workshops to define and launch collaborative experiments . . .[and] local designs collaboratively initiated that cross scales'. How then should lawyers and legal academics respond to such suggestions? In the not too distant past, Holling's prescriptions may simply have been unimaginable to lawyers, whose views on state regulation were more likely to be inspired by Hobbes' powerful story of the Leviathan (Hobbes, 1985). Fortunately, over the past decade, ideas like those proffered by Holling have been embraced and mirrored within a novel and emerging body of legal scholarship known as the new environmental governance or new governance (van der Heijden, 2013; Holley et al, 2012).

The new governance enterprise involves collaboration between a diversity of private, public and non-government stakeholders who, acting together towards commonly agreed (or mutually negotiated) goals, hope to achieve far more collectively, than individually (Holley et al, 2012, p. 4). This form of governance relies heavily upon participatory dialogue and deliberation, flexibility, inclusiveness, multi-level and integrated approaches, knowledge generation and processes of learning and adaptation (see, generally, de Búrca and Scott 2006; Holley et al, 2012, p. 4). Although new governance was once portrayed as an alternative to traditional top-down legal regulation, its ongoing evolution has now given rise to various (and still debated) interactions with environmental law (de Búrca and Scott, 2006; van der Heijden, 2011, 2012; Holley, 2016, p. 27; Trubek and Trubek, 2007; Wurzel et al, 2013). A continuum of possible relationships is beginning to emerge between law and new governance (Holley, 2016). At one end are relationships of indifference, where both law and new governance remain blind to their mutual operations (de Búrca and Scott, 2006; Holley, 2016, p. 28). In the middle of the continuum are a suite of hybrid interactions, such as law acting as a regulatory bottom line and imposing direct binding or justiciable rights that underpin new governance's softer norms; or 'the shadow of the law' being used to create an incentive for regulated parties to voluntarily produce an acceptable new governance outcome (de Búrca and Scott, 2006; Holley, 2016, p. 29). Finally, law and new governance may exist in an integrated relationship, where both are closely shaped and informed by the practices and characteristics of the other (de Búrca and Scott, 2006; Holley, 2016, p. 31). Ultimately, what is significant about the relationship between new governance and state-based law is that the law becomes simply one node, albeit a potentially important one, among many in a polycentric landscape of diffuse power and responsibility (Harlow, 2005; Rhodes, 1997).

Importantly for the purposes of this chapter, new governance's polycentric, collaborative, deliberative, integrated, multi-level and adaptive features arguably make it well suited to managing resilience by adjusting systems to stresses (or changing conditions) in a way that maintains essential system functioning (or one similar to it) (Karkkainen, 2003; Nelson et al, 2007; Redman, 2014). As discussed below, because there are a diversity of theories and practices that comprise new governance, this novel approach has not always explicitly been influenced by, or aimed to operationalise resilience, per se. However, there has been something of a rough confluence of new governance and resilience theories regarding their critiques of traditional environmental law, and their recognition of the need to better respond to uncertainty, dynamism and complexity of environmental problems and risks (Godden et al, 2013). Indeed, new governance arguably addresses critical challenges of operationalising resilience because it explicitly seeks to allow different scopes of risk and problems to be managed at different levels and engages a larger number of actors to facilitate experimentation and learning in the face of uncertainty (Engel, 2016; Klinke and Renn, 2012, p. 274; Sabel and Zeitlin, 2011). As Nourse and Shaffer (2014, pp. 125–6) explain, new governance holds this potential because it:

> bring(s) together regulators and stakeholders in iterative processes . . .[and] refocuses attention on local context while envisioning conditions for deliberative engagement among officials and stakeholders to enhance learning and coordination . . . By focusing on learning and innovation in a world of uncertainty and dynamic change, new governance theorists implicitly put the need for emergent analytics front and center.

This chapter highlights the contours of this novel new governance approach, and interrogates its strengths and weaknesses for fostering adaptability and managing resilience.

Before embarking on this analysis it is important to note that in a single chapter it is not possible to cover the breadth of global practice and debates in new environmental governance and related fields (e.g. disaster risk reduction, Djalante et al, 2011; risk governance, Hutter, 2006; risk reduction strategies, Lawrence at al, 2015) that often vary with culture, legal structures and environmental problems (see e.g. Wijbenga et al, 2008, p. 330). The chapter also does not critically engage with the concept of resilience or what this notion presupposes about the wider world (see Joseph, 2016). Rather, like much of the new governance scholarship, it proceeds on the basis that the resilience approach frames and justifies both the identification of failures in traditional environmental law and the call for innovative governance approaches (Joseph, 2016). Undeniably, new environmental governance is only one of many competing ideals that seek to provide greater flexibility and adaptive approaches to environmental law and regulation (e.g. self-regulation, process-based regulation, regulatory flexibility initiatives, cap and trade schemes, co-management and partnerships, see Holley, 2017a; Howlett, 2014, p. 190; Plummer et al, 2016; Ruhl, 2011). What sets new governance apart from these other developments is that it demands much greater levels of novel collaboration, deliberation, flexibility and adaptability (de Búrca et al, 2013; Holley et al, 2012). Even so, as an emerging approach to governance, there is a need to further clarify whether and to what extent new governance can overcome the limits of traditional law by providing more flexible and adaptive responses to environmental problems and deeper engagement of those affected by risks (Heazle et al, 2013; Holley et al, 2012; Klinke and Renn, 2012; Lawrence at al, 2015). Finally, much of the scholarship on new governance, including the work discussed here, has been developed in the fields of law, regulation and governance, rather than in the dominant strands of resilience scholarship, namely socio-ecological systems, common-pool resources and adaptive governance (cf. Cosens et al, 2014; Djalante et al, 2011; Garmestani et al, 2013; Karkkainen 2003; Techera 2012). However, these areas of resilience scholarship have only recently begun to focus on the role of law and governance in adaptability and managing resilience (Clement et al, 2015a; Cosens et al, 2014, p. 5). This chapter's exploration of new governance (through its legal and regulatory frame) accordingly may offer insights for these other areas of resilience scholarship. As Clement et al (2015a, p. 466) note, new governance thinking certainly can 'share some elements with AG [Adaptive Governance] but consider[s] more carefully the administrative limits of managing public problems and accordingly offers a way to modify AG prescriptions'.

The analysis here proceeds in three parts. The first part provides a brief overview of new governance, its growth as a new form of legal jurisprudence, its relationship to broader resilience thinking and its position as an approach that can administer and operationalise resilience. The second part then examines the advantages of new governance and its limits for adaptively managing change in social and ecological systems. The analysis reveals that although new governance holds significant promise, it has often struggled to fulfil its adaptive and flexible aspirations in practice, and overcome barriers of unequal power and resources. Finally, the third part offers some concluding thoughts and sums up the chapter by setting out emerging issues for understanding and reforming new environmental governance and its approach to managing resilience.

NEW GOVERNANCE AND RESILIENCE

New governance's polycentric, collaborative, deliberative, integrated, multi-level and adaptive approach has become increasing popular across the globe (de Búrca and Scott, 2006; van Heijden, 2015; Holley et al, 2012; Karkkainen, 2004a). At the domestic level, new governance approaches typically involve a variety of non-state actors assuming administrative, regulatory, and decision-making functions in governance processes to address some of the more complex and challenging environmental problems (Holley, 2017a, p. 748; Ostrom, 2010, p. 643). Prominent examples that fall under the sign of new governance include collaborative urban sustainability efforts in Europe, Australasia and North America in response to climate change (van Heijden, 2014); the establishment of 56 collaborative regional natural resource management bodies in Australia (Gunningham, 2009); forest governance (Parkins et al, 2016) and watershed collaborations (Brisbois and de Loë, 2016) in Canada; collaborative approaches to water management in New Zealand (Holley and Gunningham, 2011); multiple agencies and stakeholders addressing competing demands on water resources in the Bay Delta in the USA (Freeman and Farber, 2005; Holley, 2015); and more nascent attempts at collaborative processes in post-Soviet countries such as Russia's civic chambers and public councils (Sofronova et al, 2014).

Similar trends have been identified internationally (and in the interaction between international and domestic levels) with the growth of open-ended standards, multi-level webs, deliberation of international norms, and increased decisions and implementation by non-state actors (Cottrell and Trubek, 2012, p. 362; Holley, 2017a, p. 748). This has included the European Union's Water Framework Directive (Trubek and Trubek, 2007) and Forest Law Enforcement Governance and Trade initiative (Overdevest and Zeitlin, 2014); the Partnership for the Development of Environmental Law in Africa (PADELIA) (Kimani, 2010); the Inter-American Tropical Tuna Commission (de Búrca et al, 2013); management of the Great Lakes in the USA/Canada (Karkkainen, 2004b); and the Arctic Council's intergovernmental cooperation and broader knowledge community including indigenous groups and scientists (Holley, 2017a, pp. 748–9; Koivurova et al, 2015). The shift to new governance has to some extent been shaped by specific contexts and influences (de Búrca, 2010). However, generally speaking, it has come about because of the perceived capacity of its more polycentric, collaborative, deliberative, multi-level and adaptive approaches to deliver benefits in circumstances where traditional approaches cannot, not least managing resilience of complex and dynamic environmental and social systems (Holley et al, 2012, p. 4; Chaffin and Gunderson, 2016, pp. 81–2).

The notion of resilience was originally developed in the field of ecology (Holling, 1978) and subsequently explored in many other areas (see e.g. Djalante et al, 2011, p. 3). The term has been defined and applied in different ways, traversing ideas such as engineering resilience, ecological resilience, specific or general resilience, as well as a range of key concepts including panarchy, adaptability, adaptive capacity and transformability (Djalante et al, 2011; Walker et al, 2004). For present purposes, this chapter adopts one of the more common definitions of resilience, namely 'the capacity of a system to absorb disturbance and still retain its basic structure and function' (Folke, 2006; Holling, 1978; Humby, 2014, p. 90; Walker and Salt, 2006, p. iii). A system can be highly resilient if it is quite adaptable or quite resistant to change (Cosens et al, 2014; Humby 2014). This understanding does not presuppose resilience is a normative goal per se (unlike other ideals, such as ecological sustainability). Rather resilience thinking encourages governance approaches to manage the capacity of systems to cope with, adapt to, and shape change to achieve goals that are set by society (e.g. maintaining a certain system state that is environmentally sustainable) (Cosens et al, 2014, p. 8; Engel, 2016, p. 18; Pisano, 2012).

Attempts to advance, understand and think about governance approaches that can adapt to and resist change have led to a collection of diverse environmental governance theories including 'experimentalism' (de Búrca et al, 2013), 'collaborative ecosystem management' (Karkkainen, 2002), 'post sovereign environmental governance' (Karkkainen, 2004b), 'modular regulation' (Freeman and Farber, 2005), 'adaptive governance' (Chaffin and Gunderson, 2014) and 'global environmental governance' (Okereke et al, 2009). Each of these perspectives vary in their emphasis, encompassing different schools of thought and applying varying institutional and political approaches to a range of environmental problems. Experimentalism, for example, draws inspiration from pragmatism (Dewey, 1946), while collaborative ecosystem management draws on a broader mix of ideas, including ecological systems thinking and adaptive management (Berkes and Folke, 1998; Holling, 1978). However, these various environmental governance theories are increasingly viewed as bound by a shared focus on common characteristics. These include a focus on the virtues of flexibility, deliberation, integrated and multi-level management, collaboration, learning and adaptation. These common features have led a burgeoning group of scholars to collectively refer to these approaches and theories as new environmental governance (de Búrca and Scott, 2006; van der Heijden, 2015; Holley et al, 2012; Karkkainen, 2004a).

New governance has been described as falling within the broader new legal realism movement (Nourse and Shaffer, 2014). However there is no agreement on a definitive new governance 'model' per se (van der Heijden, 2013). It is mootable whether new governance adequately accounts for the practical differences *within* these evolving environmental governance examples and theories (Holley 2017a, p. 749; Karkkainen, 2004a). Certainty, using a sweeping descriptor like 'new governance' to lump different theories and practices together may twist new governance into a simple 'catchall term' (von der Porten and de Loë, 2013; Karkkainen, 2004a; Holley, 2017a, p. 749). However, considerable benefits can be gained from grouping different theories and scholarship within a new governance framework. Indeed, a generalised understanding of new governance (with apposite attention to differences) can facilitate a better understanding of what is occurring, and offers a constructive approach for testing and developing a normative vision capable of influencing the direction of sprawling environmental governance theory and its engagement with concepts of adaptive processes and resilience (Holley, 2017a, p. 749; Karkkainen, 2004a; Lobel, 2004, pp. 501–6; Walker, 2006).

There have, of course, been similar and at times overlapping attempts to combine familial approaches under different 'signs', including the notion of adaptive governance (see e.g. Djalante et al, 2011; Garmestani et al, 2008). According to Clement et al (2015b, p. 278), adaptive governance involves a family of governance approaches that have emerged as a solution to the failure of adaptive management (see also Cosens et al, 2014, p. 4; Dietz et al, 2003). There may be good reasons to adopt other organising concepts like adaptive governance, not least its direct grounding in concepts of social and ecological systems and resilience thinking (Cosens et al, 2014). However, at this stage of inquiry, the current state of knowledge and conceptual basis of adaptive governance are arguably less well developed than that of new governance (see Chaffin and Gunderson, 2016; Koontz et al, 2015). Indeed, new governance has been described as an increasingly popular form of jurisprudence that is receiving support and consideration from across the political spectrum (Alexander, 2009, p. 118; Hess, 2008, p. 450) and it stands as 'a leading contender for a new theory and approach to law' (Nourse and Shaffer, 2014, p. 144). In summary, new governance has arguably reached a conceptual maturity that makes it a useful and feasible approach for thinking about and creating flexible and adaptive arrangements for operationalising resilience. The unique advantages of new governance's adaptive and flexible approach for managing resilience are explored in the following section, before turning to consider the challenges and barriers that have arisen in practice.

NEW GOVERNANCE – ADVANTAGES AND CHALLENGES

The Advantages of New Governance for Managing Resilience

New governance is said to cope better with the dynamism, uncertainty and complexity of environmental problems than either traditional regulation or many other dominant environmental regulatory approaches. The former can easily solidify, freezing standards at a particular point in time or by adopting a one-size-fits-all approach, and in the latter case (e.g. cap and trade markets), significant post-hoc programme corrections to pollution levels and permits set from the centre can prevent new entrants or undermine security of ownership (Holley et al, 2012, p. 5). In contrast, the sort of collaborative, deliberative, multi-level, integrated and adaptive approaches contemplated by new governance have at least three potential benefits for managing resilience of ecological and social systems.

First, new governance's collaborative and multi-level institutions are said to improve the feedback and fit between knowledge, action and socio-ecological contexts (Lebel et al, 2006). New governance approaches typically seek to achieve this through a 'nested' (or polycentric) system that involves collaboration at different levels. Karkkainen's (2006) study of the Great Lakes nicely illustrates one such nested structure. As he explains, a set of basin-wide governance institutions address system problems and processes (and/or coordinate spatially differentiated parts), while more localised institutional arrangements address variable conditions at local scales – for example to account for differing conditions and stressors downstream as opposed to upstream (Karkkainen, 2006, p. 235). From the perspective of resilience, such a nested and multi-level arrangement offers significant benefits over centralised and uniform rules, because it enhances the chances that feedback from various ecological scales will be linked to the appropriate governance level, which can in turn more readily govern change (Cosens et al, 2014, p. 11). Freeman and Farber (2005, p. 891) provide a useful example of this in their study of the CalFed Bay Delta Program in the US where they describe how the Basin-wide programme involved 'problem-solving teams' that were able to be assembled from agencies and stakeholder groups to offer 'a way to meet new challenges without creating a rigid bureaucratic structure . . . [but] matching the right team with each problem'. Hill Clarvis et al (2014) similarly confirm in their study of the Water Framework Directive, how new governance better accounts for local circumstances and dynamisms by managing at transnational, national and smaller regional water management scales. These benefits have also been suggested across a range of domestic new governance approaches for biodiversity and water in Australia (Holley 2017b; Holley et al, 2012), where overarching frameworks establish broad national goals, while leaving it to subnational governments and hundreds of regional decision-making collaboratives to tailor management to unique ecological systems and problems of degradation and overuse.

Related to new governance's multi-level structure is a second purported strength, namely its capacity to enhance the types and flows of information within a system so as to reduce uncertainty, enable innovation and foster adaptation in response to changing circumstances. Unlike traditional environmental law's reliance on centralised expertise of bureaucratic agencies and legislators, new governance is able to harness the knowledge and capacities of governments, agencies, researchers, industry, NGOs, indigenous interests and community members at various scales. Lockwood et al (2012, p. 164) discuss one such approach known as the Marine Biodiversity and Resources Adaptation Research Network, where the mix of public and private stakeholders were better placed to identify knowledge gaps and create nodes of expertise for building adaptive capacity to address the impacts of climate change in the marine ecosystem. The regional organisation known as the Arctic Council also involves its own mix of state, indigenous interests, scientists and various working groups who have been able to learn from each other about how its region could better adapt to ecosystem changes (Koivurova et al, 2015). Furthermore, because new governance's multi-level arrangements aspire to information flowing between and across management scales (Ruhl, 2011, p. 1,400), the learnings and innovations from the multiple and diverse experiences of different collaborative bodies can be transmitted among many local collaborations and higher level organisations. The sharing of diverse governance responses is said to enable a more comprehensive assessment of problems and a pooling of information that can foster better adaptation strategies, reduce uncertainty and enhance the resilience of the system (Dorf and Sabel, 1998; Lockwood et al, 2012).

Arguably, the most fully formed ideal of this learning process is expressed in the theory of democratic experimentalism, which envisions a network of placed-based problem-solving groups that are explicitly experimental in nature (Karkkainen et al, 2000, pp. 693–4). These groups are minimally directed by a central body whose role is primarily to monitor and coordinate local experiments, to facilitate horizontal diffusion of best practice, peer-to-peer benchmarking and continual improvements in management techniques and the design of institutions (Karkkainen et al, 2000). Such a governance system, which is constantly monitoring its effects, diffusing information and updating its requirements, would be well suited to addressing adaptation, reducing the vulnerability of ecosystems to abrupt and uncertain change and reinforcing the resiliency of such systems (Engel, 2016). There are, however, only partial glimpses of this model operating in practice, including the EU Water Framework Directive (Scott and Holder, 2006); the National Water Initiative in Australia (Holley, 2017b); and the Forest Stewardship Council, which Overdevest and Zeitlin (2014, p. 28) note has many experimentalist features, including multi-stakeholder assemblages, deliberative decision making, principles-based standards (adaptable to national, regional and local conditions) and independent verification and adaptation of individual forest management plans.

The final benefit of new governance's unique approach over traditional environmental law is that it can increase the capacity of local communities to accept or manage change. Indeed, the direct involvement of non-government actors in deliberative styles of governance (albeit varying from local citizens to international NGOs) can foster stakeholder steering, ownership and 'buy-in' and give greater voice to marginalised and indigenous interests (as contrasted to an exclusive reliance on bureaucratic expertise in hierarchy or even price and competition in markets) (Holley et al, 2012, pp. 4–5; Karkkainen et al, 2000). This can play a particularly important role in areas with high levels of inequality, allowing governance responses to more fairly and effectively build resilience through a better understanding and incorporation of the needs and capacities of more vulnerable people (Ziervogel et al, 2016). As Kimani's (2010, p. 51) findings in the case of PADELIA illustrate, this collaborative new governance process enabled a cross-pollination of ideas between developing nations, rather than the transfer of knowledge from developed to developing contexts. This contributed to the creation of local capacity for the development and implementation of laws that would outlast the duration of the project (Kimani, 2010, pp. 50–1; Holley and Shearing, 2016, p. 563).

The engagement of non-government stakeholders can also ensure new governance responses are more successful in changing behaviour and avoiding systems crossing further into a degraded undesirable environmental regime, or succeed in crossing back into a more desirable one (Walker et al, 2004). In particular, the deliberative approaches of new governance can increase chances of local communities understanding and accepting necessary changes in their lifestyles and environment by enabling greater consideration of their rights and interests in using natural resources, as well as focusing on internalised drivers and norms, developed from social context and shared values (Bandura, 1997, p. 483; Cottrell and Trubek, 2012, p. 390; Emerson and Gerlak, 2014; Holley and Lawson, 2015). A nice illustration of such benefits comes from Njoka and Macek (2012, pp. 17–18) who comment on community-based resource management systems in the Horn of Africa. They explain how building natural resource-based resilience to address degraded soil, rangelands and watersheds benefited from community members identifying causes of degradation in a local context, considering the trends and behaviours of users, and consequently building support for change and implementation. They contrast such an approach with a resilience building strategy around a fish processing plant programme in Kenya, where the local population had little input into the system and were unmotivated to pursue the activities, leading to the pre-existing heavy fishing problem becoming compounded, rather than shifting to a new more desired ecosystem state.

New Governance Challenges and Critiques

Despite the potential benefits of new governance's features, it is important not to overlook the weaknesses and challenges of this approach. As we will see below, new governance has faced numerous criticisms, not least uncertainty over whether its proposed flexible, adaptive, multi-level, collaborative and deliberative characteristics can be effectively achieved in practice (Doremus, 2011; Driessen et al, 2012; Holley, 2017a, p. 750). Of course, it is important to remember that as an 'experimental' process, criticism and modification continues to be a feature of these developments (Holley and Shearing, 2016, p. 563). Experiments by their very nature involve attempts to govern agendas that in practice often depart significantly from what was envisioned (Holley and Shearing, 2016, p. 563). These messy realities of governance (Weir et al, 1997) are strikingly apparent in the case of new environmental governance, where at least four main challenges have limited its success in practice.

First, although there are many new governance experiments that have 'adaptive management' or 'monitoring and continuous improvement' as objectives, there has often been a lack of clear direction defining what these terms mean and what is required to implement them (Lee, 2014, p. 256; Susskind et al, 2010). For example, McDonald and Styles' (2014, p. 26) review of adaptive management finds that despite it being the dominant approach in natural resource governance, the majority of references to it are not accompanied by clear definitions of the term or the processes it involves. In the absence of this instruction, there have been significant failures or limited success in delivering experimental and adaptive models (e.g. many new governance approaches have resorted to half-hearted or conservative passive approaches to adaptive management, see Karkkainen, 2003). This is confirmed by Rijke et al's (2012) critical literature review, which identifies major constraints on the uptake of adaptive approaches as including ambiguous purposes and objectives, and uncertainty around outcomes.

The study of Susskind et al (2010) on the Glen Canyon Dam offers an instructive example of such constraints and the consequent failure to promote adaptive capacity and build resilience. Although millions of dollars were invested into collaborative and adaptive new governance processes to manage the Dam and its connected ecosystems, there was a lack of clear institutional design, direction and guidance regarding the relative priority of competing resource goals and the importance of various adaptive programme components (Susskind et al, 2010, pp. 4, 6). Multiple opportunities to foster agency and stakeholder learning, and to cultivate constructive engagement of the stakeholders were accordingly missed, producing little success in terms of stabilising or improving the quality of the downstream ecosystem (Susskind et al, 2010, p. 5). A similar example is identifiable in post-Soviet Ukraine, where attempts to establish polycentric, multi-level, collaborative and adaptive integrated water resource management have failed in practice. One cause of this failure was that the national legislation only incorporated general principles of integrated water management, leaving the detailed legal and institutional framework needed to deliver adaptive processes underdeveloped (Dombrowsky et al, 2014).

A second and related criticism of new governance arises from the tension between its flexible approach that is necessary for managing uncertainty and avoiding 'institutional arthritis' (Young, 2010, p. 378) and the traditional view that stability and predictability are central tenets of accountability and 'good' governance (Cosens et al, 2014; Karkkainen, 2003, p. 963). According to this critique, the absence of binding and objective goals and directions can allow new governance auspices to evade accountability for their work (Karkkainen, 2003, p. 963). At worst, overly flexible adaptive learning processes can lead to an abuse of process and make it difficult to hold managers accountable for promises to adapt, despite significant learning or evident need for change (Lee, 2014, p. 259). Lee (2014) finds such deficiencies in her analysis of adaptive management in Australian mining, notwithstanding that this tends to be dominated by relationships between mining and government, rather than wider collaborative processes. Doremus' review of new governance practices in the US, similarly leads her to caution that the flexibility of adaptive management may allow those who govern to maintain the status quo, effectively providing cover for governance auspices to delay imposing more politically controversial limits on economic activity (Doremus, 2011, p. 1,457). Indeed, to the extent new governance pursues open-ended decision making, it may exacerbate political asymmetries, because the groups exposed to economic costs will express their views more forcefully in deliberative and collaborative forums than those whose interests may be less direct or more representative of the public good (McDonald and Styles, 2014, p. 42).

Fortunately, new governance scholarship is increasingly cognisant of many of the above accountability concerns. A range of scholars have begun to argue that new governance needs to exist in hybrid form within conventional forms of law, not least to prevent abuse but also to incentivise actors' genuine engagement in the adaptive new governance enterprise (de Búrca et al, 2013; Craig, 2009; Garmestani et al, 2013; Holley and Gunningham, 2011). This includes proposals for minimal legal baselines to be set, albeit periodically revised based on the benchmarked success or failings of collaborative experiments at local levels (see Doelle and Lahey, 2015, p. 82; Hill Clarvis et al, 2014, pp. 101–2). With legal remedies in place, these baselines can guard against new governance's provisional decision-making acting as a form of covert deregulation (Trubek and Trubek, 2007). Nonetheless, it has often proven difficult in practice to set objectives and statutory baselines that navigate the 'thin green line' between too much specificity (which can stymie flexible revision of targets and marginalise local context) and overgeneralisation (which can invite bottom lines to be ignored and invite abuse) (see Doremus et al, 2011, p. 6; Holley, 2010; Lee, 2014; McDonald and Styles, 2014, p. 42).

A third major challenge for new governance has been securing adequate resourcing to pursue the requisite adaptive, collaborative, deliberative and multi-level approaches central to managing resilience. New governance's collaborative approach is often seen as a way to maximise the use of existing resources, or harness new ones in the steering and rowing of governance (Osborne and Gaebler, 1993). However, the reality is that new governance approaches typical require more, rather than less public funding. The study by Holley et al (2012) of six new governance approaches in Australia and New Zealand finds that even in these relatively affluent nations where billions of dollars had been invested in new governance, inadequacies in funding caused fundamental weaknesses. This included stymieing effective monitoring and information sharing required to achieve adaptive learning aspirations, and limiting the knowledge benefits obtained through collaboration and deliberation. The latter is of particular concern, as without sufficient funding to support the collaborative and deliberative participation of more marginalised interests, such as indigenous peoples, new governance approaches may simply reproduce existing conditions and inequality (Holley and Gunningham, 2011; Lane and Williams, 2008; Jackson et al, 2015). Put simply, those who are more powerful and resourceful actors, such as large industries and global corporations, will be over-represented or win out in deliberative decision-making (Chaffin et al, 2014; Brisbois and de Loë, 2016).

Another resource-intensive, but under-supported new governance feature is the costs associated with monitoring ecological conditions and implementing information sharing. Doremus (2011) argues that information is a threshold problem for learning and adaptive processes like those in new governance. Without information, learning is unlikely to be feasible, and it makes little sense to 'worry about whether managers want to learn, can be forced to learn or can use knowledge they acquire' (Doremus, 2011, p. 1,458). As discussed above, the increased involvement of non-government actors in multi-level new governance arrangements can substantially enhance the local and regional knowledge and the flow of information in decision-making. However, when seeking to manage complex and non-linear systems, achieving successful adaptive processes will typically require much more detailed monitoring and modelling of resources, conditions and impacts of management actions. This is a challenge because scientific knowledge of potential outcomes and human interventions in natural processes are still subject to significant knowledge gaps (Emerson and Gerlak, 2014, p. 561; Klinke and Renn, 2012, p. 276). Australia's water reforms provide a useful illustration here. Despite billions of dollars being invested in monitoring and infrastructure, the monitoring and adaption of collaborative catchment plans has been undermined by limited funding for targeted baseline assessments of water conditions, as well as the ongoing evaluation and reporting of water plan objectives (NWC, 2013, 2014, p. 404).

Even when information is available, a fourth and final challenge for new governance is whether government and non-government actors have the necessary capacity or willingness to gather, analyse, share and collaboratively act on information about their impacts on social and ecological systems (Sturm, 2006, p. 327). The study by Holley and Sinclair (2011) of Australian natural resource management bodies exposes many of these challenges. Despite being charged with adaptive management tasks, these collaborative bodies largely struggled to fulfil their functions. The authors (Holley and Sinclair, 2011) argue this is because of, among other things, insufficient internal expertise to conduct adaptive management, the sheer complexity and scope of the environmental problems, and state government agencies being either unwilling or unable to provide direct input or support for data. Fostering the necessary capacity or willingness to pursue new governance features is perhaps even more difficult in countries where governors have an entrenched history of highly centralised and hierarchical governance regimes, such as many post-Soviet nations (Sofronova et al, 2014). For example, in Belarus, there is evidence of an emerging new governance system of polycentric and multi-levelled forest management, which engages international and domestic non-governmental organisations and diverse state bodies from forest, biodiversity conservation, land and other relevant types of management (Banaszak et al, 2010). However, practitioners and policymakers' low connectivity, communication and willingness of cooperation have largely prevented it from working effectively (Banaszak et al, 2010).

CONCLUDING REMARKS

Hierarchical environmental law implemented by agencies and enforced by courts has played an indispensable role in protecting our environment, economy and society. Yet these tools have proven ill-suited to managing many of the most confounding environmental risks and problems that confront the world today. Problems like biodiversity, climate change impacts and risks, water scarcity and natural resource degradation are fraught with complexity, severe knowledge gaps, unintended consequences, and dynamic social and ecological systems. This has necessitated a shift in thinking and practice towards new responses to these environmental challenges. One of the catalysts of this rethinking has been resilience theory, which acknowledges the critical role of cross-scale dynamics, disequilibrium in socio-ecological systems and the capacity of systems to withstand internal or external change, but remain within their same regimes (Garmestani et al, 2013). This chapter has explored one of the more novel governance innovations thought to be capable of operationalising resilience, namely new environmental governance. Examples of new governance were examined and key benefits to managing resilience were explored. These advantages included: fostering problem solving that is contextualised and responsive to circumstances at and across multiple scales, both vertical from local to international, and horizontal; and enhancing the types and flow of information within a system so as to enable innovation and the adaptation of rules in response to changing circumstances; and increasing the capacity of local communities to accept or manage change.

Recent debates were also highlighted, with a focus on whether new governance can deliver on its promised benefits to foster resilience by enabling systems to better cope with, adapt to and shape change (Pisano, 2012). Four key overlapping challenges were identified, namely: a lack of clear direction for guiding and implementing adaptive practices; risks of accountability deficits arising from new governance's flexibility for managing uncertainty; inadequate resourcing to pursue requisite flexible, adaptive and collaborative structures; and an absence of interest or capacity to gather, analyse, share and collaboratively act on information. Given these potential challenges, it is important to caution against seeing new governance as a panacea for managing resilience in response to environmental problems and risks (Holley, 2017a, p. 751). The concept of resilience has come from the natural sciences, however its implementation through new governance is still developing and adjusting. Many of the challenges highlighted in the chapter resonate with concerns about resilience itself, including limitations of asymmetrical power arrangements, limited information (Aldunce et al, 2015, pp. 8–9) as well as concerns it can postpone necessary changes (Diprose, 2015, pp. 49, 53). At a broader level, it is also arguable that both new governance and resilience have been heralded by their respective camps as new important archetypes, with the result that they are now both getting pushed to represent more than they can deliver in practice (Olsson et al, 2015).

There is, however, still a long way to go to understand when and whether new governance may 'work', particularly considering the complexity of global problems and institutions, inequality and differences in resources, economic development (e.g. between developed and developing countries) and political arrangements (e.g. between the developed and the post-communist countries). As already suggested, this will be a long journey because new governance is a continuing social experiment that is transiting from a period of testing by trial and error to one of consolidation and refinement (Holley, 2017a, p. 751). But the success of new governance's mature stages will depend principally upon heeding the lessons of earlier successes and failures, and drawing broader lessons from them to make new governance work in practice (Holley, 2017a, p. 752).

A range of scholars are increasingly turning their mind to developing these lessons and identifying principles and conditions under which new governance appears more likely to overcome the above barriers and increase its potential as a tool for managing change. Such suggestions include: selection and training of governors in information use and sharing (Doremus, 2011, p. 1,462); utilising law to more clearly define the content of adaptive processes, set substantive objectives and standards and establish legally enforceable obligations to monitor and pursue adaptation (Doremus, 2011; Lee, 2014; McDonald and Styles, 2014); and enhancing collaboration and information generation by designating significant funding to the new governance enterprise (Garmestani et al, 2014; Holley et al, 2012). In addition to using funding to better support and build the capacity of stakeholders to participate, von der Porten and de Loë (2014) usefully challenge new governance to also integrate concepts from indigenous governance, including the need to recognise indigenous nationhood, *sui generis* rights and indigenous self-determination.

While such recommendations can help advance new governance thinking and practice, it is an enormously complex and far-reaching undertaking for any governance system (be it new governance or otherwise) to manage resilience. Doing it right may very well require a foundational realignment of not just the entirety of natural resource and environmental law and policy (Karkkainen, 2006, p. 225), but perhaps even global patterns of socio-economic organisation (von der Ponten and de Loë, 2016). Moreover, with growing recognition that humans are the now the key drivers for change in the planetary system (Biermann, 2014, p. 57; Pattberg and Widerberg, 2015), we may need not only an increased attention to new governance, but entirely new ways of governing the Anthropocene, including orchestrating the increasingly complex legal, regulatory and governance approaches and actors at local, national and international levels (Gunningham and Holley, 2016; Pattberg and Widerberg, 2015, pp. 689, 693; Stevenson and Dryzek, 2014).

In summary, the recent shift to new governance remains a work in progress, and the journey of exploring new ways of thinking about, and creating arrangements for, governing complex systems has only just begun. This chapter has pointed to ways in which new governance can work, but also suggested we find new ways to do things better when it doesn't work (Holley, 2017a, p. 751). Beyond pragmatic concerns, new governance is likely to continue to attract attention in environmental legal scholarship (Nourse and Shaffer, 2014). At a broad level, there is need for further conceptual refinement and clarity regarding the benefits and drawbacks of new governance's 'theoretical multiplicity' and how it can and should relate to other fields relevant to resilience and adaptation, not least adaptive governance (see e.g. Karpouzoglou et al, 2016). Developing a clearer picture of the increasingly crowded space of environmental governance and resilience is not only important conceptually and descriptively, but it can also help us normatively identify and build more effective and fair governance systems for fostering social and ecological resilience in the future (Holley and Shearing, 2016).

8. Science and the law: how will developments in attribution science affect how the law addresses compensation for climate change effects?

Lindene Patton and Felicia H. Barnes

INTRODUCTION

The scientific community has largely settled the question of whether changes to the earth's climate are occurring, but the legal community has not reached consensus on how to address these changes or their resulting risks or damages. This is not surprising, given the law's structural and procedural emphasis on certainty and predictability, and discouragement of rapid change or instability, contrasted with science's open embrace of change and reconsideration of previous findings. These tensions are particularly evident in areas rife with scientific complexity, like global climate change. This chapter discusses the gap between science and the law in the climate change arena and how it has impacted attempts to address the risks, losses and damages related to climate change in a more comprehensive fashion. Adding to this already complex area are recent attribution science developments that seek to determine if the magnitude or frequency of an event has been changed by anthropogenically induced climate change.[1] Improvements in attribution science tee up complex questions regarding how to allocate 'damages' from climate change-related effects.

1 The Intergovernmental Panel on Climate Change (IPCC, 2014a) defines attribution as 'the process of evaluating the relative contributions of multiple causal factors to a change or event with an assignment of statistical confidence' <https://www.ipcc.ch/pdf/assessment-report/ar5/wg2/WGIIAR5-AnnexII_FINAL.pdf> accessed 2 June 2016. The National Academies of Sciences, Engineering and Medicine (2016) use the same definition (hereafter 'NAS, 2016') <http://www.nap.edu/catalog/21852/attribution-of-extreme-weather-events-in-the-context-of-climate-change>accessed

The subject of attribution and related liability cannot be completely discussed without considering insurance, a financial risk management tool that is pivotal in society because it addresses liability. As such, this chapter also addresses the role of insurance in responding to climate-related impacts and the added complexity climate change brings to the insurance process. Insurance is a special type of contract that relies heavily on the law for interpretation – and in turn, in many cases, on science for its triggering events. Trends documented by (re)insurers and their regulators note that less of overall physical damages arising out of climatic events, especially extreme ones, is being insured by exposed asset owners (see, e.g., US Senate Homeland Security and Government Affairs Committee, 2014). Consequently, asset owners and sovereigns are retaining more extreme weather and basic climate-related risks. Credit rating institutions are also noting this trend has gone far enough to create potential industry and sovereign credit risks when extreme weather events manifest (Standard and Poor's Rating Services, 2015a; 2015b). In other words, the trend suggests that less and less *ex ante* funding exists for catastrophic climate-related and extreme weather event-related loss and damage – setting the stage for increasing pressure on, and interest in, climate change science and socio-economic attribution and allocation theory. If the gap between *ex ante* financing of, and experienced loss and damage from, climate change-related events becomes too large, insurance and sovereign resources will not likely be adequate to cover all costs in the short term. Insurance may play an integral role in closing this climate resilience gap in order to manage these risks efficiently, particularly if insurance is involved up front, rather than in a litigation setting.

THE LAW AND CLIMATE SCIENCE: WHY ISN'T THE LAW USED CONSISTENTLY TO ADDRESS CLIMATE CHANGE IMPACTS?

Both science and the law are important tools for dealing with existing and future social, economic and environmental conditions. But they

---

2 June 2016. See also NAS (2016, p. 8) noting the 'importance of framing any attribution question' and stating it is poor framing to ask 'was a given observed weather event caused by climate change?' 'There can be a tendency in some quarters to want to confidently attribute extremes to anthropogenic climate change in the absence of scientific consensus or to argue that it isn't possible to link individual extreme events with anthropogenic climate change, neither of which is correct' (Stott et al, 2016, p. 24).

have important differences, particularly with respect to their treatment of uncertainty and change. Thus far, these differences have prevented traditional legal theories – such as civil tort claims for damages, litigation using statutory rights or national regulation – from providing a means for addressing climate change effects in a meaningful, comprehensive way. Improvements in attribution science may change this landscape. And throughout this complex area, difficult questions remain about how damages, if appropriate, would be assessed.

The Gap between Science and Law

On a conceptual basis, the differences between science and the law help partially explain why traditional legal paths have not addressed climate change effects. The law provides certainty in the face of unpredictable events. Science seeks to understand events and processes that may be unpredictable. The law celebrates consistency, predictability and fairness; science celebrates chaos, uniqueness, change and repeatability. While both the law and science are rooted in the pursuit of the truth (and how truth is discovered, i.e. 'proof'), they do not share a common method for evaluating truth. Many areas of science rely on the 95 per cent confidence as their standard (see generally Bradley, 2011). The law typically does not require that level of confidence, often utilising a 'more likely than not' (i.e. 51 per cent threshold) to determine key facts and ascertain liability.[2] And the end points of the legal and scientific processes are different. The law seeks a final determination, with limits on when an issue can be revisited (Dyson, 2011). But science expects no such finality. Because it seeks to understand the world around it based upon current knowledge and technology, science instead expects and demands that it will learn more continuously – learning that may change prior understanding, consensus and determinations.

The gap between science and law is also the result of different approaches to dealing with uncertainty.[3] The law and the social and economic

---

[2] Orloff and Stedinger (1983, p. 1159), noting that the burden of persuasion in most civil cases in the United States 'requires demonstrating that the existence of the contested fact is more probable than its nonexistence'; House of Lords (2008), many civil law countries require a more subjective standard of proof even further from a 95 per cent confidence interval. See Clermont and Sherwin (2002, p. 243), 'In civil-law countries . . . a civil claimant must in effect convince the trier of fact that the claimant's assertions are true'; 'On the Continent, proof is understood as a strictly subjective impression in the judge's mind. By contrast, in American law, proof is an objective concept' (Engel, 2009, p. 436).

[3] 'Law was one of the first of society's endeavors in which things appeared as neither completely true nor completely untrue. Aristotelian two-valued logic

structures it supports are all based on societal agreements regarding morality, social norms and common social experiences.[4] The law effectively memorialises collectively what we 'know' and what we 'should have known' based upon experience. But when common experience is a poor guide for future conditions, the law can be slow to adapt to new risks. In the case of climate change, the disciplines of law and science struggle mightily to find common ground on many fundamental questions, such as what the climate used to be like, what it is today and what it is likely to be like in the future. And it is additionally difficult for the law to address climate change effects comprehensively when the science is still developing, particularly on a granular scale.

In the climate change context, this struggle is demonstrated by upsets to the assumption of stationarity, which is the concept that the water cycle functions as a consistent pattern. Many parts of the law assume that the history of climatic patterns, including the water cycle, is a useful predictor for the expected future environment. Climate change challenges this notion.[5] Although, of course, such assertions are based at least in part on indirect indicators, models and measurements that, however prolific, are nonetheless bedevilled by uncertainties in data collection and analysis.[6]

And even if the law recognises change is happening, defining and

---

did not work for such partial truths . . . The prevailing but contested view is that fact-finders should determine facts by this line of probabilistic reasoning: although given imperfect evidence, they should ask themselves what they think the chances are that the burdened party would be right if the truth were somehow to become known' (Clermont, 2013, pp. 1069–70).

4 For example, tort law is generally thought of as largely 'reflect[ing] social values and norms already in existence in the culture. . . The tort rule confirms or articulates social ideals and perhaps reinforces them by imposing liability' (Dobbs, 2000, p. 30).

5 See Milly et al (2008, p. 573) 'In view of the magnitude and ubiquity of the hydroclimatic change apparently now under way, . . . we assert that stationarity is dead and should no longer serve as a central, default assumption in water-resource risk assessment and planning. Finding a suitable successor is crucial for human adaptation to changing climate'; Milly et al (2015); 'We do not suggest that the "suitable successor" [Milly et al, 2008] to stationarity has been found. Rather we continue to regard finding such a suitable successor as a major challenge to the community of hydrologists and water resource engineers.'

6 Surminski and Lopez (2015, pp. 267–77); Milly et al (2015) noting that due to disagreements, biases, and imperfections with climate models, projections are 'samples of possible futures, subject to errors, and conditioned on assumed trajectories of atmospheric composition' (Milly et al, 2015, p. 7787), and thus using these results requires considering reasonable error estimates; 'In a nonstationary world, continuity of observations is critical. . . [W]e must use long-term hydrologic observations to help us evaluate, on an ongoing basis, how the changing atmosphere

accounting for that change is quite complicated, both for scientific and legal reasons. Scientifically, it can be tricky because different regions of the world have different capacities for adaptation to extreme weather and other events associated with climate change. Adaptation variation even exists within smaller socio-economic or political structures, based upon building stock conditions, infrastructure and other characteristics. Thus, extreme weather events with the same physical characteristics can have wildly different impacts (Botts, 2014; Grannis, 2011). These differences can present themselves even in the lateral or vertical space of a few feet (less than a metre). Thus for a variety of factual reasons, calculating for this under the law in any objective manner can be difficult, if not impossible – raising the spectre of political or social imperatives overwriting or compensating for gaps in data and calculations.

Finally, incorporating information about climate change into legal proceedings and documents is a complex endeavour. This is particularly relevant in the insurance realm. Proof of climate change and who knew what and when affects the interpretation and operation of insurance products (i.e. contracts) in unique ways – for both property and casualty products. In particular, if a prospective insured declares in an application that no actions have occurred or are in process that are likely to trigger coverage, but at the time of the application the prospective insured was indeed aware of such conditions, such actions may constitute fraud in the application and could later void all or part of the coverage. And, in the case of the insured and injured third party, when individuals suffer damage, especially where the individual does not believe their actions caused or contributed to their damages and suffering, they will often look to insurance to pay – or to determine what other party might be responsible for their damage and seek recovery from that party's insurance.

Current State of Climate Law

Laws and regulations seeking to address climate change have expanded significantly in recent years, spanning international, national and sub-national jurisdictions and traversing numerous legal disciplines, including environmental regulations, common law causes of action and reporting standards. Politics and publicity have fostered a high degree of awareness about climate change and its prospective impacts. Yet so far, none of these avenues has created a consistent or comprehensive method

---

is changing hydrologic processes' (internal quotation omitted) (Milly et al, 2015, p. 7788).

for addressing climate change effects or compensating victims of alleged climate-related damages, largely due to issues of political will, causation and justiciability.

The steady increase of extreme weather losses and improvements in attribution science are likely to drive the next wave of climate change litigation. This next area will likely focus on legal areas without justiciability problems, such as those against people who had special knowledge about climate-related risk but did not share or disclose such knowledge. These lawsuits will likely be influenced by the state of attribution science, which will be relevant in evaluation of causation issues as well as allocation of damages.

Recent Advances in Climate Science

Attribution science seeks to 'estimate how much climate change has affected an individual event's magnitude or probability of occurrence'.[7] Attribution science has made significant strides in recent years, but important uncertainties and limitations remain.[8] Extreme event types with the strongest results have lengthy observational records providing historical context, sufficiently accurate climate modelling and have little or no confounding from non-meteorological factors, such as the state of infrastructure or planning (NAS, 2016, pp. 5–6). Scientists report increasing confidence for anthropogenic influence on extreme temperature events (NAS, 2016, pp. 6–9; Herring et al, 2016; Stott et al, 2016, p. 37; Herring et al, 2015). Scientists express less confidence for extreme precipitation events, droughts, storms and wildfires.[9]

---

[7] NAS (2016); see also Stott et al (2016, pp. 24–5): 'Event attribution studies have sought to determine to whether anthropogenic climate change has altered the probability or magnitude of particular events. Early examples include the European summer heat wave of 2003 that killed many thousands of people and the flooding in the UK in autumn, 2000' (internal citations omitted); discussing methodologies of different attribution studies (Stott et al, 2016, pp. 25–32).

[8] NAS (2016) noting the importance of framing the research question, identifying assumptions and estimating uncertainties; Stott et al (2016) noting 'remaining scientific uncertainties' and 'patchy' geographical information on extreme events; 'Studies show clear evidence for human influence on some events and little evidence for human influence on others and in some cases draw seemingly conflicting conclusions due to differences in the way the attribution question has been framed' (internal citations omitted) (Stott et al, 2016, p. 25). Remaining uncertainties about specific climate change trends also require additional research. See e.g. Fyfe (2016).

[9] NAS (2016, pp. 6–9) concluding that the highest confidence exists for extreme heat and cold events, next highest is for hydrological drought and heavy

These advances in attribution science are documented in the progression of peer-reviewed reports produced by the *Bulletin of the American Meteorological Society* (BAMS). Since 2012, BAMS has published an annual review of the previous year's extreme weather events from a climate perspective. These reviews show increasing certainty in their results and an evolution of scientific thinking on this issue such that it is now widely accepted that attribution statements about individual weather or climate events are possible, provided proper account is taken of the probabilistic nature of attribution. For example, the 2012 report only went so far as to say that attribution analyses 'have the *potential* to inform the necessary training and adaption options for societies in dealing with the punches weather and climate extremes throw their way' (Peterson, 2012, p. 1,062) (emphasis added). The hesitation shown throughout the 2012 report is in marked contrast to the research and conclusions of the 2016 and 2015 reports. The 2016 report found '"[w]ithout exception" that all the heat-related events studied in this year's report were found to have been made more intense or likely due to human-induced climate change, and this was discernible even for those events strongly influenced by the 2015 El Niño.' (Herring et al, 2016, p. Sii). Similarly, the 2015 report concluded that the preponderance of the evidence regarding heatwaves showed an impact from human-caused climate change (Herring et al, 2015, p. S168). The supporting studies use strong language to describe their results, such as a study on the East African drought which concluded that the temperature anomalies 'appear extremely unlikely without anthropogenic warming' (Herring et al, 2015, p. S78). Similarly, a study on the Argentinian heatwave of December 2013 concluded it 'was likely caused in part by anthropogenic forcings' (Herring et al, 2015, p. S44).

---

precipitation, and stating that there is 'little or no confidence in the attribution of severe convective storms and extratropical cyclones'; 'Research to date has shown much clearer evidence for human influence on extreme temperature events than extreme precipitation events, droughts, and storms . . . For extreme precipitation events, droughts, and storms, the evidence is much more mixed. The observational basis is less secure, climate models can struggle to capture relevant features of the events, and different methods of framing attribution questions can reduce contrasting results' (Stott et al, 2016, p. 37); '[R]esults remain subject to substantial uncertainty, with greater levels of uncertainty for events that are not directly temperature related. The conclusions drawn also depend, in general, on choices made when selecting the events, framing the questions asked about the role of climate change, designing the modeling setup, and selecting statistical tools to quantify uncertainty' (NAS, 2016, p. 1); '[A]s the science advances we hope to see more papers connected a line between climate change and impacts, not only for heat but also for other event types.' (Herring et al, 2016, p. S2).

Additionally, the 2016 and 2015 reports included studies covering a larger geographic scope, whereas prior reports had 'some gaps in South America and much of Africa' (Stott et al, 2016, p. 33). The 2016 report included multiple studies from Africa (Herring et al, 2016, p. S2). And the 2015 report discussed the influence of human activities, including greenhouse gas emissions, had on specific extreme weather events in 2014, including a water shortage in Brazil, a heatwave in Argentina, and drought in East Africa. (BAMS, 2015).

Work is already underway on the next level of attribution research. For instance, more frequent attribution analyses are on their way.[10] According to Climate Central's chief scientist, Heidi Cullen, there are plans to use 'seasonal forecasts to compare extreme weather events as they happen with the very same weather events in a world that might have been without climate change', in pursuit of their goal 'to give a first, scientifically based answer to the question whether and to what extent climate change played a role in the probability of occurrence of the event in real time'.[11] Efforts are also underway to develop broader data sources covering geographical areas in a more consistent fashion. For example, Climate Central and Oxford University's Environmental Change Institute employ crowdsourcing type tactics to develop additional data and analytics for their world weather attribution project.[12] The European Climate and Weather Events: Interpretation and Attribution (EUCLEIA) is developing an operational attribution system for Europe.[13]

Even with these advances in attribution science, however, it is important to keep in mind that extreme events typically have a natural variability component. The role of this natural variability is sufficiently important that the National Academies of Sciences (NAS) concluded recently that there usually cannot be a 'definitive answer to the commonly asked question of whether climate change "caused" a particular event' (NAS, 2016, p. 9). Further, the NAS cautioned that studies regarding attribution for individual events are not appropriately used to describe how climate change impacts the entirety of extreme events.[14]

---

10 Some believe the BAMS reports are 'too late to be relevant on the timescales when the media are asking questions about causality of damaging weather and climate events', and their ad hoc nature has resulted in patchy geographic coverage and random selection of events, limiting 'the ability to draw wider conclusions for the year in question' (Stott et al, 2016, p. 37).

11 See <http://www.climatecentral.org> [accessed 2 June 2016] and <http://climateprediction.net> [accessed 2 June 2016].

12 See <http://climateprediction.net> [accessed 2 June 2016].

13 See <http://www.eucleia.eu> [accessed 2 June 2016].

14 NAS (2016, p. 10) notes that '[e]vents that have been selected for attribution studies to date are not a representative sample', and that 'counts of available attri-

Developments in Theories for Damage Allocation

All of these scientific developments have the potential to inform and move the legal liability discussion about climate change. By informing the discussion about risks to both the most vulnerable and the most developed, such developments affect our understanding of what conditions are reasonably to be expected in the future and consequently what can be done to improve resilience.

Attribution Science and Policy Issues Regarding Damage Allocation

There are multiple complex questions in the damages calculations area. How to assess 'loss and damage' is an emerging legal field (Surminski and Lopez, 2015, section 2.2) and a focal point of the multilateral negotiations under the United Nations Framework Convention on Climate Change (UNFCCC). Further complicating it is the physical reality of the kinds of impacts at issue. Physically similar extreme events can result in very different impacts based on where and when they occur. Consequently, the associated loss and damage from these events can vary markedly. For example, a small, low-lying island nation could see its shorelines vanish under even the most modest of sea-level rise scenarios. A wealthy industrialised nation surrounded by state-of-the-art seawalls might not. From a certain perspective, plaintiffs injured on the island nation would have more viable claims to damages than those in the nation with more advanced resilience technology. What if, however, the plaintiffs are not damaged alone – but are part of a community under a sovereign with duties to protect and support the community? Isn't there a difference between a solitary plaintiff and a large population under a sovereign government actively engaged in the protection of its health and welfare?

Additionally, climate change is a global issue, and the emissions allegedly causing climate change derive from products and services provided by both private actors and sovereigns, as well as a natural carbon cycle subject to a multitude of variables. Both sovereigns and private actors have derived pecuniary benefits from the activities that produce greenhouse gases. Given that sovereigns are entrusted with certain obligations to protect constituents from harm, an important question is what duty these sovereigns owe their citizens to assure sufficient resilience to effects

---

bution studies with either positive, negative, or neutral results are not expected to give a reliable indication of the overall importance of human influence on extreme events'.

of climate change. Should damage calculations account for some level of obligation or duty of their sovereigns to take action to invest in resilience? And if attribution science is sufficient to make certain hazards and associated damages obvious, this prompts questions about whether injured parties have a duty to protect themselves.

Further, for certain potential plaintiffs, such as island nations, both the kind and extent of damages may be deemed foreseeable in the coming years as a result of the developments in attribution science. Yet requiring full payment of all damages in a kind of 'polluter pays' scheme would be a dramatic shift from current legal approaches to climate change damages and is likely to be resisted. It also may, in any event, prove politically untenable and serve only to mark yet another destabilising failure in the ongoing climate policy debate at the international level. That is, while these questions may seem provocative, their potential answers (or lack thereof) are, in many respects, more so.

Current Damage Allocation Proposals

Substantial developments have been made in the areas of quantification of emissions (Heede, 2014) and theories on legal damage allocation. A series of methodologies have been developed to ascertain damages directly or indirectly caused by an event attributable to greenhouse gas emissions. These methods have neither used attribution science as a basis nor have they followed the common law approach in determining damages.

Major international climate policy dialogues on the subject of 'loss and damage' have thus far looked past a polluter-pays approach and instead focused on various forms of contract or statutorily subsidised disaster risk reduction, including through the Green Climate Fund's dual emphasis on adaptation and mitigation.[15] Other suggested damage methods have used

---

15 See e.g. United Nations Framework Convention on Climate Change 2016 <http://unfccc.int/cooperation_and_support/financial_mechanism/green_climate_fund/items/5869.php> [accessed 2 June 2016]; United Nations Framework Convention on Climate Change. 2015. Report of the Adaptation Committee, Decision 4/CP.21, http://unfccc.int/resource/docs/2015/cop21/eng/10a02.pdf#page=4 [accessed 7 June 2016]; Adaptation Fund, 'Projects & Programmes', <https://www.adaptation-fund.org> [accessed 2 June 2016]. This may be motivated, in part, by practical concerns about the total financial burden climate change could impose. Attribution science may be helpful in targeting damage estimates to make them more manageable. See Pinninti (2014, p. 31): 'The estimates of loss and damage due to climate change (whichever source used) are very high; these are too high to be paid by the main contributors of climate change (historically and/or currently). The purpose of deriving more precise estimates is to seek some

a theoretical market price for carbon dioxide emissions or a polluter-pays model of total damages.

For instance, a KPMG International (2012, p. 13) report indicates 'the world's 3,000 largest public companies by market capitalization were estimated to be causing US $2.15 trillion of environmental damage annually'. This calculation used a synthetic market price for carbon (an estimated cost of carbon per ton in a hypothetical market) to estimate damages from carbon and other environmental pollutants and harms. This approach has no relation to actual damage, as it is based on a theoretical market price. Its translation into litigation would be difficult to achieve under the current recognised common-law legal theorem.

Another approach was taken in a 2014 report by the Centre for Policy Alternative and the West Coast Environmental Law Institute. This report set forth a methodology and, using that methodology, evaluated the total potential liability for damages attributable to the share of greenhouse gas emissions from businesses of five oil and gas companies currently trading on the Toronto Stock Exchange: EnCana, Suncor, Canadian Natural Resources (CNR), Talisman and Husky (Gage and Byers, 2014). However, this methodology looked to add all damages and then apportioned the damages by share of total emissions. This kind of polluter-pays approach is more akin to environmental statutes such as the Comprehensive Environmental Response, Compensation and Liability Act of 1980 (CERCLA). This kind of method has neither been incorporated into tort law nor used in a specific case. As it does not follow the typical common-law approach, it is also unlikely to be used in litigation in the future.

LOSS AND ATTRIBUTION: THE RELEVANCE OF THE GROWING CLIMATE RESILIENCE GAP

To avoid unexpected, black-swan type loss and damage claims related to climate change, adaptation of, and improved resilience to, assets and socio-economic structures is essential. Science, especially attribution

---

sense of proportionality of cause-and-effect and loss-and-damage so that vulnerable countries obtain compensation as partial relief. Since full *ex ante* restoration of assets and resources is not contemplated under any of the current and proposed laws at the international levels, it is prudent to seek compensation mechanisms resources that cater to short-term and long-term aspects of DDR and CCA in the vulnerable countries that have low levels of infrastructure and capacities to address adverse impacts of climate change.'

science, can aid society by informing estimates of the increased physical forces (energy) that can be expected with climate change. Further analytics can project expected damage and loss based on current trends or based on additional investments. The result creates the basis for a cost-benefit analysis that could be considered in the evaluation of the reasonableness (or another standard of care) of the behaviour of a party with a duty to consider the impacts of failure on the persons relying on the investment – whether in a physical asset or a financial instrument. Thus, insurance will be involved in losses and damages related to climate change one way or another – either as a risk manager or in litigation. It is most economically efficient if insurance is involved up front, intentionally as an expert advisor and *ex ante* finance partner, rather than in a litigation setting.

The Growing Climate Resilience Gap

For a society to function sustainably, resilience is essential.[16] The 'climate resilience gap' is the divergence between the level of protection afforded to assets, people and communities and the level of protection that is required to reduce climate change-related losses to assure resilience. The 'climate resilience gap' can often be expressed in terms of financial and economic losses that cause disruption, which may or may not be absorbed by a system, community or society after a weather-related catastrophe.

Evidence shows that the climate resilience gap is growing. The frequency and severity of climate-driven natural disasters is increasing,[17] with rapid growth of both the number of people and assets in harm's way. The percentage of natural disaster damage that is insured is decreasing when

---

16 One major component of resilience is the capacity of society's assets or its built environment to withstand or quickly recover from weather-related catastrophes. For example, the U.N. Office for Disaster Risk Reduction defines resilience as 'the ability of a system, community, or society exposed to hazards to resist, absorb, accommodate to, and recover from the effects of hazard in a timely and efficient manner, including through the preservation and restoration of its essential basic structures and functions' U.N. Office for Disaster Risk Reduction (2016).

17 See e.g. Munich Re (2016a), <https://www.munichre.com/site/wrap/get/documents_E1831215213/mram/assetpool.munichreamerica.wrap/PDF/07Press/2015_natural_catastrophe_losses_US_010416.pdf>[accessed 2 June 2016]; Munich Re (2016b), <https://www.munichre.com/site/wrap/get/documents_E1656163460/mram/assetpool.munichreamerica.wrap/PDF/07Press/2015_World_map_of_nat_cats.pdf> [accessed 2 June 2016]; Pinninti (2014, p. 13): 'Since 1981, economic loss from disasters is growing faster than GDP per capita in the OECD countries. This means that the risk of losing wealth in weather-related disasters is now exceeding the rate at which wealth itself is being created.'

the magnitude of the loss trips aggregate management mechanisms of the industry – either individually or regionally.[18] In other words, the amount of uninsured losses is growing and increasingly being covered by government catastrophe funds (Michel-Kerjan, 2015, pp. 2–4), thus contributing to a greater climate resilience gap. Uninsured losses largely drive the subsequent macroeconomic cost because sufficiently insured events are inconsequential in terms of forgone output (von Peter et al, 2012; CEBR, 2012). High potential risks could become uninsurable as a result of volatility and/or unaffordability (European Commission, 2013, p. 5).

The climate resilience gap presents a global threat to economic sustainability. It is present in both the developed[19] and developing world.[20] And this gap is growing.[21] If the gap between *ex ante* financing of, and experienced loss and damage from, climate change-related events becomes too large, insurance and sovereign resources will likely be inadequate to cover all costs in the short term. In fact, rating agencies are now articulating the potential expected credit risk downgrades for industry and sovereigns should extreme events manifest. Further investment in resilience is required to manage these risks efficiently (Build Strong Coalition, 2015).

The climate resilience gap is likely to drive continued tort litigation –

---

18 See note 17.

19 See generally, Notre Dame Global Adaptation Index (2014a) (2014b), developed markets represent the largest source of insurance premiums globally, but they also represent the largest absolute insured loss source. For example, Munich Re NatCatSERVICE data show that the number of loss-relevant weather catastrophes has increased dramatically since 1980, globally and in North America; Munich Re (2012), in North America, the annual average number of natural catastrophe events (primarily, weather-related) has risen by four-fold, from 50 to 200 in the past 30 years; Munich Re (2012), Figure 3, in the United States, a recently released report identifies that both the frequency and magnitude of federal disaster relief for events causing loss in excess of $1B USD is increasing at a significant rate and that federal disaster relief expenditures alone (which excludes supplementary charitable, state and local costs) over the past three years have risen to $400 per household – more than a four-fold increase over the past 30 years; Weiss and Weidman (2013), for the European Union, while the total number of events increased slightly less than the 2.5 factor average for the 1980–2010 time frame, the loss cost impacts to governments and their citizens, especially when considered in the context of climate change, are considered to be of significant fiscal concern; European Environment Agency (2012); see also Quinto (2012, pp. 30–77) surveying different state and insurance options for several European countries and the US and concluding that 'comprehensive insurance against natural hazards, based on statutory insurance, represents a necessity today and all the more so in the future' due to climate change.

20 See generally, Notre Dame Global Adaptation Index (2014a) (2014b).

21 See note 17.

just as similar gaps between losses and protection have driven litigation in other areas, such as asbestos, hazardous waste and pharmaceuticals. In other words, increasing losses place additional stress on an increasingly pressing question: who should pay for loss and damages that can be attributed to greenhouse gas emissions? Insurers will be involved in the societal discussions about climate change resilience, just as they were in asbestos, pharmaceutical and other environmental issues. Insurance may find itself on both the solutions side and the defence side. As attribution science develops, insurers would be wise to consider how these trends will impact their position as insurer of emitters and developer of multi-lateral solutions.

How Will Developments in Attribution Science Affect Efforts to Address and Close the Climate Resilience Gap?

One way that insurance can be involved in bridging the climate resilience gap, thus allowing for a more efficient use of resources, is through improving resilience. Commentators have often suggested that insurance and government are uniquely positioned to help improve resilience to, and mitigate the risks arising out of, the frequency of extreme weather events, especially those caused by, or contributed to, by climate change. While it may be true that insurance and government can work to improve resilience,[22] insurance and government aid have fundamentally distinct social and economic functions – as such their roles, capabilities and capacities should not be conflated. Attribution science can be used by both governments and insurers to ascertain how best to use their differing resources to fill the climate resilience gap.

Differing Roles of Disaster Response and Insurance in Addressing the Climate Resilience Gap

Disaster response and insurance perform distinct functions for society. Both are essential and often work together. But nonetheless, they perform different roles to meet different goals. The purpose of disaster response and recovery efforts is largely to return people and society back to basic levels of functionality. Government aid is a tool which allows sovereign or multi-lateral sourced funds *ex post* to pay for typically public goods and

---

22 See e.g. Lloyd's (2015), <http://www.lloyds.com/cityriskindex> [accessed 2 June 2016], 'A 1% rise in insurance penetration translates into a 13% reduction in uninsured losses – a 22% reduction in taxpayers' contribution following a disaster.'

services that individual beneficiaries could not otherwise afford – such as shared transportation, water or power systems. The purpose of insurance, however, is to turn the damaged party to his/her condition prior to the loss event. Insurance is an *ex ante* risk financing and management tool.

Insurance can create instruments and facilities to pool funds to pay for fortuitous loss and damage to shared and individually owned assets. But when fortuity[23] diminishes (as certainty of loss increases due to improved understanding of climate science-related extreme event impacts), insurance no longer functions as a stand-alone solution to loss and damage. In short, the resilience of the assets must be improved. If the owners of the assets cannot afford to pay for improvement to an appropriate level of resilience where loss and damage from extreme events once again become fortuitous, then government aid must bridge the gap to pay for such improvements.

The interplay between disaster relief and insurance can significantly impact the effectiveness of both. As an *ex ante* tool, insurance can create incentives to reduce risk. And the effectiveness of government aid is increased if risks are first minimised through insurance (Michel-Kerjan, 2015, p. 6). But the knowledge that disaster relief is available may diminish the strength of the incentive to reduce risk, creating a moral hazard (Michel-Kerjan, 2015, p. 6). Consequently, the welfare value of insurance is impacted by the interaction between four factors – 'the increasing severity of the catastrophes, the rising trend of government aid, the substitution of government insurance for private insurance and the incentive of homeowners and even the government itself not to mitigate the underlying risks' (Dwight and Russell, 2013).

How Can the Attribution Science Inform Investment Decisions about Resilience?

Attribution science can inform policy makers, professionals and investors about how much 'additional' resilience is required to minimise damage caused by expected extreme weather events to a level that assures economic stability or another socio-economic goal.

---

[23] The fortuity doctrine states that insurance will not cover 'losses that the policyholder knows of, planned, intended, or is aware are substantially certain to occur' (Zalma, 2007, p. 409); '[A] fortuitous event is an event which, so far as the parties to the contract are aware, is dependent on chance. It may be beyond the power of any human being to bring to pass; it may be within the control of third persons, provided that the fact is unknown to the parties. The thrust of the definition is that the occurrence be unplanned and unintentional in nature' (Zalma, 2007, p. 1932) (quoting *Restatement of Contracts*, Section 291, cmt. a (1932)).

Government regulation is one way built assets can be made resilient to the physical, climate or extreme weather event-related stresses to which they are exposed. A prime example is strict building codes and zoning. In brief, building codes can legally require that certain safety standards be implemented. To ensure these codes actually bolster protection, public and private actors must invest in built environments, such as government investments in public infrastructure like streets or a homeowner retrofitting her house against flooding. *Ex ante* and *ex post* investments that fortify structures and financial protection can be encouraged and enabled by insurance.

Many legal issues of defence to coverage could present if a government does not put in place zoning and building codes which support resilience. With advances in attribution science, it is becoming more plausible that insufficiently protective building codes or zoning rules could be determined to be a contributing factor to loss and damage. This is of particular concern if the loss is of a type that attribution science shows is increasingly likely, in part or in whole, because of climate change.

Insurance is an *ex ante* financial instrument that can help societies and individuals prepare for catastrophes. Insurance helps mitigate the effects of disasters on households and the broader economy, it establishes baseline costs and it places a price on risks that can allow comparison of multiple risk management options.

Insurance, through the post-loss claims payment process, can facilitate timely restoration without the delays often experienced with disaster response (von Peter et al., 2012). The amount of indemnification provided by private insurance will typically reflect the loss/damage to the insured asset based upon insurable interest and value, rather than the arbitrary amount typically set by government insurance programmes or disaster recovery programmes. As such, insurance can provide both *ex ante* risk mitigation market welfare benefit, as well as *ex post* market welfare benefit through disaster recovery claim payments, and when combined with government disaster recovery efforts can be both economically beneficial and facilitate post-event restoration within short periods (von Peter et al, 2012). Contrast that performance with that of disaster relief done without insurance, which can result in multi-decadenal economic loss (von Peter et al, 2012).

New Products May Fill Specific Governance Gaps or Improve Resilience for Targeted Classes

Blended insurance products or alternative financial instruments sold by insurers can be used to narrow the climate resilience gap, and these products will improve and become more useful as attribution science improves. In particular, parametric insurance products, including forecast insurance, may be important to filling specific resilience gaps and will likely be affected by improvements in attribution science.

Parametric insurance typically relies on an objective measure of a physical event as the sole basis for triggering insurance payouts. Such measures include wind speed, excess rainfall measured by weather station and other items measured by satellite data. No proof of loss is required: payment is triggered by the happening of the covered events. Covered events often correspond to certain characteristics of extreme weather events or natural catastrophes. Parametric products can be deployed to generate payments that can be applied to restore assets to their condition prior to the loss or to an improved resilient state. Alternatively, they can be deployed to generate payments in amounts that do not reflect loss and damage but merely supply sufficient cash flow to stabilise government institutions so they may begin to recover and perform their jobs, which may include some disaster recovery and rebuilding (or not). Parametric insurance may hold value in managing business interruptions, addressing the consequential losses and costs of a disaster. Business interruption insurance lags behind property and life insurances in low-income countries, at least in part because of the challenges of adverse selection, moral hazard and loss adjustment for this coverage. Protecting against production risks with index insurance may be a natural complement to the asset protection provided by property insurance that may be (somewhat) more readily available in low-income countries.

Parametric insurance is being used increasingly to manage disaster risk in low-income countries, although it is not widely used, particularly when compared to the loss and damage caused by predicted events that trigger the programme. For example, a large group of Caribbean states are insuring against earthquakes and windstorms to reduce sovereign risk.[24] Additionally, the World Food Programme insured against drought in Ethiopia in 2006, demonstrating the potential of index insurance to enhance the provision of emergency food aid (Alderman and Haque, 2007, pp. 15–17). Following these examples, a large set of African countries are developing a regional disaster financing pool to address disaster risks and food insecurity.[25] There are also several examples of private sector

---

[24] Caribbean Catastrophe Risk Insurance Facility (CCRIF) (2015), <http://www.ccrif.org/sites/default/files/publications/CCRIFSPC_Annual_Report_2014_2015.pdf> [accessed 2 June 2016].

[25] See the African Risk Capacity website for up-to-date information, <http://www.africanriskcapacity.org> [accessed 2 June 2016].

deployment of parametric insurance.[26] For example, a microfinance institution in Peru is protecting against catastrophic flooding using El Niño insurance in order to increase its outreach to vulnerable, under-served markets (Collier and Skees, 2012).

One particular kind of parametric insurance, forecast insurance, may have particular relevance to advancing adaptation. The Peru example above acts as a test case of forecast insurance, which may be much more broadly applicable. El Niño is but one example of how global circulation patterns, called *teleconnections*, can dramatically affect regional climate conditions. El Niño is the result of disruptions in the teleconnection El Niño Southern Oscillation (ENSO), which describes atmospheric pressures that determine ocean and air circulation across the equatorial Pacific.[27] Interestingly, information on the teleconnection predates regional climate events. The disaster index used for El Niño insurance in Peru is the ocean temperature in a portion of the ENSO zone. As an El Niño event emerges, these ocean temperatures increase before catastrophic flooding occurs in Peru. As a result, the El Niño insurance is structured to pay policyholders *before* the disaster occurs. To our knowledge El Niño insurance is the first regulated forecast insurance in the world (Collier and Skees, 2012).

Forecast insurance may reduce losses through short-term loss prevention measures because it can enhance the ability of decision makers to adjust as warning signs of an impending event emerge. For example, a higher likelihood of windstorms motivates a business manager to relocate valuable inventory away from coastal regions. Also, a producer could adjust to emerging drought conditions by changing cropping strategies from corn to wheat in an agricultural season.

Forecast insurance may also motivate longer-term adaptation. Teleconnections have annual or even multiannual cycles, such that protecting against their extreme oscillations using forecast insurance may

---

[26] See Murphy et al (2011) for a broad overview of work in index insurance. Horn of Africa Risk Transfer for Adaptation (HARITA) and its successor project R4 (Rural Resilience Initiative) used parametric insurance as a means to structure payments tied to crop yield. See also Oxfam America (2012) and Oxfam America and United Nations World Food Programme (2016), R4 Rural Resilience Initiative's quarterly report (October–December 2015), <http://documents.wfp.org/stellent/groups/public/documents/newsroom/wfp281956.pdf> [accessed 2 June 2016].

[27] Other important teleconnections include the North Atlantic Oscillation, which influences rainfall in Western Europe and West Africa, the Arctic Oscillation, affecting winter conditions in many areas of the northern hemisphere, and the Indian Ocean Dipole, influencing the monsoon season in India and rainfall in Australia and South East Asia.

motivate more permanent adaptation. Continuing with the agricultural producer example, an expectation of more persistent dry conditions motivates the producer to convert agricultural land for livestock use. Also, faced with a forecast of a wetter season with intense rain and believing this risk will continue, an infrastructure manager could use an insurance payout to fund a project improving drainage systems on important roadways. More research is needed to identify the potential value of forecast insurance in this context.

Private Insurance, Government Disaster Response, Attribution and Tort Litigation

With the increasing share of disaster recovery costs being borne by governments and their taxpayers, consumers are finding that disaster relief is not functionally equivalent to private insurance. In other words, they are finding themselves either uncompensated for loss or compensated with great delay. And, delay could in fact worsen damages. Further, history suggests that when losses become big enough, tort litigation proceeds. The developments in the climate liability area are consistent with such a pattern. Thus, the climate resilience gap matters because the existence of the gap itself may drive litigation. This situation begs the question: how should these costs be paid, and by whom? Resolving this issue within the confines of the UNFCCC has proved challenging. Resolving it in a court of law is likely to be even more complex – with defendants likely to argue a multitude of bases for defence to liability, including, but not limited to, multiple or concurrent causation of loss and failure to mitigate damages arising out of an (obvious) hazard.

The insurance industry can act as a bridge between the public and private sectors in addressing risk awareness, physical resilience and financial preparedness (World Economic Forum, 2011) – but doing so requires a real partnership and an agreement on a path forward. If attribution science is used to take up capital capacity of the insurance industry in tort litigation defence and indemnity costs, then that capacity will not be available to facilitate processes focused on improving resilience today.

Notably, there is no push from experts to use casualty coverage of any type to address climate change loss and damage as liability. It appears to be accepted that attempting to manage climate change-related risk through a tort liability mechanism is a tool of last resort. In fact, experts argue that:

> . . . insurance should not be viewed as a form of compensation for victims of climate change, but instead in the classical view, as a risk-sharing mechanism

> or form of solidarity. Indeed, since insurance can help to preserve the global financial and social system, it is a risk reduction tool, not simply a risk-sharing one. (Silver and Dlugolecki, 2009)

CONCLUSION AND POSSIBLE FUTURE DEVELOPMENTS

Attribution science itself is complex, and its effects on legal processes may be even more so. Advances in attribution science, though useful, will not 'solve' the problems associated with loss and damage caused in whole or in part by climate change. And in fact, improvements in attribution science may shift the very hard discussion about what to do to protect society in the face of climate change. Instead of focusing on the science, attention may pivot to public policy in the face of that science. The practical reality is that three conditions will likely push the framing of future legal developments and risk reduction and management discussions:

- Developments in attribution science;
- Specific extreme events affecting highly developed economies that are insufficiently resilient (thus focusing the 'who pays' question on a demographic that can pay to push the analytics); and
- Communication of validated science in a manner that engages the public and links to specific outcomes in the political/policy realm.

In raising the question of who should pay, improvements in attribution science will likely raise a series of very difficult social and economic issues. Closing the climate resilience gap requires both government aid and insurance, but how to use them together implicates complicated value judgements and economic assessments. Should government aid programmes treat climate change losses the same as all other losses? Do fairness concerns support a different aid distribution, and what if that distribution fails to promote risk reduction measures needed in the face of trends shown by attribution science? What trade-offs will be required between economic and equity concerns? Will economic pressures compel a heavier focus on non-aid governmental actions, such as building codes and zoning? Will governments seek to reduce their direct relief efforts by creating or expanding mandatory or government subsidised insurance programmes? Will otherwise uninsurable assets be improved through government programmes to balance equity concerns with economic realities? The challenges will be significant. A more serious and disciplined discussion must be had regarding the calculation of damages in order to have this conversation.

9. Dialogue strategies for socio-ecological resilience and sustainability in China

Hua Wang

THE ISSUE AND CONTEXT

Socio-ecological resilience and sustainability have long been serious issues in China. Along with the rapid economic development in the past three decades in China, environmental qualities of air, water and soil have continuously and seriously deteriorated. Health risks caused by pollution have recently reached historically high points, and related social conflicts occur frequently throughout China. Major environmental accidents occur increasingly. Between 2008 and 2011, there were 568 serious environmental accidents in China, which more than tripled in the three years from 2012 to 2014 at 542, 712 and 471 accidents respectively. More than half of the accidents involved toxic chemicals, which caused serious damage to human health. Social conflicts caused by environmental problems, that are mostly introduced by the construction of industrial facilities and urban infrastructure, discharge and emission of industrial pollutants and hazardous wastes, and pollution accidents, are increasing rapidly. Between 2007 and 2014, there were several massive demonstrations against the construction of Para-xylene[1] facilities in the cities of Xiamen, Dalian, Ningbo and Maoming, among others. Thousands of community demonstrations occurred against local pollution factories that were identified as sources of health problems. Such environmental issues can hardly be prevented or solved by traditional government regulations, because almost all of those

1 Para-xylene (PX) serves as a significant and basic chemical and has enjoyed extensive application in many fields of chemical production, such as chemical fibre, synthetic resin, pesticide, medicine and plastics. Currently PX is mainly used for producing pure terephthalic acid (PTA) and then producing polyester, as well as used as raw material for solvents, medicine, spice and printing ink. China is the world's largest country in terms of producing, importing and consuming PX.

conflicts involve multiple stakeholders, relating to different government departments, and affect large populations.

Although the concept of socio-ecological resilience has not been discussed as widely as that of socio-ecological sustainability, government regulations have been developed and implemented to address both issues of resilience and sustainability. Environmental standards concerning emissions and technology have been developed and enforced. For example, policies on pollution discharge and emission permits have been designed and implemented, and information disclosure and public participation strategies have been adopted for several years. Those policies and strategies have helped address both issues of socio-ecological resilience and sustainability to a certain extent. However, there are serious flaws in the government regulations. Effective social instruments need to be further developed, to significantly enhance socio-ecological resilience and sustainability in China.

According to Chinese laws, it is the local governments that are responsible for environmental qualities in China, while the central and the provincial governments provide regulations and policy guidance. Environmental enforcement by the local governments, however, is notoriously weak in China for technical and financial reasons. But more importantly, the political will of the local governments is often limited. There are no strong incentives for the local governments to protect the environment in China. The inducement for promoting economic growth in the local regions outweighs the pressure from the higher level governments for environmental protection.[2] There is no adequate channel or mechanism for local citizens to compel local governments to safeguard the environment. However, there are strong incentives for local governments to protect the interests of polluting or environmentally destructive firms that can contribute to local economic growth and the budgets of local governments. Fiscal decentralisation in China has meant that local governments rely heavily on revenues from local companies. This is one reason why public service provision is inadequate or unsatisfactory in most areas of China especially in remote areas.

Legal recourse in China is also inadequate for environmental protection. Until recently, polluting firms were barely penalised by the court. In theory, citizens can sue a company violating environmental regulations. However, with protection of enterprises by local governments, it is very difficult for the suits to succeed. Even if a polluting company loses a

[2] The recent energy saving and pollution reduction programme is an exception, where strong administrative measures have been used by the central government.

lawsuit, it still can escape legal punishment, as a large number of court orders have not been enforced in China.

There have been a growing number of environmental NGOs emerging recently in China, but these are weak in general. They lack financial, technical and, more importantly, legal and political support: environmental NGOs have to work in co-operation with local governments. Until recently, the public, NGOs or individual citizens, lacked access to environmental information and, therefore, could not effectively participate in environmental management, even though the rights of participation have been clearly defined in relevant laws and regulations in China. A regulation on public participation in environmental impact assessment was enacted by the central government in 2006 and one on environmental information disclosure has been in effect since 2008. These two regulations support Chinese citizens and environmental NGOs participating in local environmental governance but less effectively than expected. As the public's rights of access to information, to participate in environmental management, to sue companies, to express opinions and to organise activities against pollution have been more or less well defined by Chinese laws and regulations, it is anticipated that a grassroots environmental movement will gradually take shape. A bottom-up, community-based environmental management mechanism will form a complementary force to the traditional, top-down, central government-initiated environmental programmes with all the limits on their impacts noted above.

Broadly defined, a community in China can be a village, part of an urban district or a town. Community leaders are generally publicly elected or hired, full-time civil servants. The central government of China is promoting self-governance by the community and for the community. Community-driven development and self-management are strongly encouraged by the central government. However, most community leaders lack knowledge, skill and means in community self-management. They mostly perform their duties in a traditional way, which is to help the government implement certain programmes.

Community participation in development in China began in the late 1980s, when international organisations and foreign NGOs supported a number of projects in community participation in China, but its development in China is slow, given the limited incentives for government officials to engage in the goals of community participation. The Chinese government is unfamiliar with participatory democracy, lacking the capability to implement as well as lacking commitment to building its capacity. Unlike other countries, the partnership of community participation in China inevitably involves the government rather than a civil society, and the interface is restricted to government officials rather than community workers. However, recently the central government of China has issued a number of policy documents which call for public and community participation in public management, and the political leaders have emphasised the importance of having the public and the communities involved in public affairs, particularly in environmental protection.

While there seems neither lack of political will of the central government nor lack of legal bases for the public and community to participate in development and environmental protection nowadays in China, the key challenges remain designing proper mechanisms that are feasible, effective and with low cost for the public and community to contribute to the course of socio-ecological sustainability and resilience. Public hearings are one approach widely used in China, but the effectiveness of this approach is limited (CECE, 2009), and stakeholder dialogues may be a better avenue within the Chinese context.

THE APPROACH

Background

Stakeholder dialogue has been employed extensively by business communities, to share information and concerns and develop better mutual understandings, to find areas of agreement and negotiate on terms of contracts and to manage a joint decision-making process.[3] It is a process of discussion and/or decision-making among different parties with different interests and values at stake in a particular situation. In practice, this usually takes the form of a meeting or series of meetings, at which companies, government departments and experts are helped to work together towards mutually acceptable conclusions. It can help identify and avert problems before they arise, can help collaboration to alleviate sources of dispute and can establish effective communication to clarify and resolve disputes. Stakeholder dialogues are usually facilitated by independent facilitators in order to ensure that no one group or person dominates proceedings and that the record of the meeting is an accurate reflection of the discussion. It should be an inclusive process to ensure anyone with a stake in the issue is involved in the dialogue, and every participant is considered equal.

---

[3] For more materials about this approach, see the Environment Council's website <www.the-environment-council.org.uk> and the website of the Global Dialogue on Water, Food and Environment: <www.iwmi.cgiar.org/dialogue> where extensive discussions on the dialogue approach are provided.

Stakeholder dialogue has also been employed for public management (Stoll-Kleemann and Welp, 2006). It is in line with the general trend towards decentralised resource management and recognition of the failures of overly bureaucratic approaches. In the arena of public management, stakeholder dialogue has so far been mostly applied to environmental and natural resources management in developed countries.[4]

Stakeholder dialogue can take place at different levels – global, international, national, local, and even of enterprises or of projects, and may appear in various formats. Some involve institutional arrangements that formalise participation of stakeholders.[5] Stakeholder dialogue may also be focused on specific decisions and projects, for example through environmental and social impact assessment processes. A recent trend in many countries has been to hold public hearings, at which those with concerns can access information and air their views. The effectiveness of such processes depends on the context in which they are run. At another level, stakeholder dialogue may focus on governance arrangements and broad principles: the World Commission on Dams was the most ambitious stakeholder dialogue relevant to river basins ever to be convened.[6]

At the community level, stakeholder dialogue can aim to prevent, manage or resolve disputes among stakeholders within a community. It can be a regular programme which involves organisation of periodic

---

4 One example is that the Environment Council in UK helped the Environment Agency Wales bring together key stakeholders to resolve long-standing conflicts around the Trecatti landfill site. Two large open meetings were held in 2002 to identify concerns and decide the best process to resolve them. Participants included local residents, local community groups, Biffa Waste Services (the site operator), the Environment Agency Wales, the National Assembly for Wales, local authorities, local businesses and the Bro Taff Health Authority. Concerns raised included health and safety, monitoring the site, local communication and socio-economic impacts. Participants agreed to set up a representative working group to discuss concerns in more detail and make recommendations on how they could be addressed. The main stakeholder group has since met again and agreed that the working group should continue their work. For more information, see <www.the-environment-council.org.uk>

5 For example, the Murray Darling Basin Initiative of Australia provides for the Community Advisory Committee to attend all Murray Darling Basin Council meetings and to liaise with the Murray Darling Basin Commission. A new Indigenous Policy Office at the Commission allows for representation of indigenous interests. It needs to be recognised that these stakeholder opportunities are the outcome of years of negotiation and less inclusive decision-making, and the terms of involvement are continuously being evaluated and periodically re-negotiated. For more details, see website: <www.mdbc.gov.au>

6 See website: <www.mdbc.gov.au>

community meetings, preparation for meetings and follow-up actions. The meetings may be held in a form of roundtable where all participants are treated as equally important. The literature has explored a variety of factors on whether this kind of bargaining among stakeholders can reduce inefficiencies from externalities, taking into account existing distributions of economic and political power and real-world frictions in bargaining.

Given the current institutions in China, this author believes that introducing the stakeholder dialogue approach into China is feasible and effective in terms of improving public institutions and solving current social and environmental issues in China. Since 2000, this author has been designing and implementing a stakeholder dialogue strategy in China at the community level, in order to help solve certain environmental and social problems. The questions are: what kind of dialogue models can be feasibly designed and be effective in helping solve the environmental and social issues that the communities are facing?; and how they should be implemented and institutionalised?

Along with the movement waged by the central government in building a harmonious society, various stakeholder dialogue programmes at the community level have been designed and implemented in dozens of Chinese municipalities, with this author's guidance.[7] While the community roundtable dialogue approach has been designed and applied mostly to solving local environmental conflicts in China at this stage, it is expected that ultimately it can help solve other social and public governance issues throughout the country.

Design

The design and implementation of community environmental dialogue started with a research project on the industrial pollution control of small enterprises in rural China in 2000. While the industrial pollution control policies practised in China are generally designed for urban and state-owned industrial enterprises, millions of relatively small, non-state-owned enterprises, mostly located in the countryside have successfully avoided the scrutiny of the regulatory system. Pollution generated by those so-called Township-Village Industrial Enterprises (TVIE) caused tremendous economic damage and social conflicts. In order to help China resolve its environmental and social problems caused by TVIE

---

[7] Financial support was provided by the World Bank and Chinese government. This author introduced the ideas, provided guidelines and training, and facilitated the design and implementation.

pollution, the World Bank sponsored a policy research project in 2000. One of the project activities is to test the feasibility and effectiveness of the stakeholder dialogue approach. Since then the community roundtable dialogue approach in the Chinese context has been evolving and improving, even though the principles have not been changed significantly.

Specifically, in addition to following the general principles of the stakeholder dialogue approach such as equality, openness and fairness, the community environmental roundtable dialogue programmes designed in China[8] have the following major aspects:

1. Community leaders (and sometimes local environmental coordinators) organise environmental roundtables, with participants that include relevant government agency representatives, relevant polluting company managers, community residents (especially pollution victims) as well as representatives from environmental NGOs, technical institutions and the mass media.
2. During the meetings, government representatives report on the current socio-economic and environmental situations of the community and the future actions and/or policies on the issues involved. Both costs and benefits are presented.
3. The polluting company managers report to the meeting on what the current pollution control status is of their respective companies, what they did in the past, what are the future plans and what are the difficulties.
4. Environmental authorities and technical persons give comments on each company's performance, based on the information available to them.
5. Community representatives as well as pollution victims take turns to offer their comments, enquiries and demands as well as suggestions.
6. Government leaders and the company managers give feedback, including explanations, promises and the like.
7. Community workers, who chair the meetings, give summaries of the major points discussed, the agreements reached as well as the future actions that should be taken. The representatives of stakeholders may sign an agreement whenever possible.
8. Community workers follow up on the major issues and prepare for the next dialogue meeting, including collecting reports from the government agencies and the companies, and disclosing them to the public before the next dialogue meeting.

---

[8] For the detailed principles and procedures, see CECE (2009).

Implementation

The stakeholder dialogue approach was first tested on the pollution issues of TVIE in nine towns in Jiangsu, Guizhou and Tianjin in 2000. Because it is perceived as feasible and effective, the programme has since been gradually expanded to cover environmental issues in other areas. In 2002, two counties in Jiangsu tried to institutionalise the dialogue strategy, and in 2004, a number of other cities in Jiangsu piloted the approach. In 2005, the Jiangsu Provincial Department of Environmental Protection (EPD) started working on its environmental dialogue programme more systematically, and in 2007 a formal call for province-wide implementation of the environmental dialogue strategy was made by Jiangsu EPD.

Chongqing Municipal Government started working on the roundtable dialogue approach in 2004, and since then, various formats of stakeholder dialogue have been tried and hundreds of community roundtable dialogues have been organised. The Centre for Environmental Communication and Education of the Ministry of Environmental Protection started working on community environmental roundtable dialogue in 2005 and now the dialogue work has been integrated into the Centre's Green Community Programme.

As of 2016, more than 30 municipalities in 15 provinces have started practising the community environmental roundtable dialogue. The topic of dialogue has also gone beyond industrial pollution control. The dialogue strategy has been applied to neighbourhood issues like rubbish collection, pollution control of restaurants, construction sites, river basin management, etc. The dialogue strategy has also been used to help solve some social conflicts at the community level such as urban construction resettlements. Mass media at all levels in China have widely reported the dialogue programmes. A few cases are presented below in order to further illustrate the approach.[9]

Cases

Case 1: Urban solid wastes (Wanshen City, Chongqing Municipality)

Wanshen City, located in Chongqing Municipality, is an urban area developed from mining industries, covering 566 square kilometres and with a population of more than 300,000. Most of the residents have some relationship with the mining industries. Due to the privatisation

---

[9] See CECE (2009) for more cases and implementation guidelines.

of the mining industries and the reform of social responsibilities of corporations, social and environmental issues in Wanshen had been enormous. Prior to 2005, complaints and conflicts between the residents, government agencies and the industries were becoming increasingly serious. In 2004, this author introduced the stakeholder dialogue experiments that he was conducting in China to one of the high-level officials of the Chongqing Municipal Government. As a result, a joint effort in designing and implementing stakeholder roundtable dialogue in Chongqing was launched by the World Bank and Chongq'ing Municipal Government in 2005, where Wanshen was selected as one of the areas piloting the dialogue approach.

Among the first roundtable dialogues conducted in Wanshen was one on rubbish collection in Heping Village of Donglin District on 15 March 2006. The key environmental issue was that litter was scattered in the streets due to an insufficient number of litter bins. Though the issue was simple, the solution was less so. The first difficulty was that there were no clearly defined agencies responsible for the issue. Any number of government units and corporate entities could have taken some responsibility, but all gave one excuse or another. After about two hours of discussions, two units – one in the government sector and the other, a school within the village, volunteered to take action. While it was too expensive to distribute plastic litter bins in the streets as used in better-off areas, it was decided at the roundtable meeting to use bricks and cement to build static litter bins which are much cheaper. Consequently, a long-standing, complicated public management issue was resolved. The harsh exchanges at the start of the roundtable dialogue ended amicably with grateful thanks by the end of the meeting.

There have since been 220 dialogue meetings organised by local community workers in Donglin District and reportedly 350 public management issues were solved this way. It would have been unthinkable that these could be solved through traditional public management. Mutual understandings between the different stakeholders and the stakeholders' understandings in various public issues have significantly improved. Now the citizens in the area are familiar with requesting dialogues whenever they have a public issue, rather than filing complaints or having public protests as they traditionally did. Another example is the resettlement caused by the new urban construction projects in Donglin. Initially, 78 households had serious complaints against the government and were unwilling to accept the resettlement packages offered. After a series of roundtable dialogues, there were no more household complaints as the issue was finally successfully resolved.

Case 2: Industrial pollution control (Jiangyan City, Jiangsu Province)[10]

Jiangyan, a city in Taizhou Municipality of Jiangsu Province, is located between Shanghai and Nanjing, on the northern side of the Yangtze River. It covers about 1,000 square kilometres and has a population of 910,000. A modestly well-developed area in Jiangsu, one of the richest provinces in China, Jiangyan enjoyed fast economic growth in the past two decades. However, its people also suffered from serious industrial pollution, which brought a colossal amount of complaints from the citizens that sometimes resulted in public protests. The major pollution sources were small metal-processing companies, which provided a significant number of jobs to local residents as well as tax revenues to the local government. Jiangyan city's environmental authorities made great efforts to enforce relevant environmental regulations and won a national award for its outstanding performance in environmental inspection in 2007. However, the environmental quality was still far from satisfactory to its citizens and the environmental authority was too weak to bring those polluters into compliance, due to various political, economic and technical reasons.

In 2006, Jiangyan was selected to be one of the pilot areas for the environmental stakeholder roundtable dialogue programme which was jointly sponsored by the World Bank and Jiangsu Environmental Protection Department. A number of environmental officers and community leaders of Jiangyan city received training on the stakeholder dialogue approach, provided by this author and the project team members. Following the training, the environmental protection bureau began organising the first roundtable dialogue meeting on 10 January 2007, on pollution issues generated by the non-ferrous metal industries, which received the most citizen complaints. The polluting firms' managers were not in a position to reject requests for further reduction in pollution from the local citizens as they were mostly the neighbours of the firm managers, and particularly, when they were also confronted by the mass media during the dialogue meetings. While trying to explain the difficulties in reducing pollution, almost all of the firm managers promised to invest more facilities in pollution abatement, and they did do so after the dialogue meeting.

Due to the perceived effectiveness of the dialogue approach, dozens of dialogue meetings have been organised in Jiangyan since the first roundtable dialogue. Various environmental issues besides industrial pollution have been covered, including pollution from the service sector, air

---

10 Source: documents submitted by Jiangyan Municipal Environmental Protection Bureau.

pollution from burning rice and wheat straw in the fields, solid wastes in residential districts and water pollution from livestock farms.

An important feature of the environmental dialogue approach designed and implemented in Jiangyan is the establishment of an environmental NGO in the city. From the start, the dialogue organisers, mostly government environmental officers, realised that such dialogues should be organised by an NGO that is independent of the government. Encouraged by the government, an environmental NGO, called Jiangyan Environ-Eco Family, was established and registered on 4 June 2008. A former deputy mayor of Jiangyan City, who had been in charge of environmental protection in Jiangyan for many years, Zichen Shen, was elected to be president of the Eco Family. By the end of 2008, the Eco Family established 16 chapters that covered all towns in Jiangyan and had about 300 members, comprising respected senior citizens, active public workers and young volunteers. Dozens of roundtable dialogues have been organised by the Eco Family on various social and environmental issues that were deemed important to local people. There was thus a relatively satisfactory balance between economic development and socio-environmental protection.

Case 3: Restaurant pollution control (Jiangsu and Hebei)

Huarun Village, a residential community established in 2001, is located in the Jingkou District of Zhenjiang City, a well-developed municipality of Jiangsu Province. Huarun Village occupies 0.35 square kilometres of land and includes 63 residential buildings, for about 6,000 residents or 2,500 households. As in many Chinese cities, street-facing ground floors of buildings are sometimes used for businesses including that of restaurants. One example is the Junhong Noodle House. With the expansion of its business, the cooking smells, especially that of fish, the smoke and the noise from the stove blower affect residents who live above the restaurant as well as those who live nearby. The neighbours had often complained to the restaurant and to the government authority – the district environmental protection bureau (EPB). The EPB investigated the case and asked that the Junhong Noodle House deal with the complainants' issues. However, the operation of the restaurant was for the most part legally permitted, and there was little else the EPB could do. The conflict between the local residents and the restaurant accrued with diminishing trust in the district EPB's effectiveness.

To solve the pollution issue caused by the Junhong Noodle House and the attendant friction between the restaurant and the local residents, the community leader of Huarun Village organised a community roundtable on 6 September 2007, attended by seven representatives of local residents, two from the Junhong Noodle House and two government officials.

During the meeting, the community leader first summarised the issues that brought about the meeting. One representative of the restaurant expressed his regrets about the dispute and his willingness to solve the problem, but also emphasised his difficulties in trying to improve the situation. The representatives of the local residents expressed their demands for improvements, and also offered suggestions which included: replacing coal with gas so that the noise and the smoke would be significantly reduced; building a new sewage pipe solely for the restaurant's waste water discharge so that the odour of its waste water did not enter the sewage pipe that was for household use; relocating the raw fish processing to outside of the community; not occupying the street for business purposes; and relocating the air conditioner to reduce its noise. Some of the representatives of residents and the government also offered personal help to implement these suggestions. After several rounds of negotiations, the three parties – the restaurant, the government and the residents – reached an agreement which incorporated all the major suggestions made by the residents, and the representatives of the three parties signed the agreement.

A few months later, on 19 December 2007, the community leader organised another roundtable dialogue with the same participants to review the implementation of the above mentioned agreement. Five of the six items on the agreement had been realised, except the one on replacing coal with gas, because of its significant financial implication – the Junhong Noodle House had difficulty in negotiating a deal with the gas company. However, with help from the roundtable participants, the restaurant was able to have a gas stove provided by the gas company at a significantly reduced price. In less than two weeks, i.e. by 31 December 2007, all the major issues raised by the residents with regard to the pollution caused by the Junhong Noodle House had been resolved. All parties involved were satisfied with the final outcome.

Restaurant pollution has been a serious issue in almost all cities in China, and several roundtable dialogues have been organised in other cities. Another typical one can be found in Qinhuangdao, Hebei Province, where pollution and poverty were intertwined.

The residents in the Hejianli Community of Qinhuangdao City suffered from serious pollution issues caused by two restaurants located in buildings #15 and #18 prior to 2008. In late 2006, a poor man, Mr Ma, an unemployed worker, rented a room on the ground floor of building #15 and started a small restaurant to make a living. In early 2008, another poor, unemployed man, Mr Sun, followed suit with a small restaurant on the ground floor of building #18. Both restaurants produced tasty local food, but at the same time generated intolerable pollution: noise, from the stove blower starting as early as 4am when most of the residents living above the restaurant were still sleeping; smoke from the cooking; and human waste as there is no public latrine nearby. Complaints and even violent reactions from residents above the premises occurred against the operations of the two restaurants.

The community workers conducted a survey in early May 2008 on the most serious issues that affected the community, and found that the pollution generated by the two restaurants was top of the list. On 26 May 2008, the community workers organised a stakeholder roundtable dialogue, where representatives of the government, the local residents and the restaurant owners and their financial providers sat together to discuss the problems. After strident debates and tough negotiations, agreements were reached finally which involved either shutting down or relocating the two restaurants, and that their respective financiers returned the deposits of the restaurant owners. The community workers and some residents in the community also began to look for ways to help the two families. Mr Ma received help to start a spa, managed by his son, and Mr Sun opened a shop selling irons, which allowed them both to earn an income. On 24 June 2008, the community workers organised the second dialogue meeting where some minor remaining issues were solved.

SURVEY ANALYSIS

The Survey

In order to evaluate the impacts and to improve the design and implementation of the dialogue programmes, a survey was conducted in December 2007 among 200 individuals who had participated in the roundtable dialogues. The survey questionnaire which was to be completed anonymously included six sections: background information of the individual's participation in the dialogues; dialogue design and operation; information exchange; impact evaluation; programme expansion; and personal information. It was in simple multiple choice forms to avoid potential difficulties in answering them. The survey was developed in consultation with a number of dialogue participants and was conducted with the assistance of an independent research institute in China and community workers of four municipalities (Chongqing, Tianjin, Chifeng and Shenyang) where the roundtable dialogues were tested. Two hundred questionnaires were distributed to all participants in the dialogues organised by community workers. The completed questionnaires were returned to the research institute in postage-paid envelopes.

Survey Participants

The survey results showed that about 82 per cent of the respondents had taken part in the dialogue only once, 12 per cent had participated twice and the remaining 6 per cent had been involved more often. Ten per cent of the respondents were dialogue organisers, 15 per cent were government representatives, 10 per cent were from the enterprises, 52 per cent were residents and the remaining 13 per cent came from NGOs and the media. Fifty-six per cent of the dialogues were related to pollution issues caused by enterprises. Seventy-nine per cent of respondents felt the dialogue topics dealt with extremely urgent issues.

Thirty-five per cent of survey respondents were from Chongqing, 23 per cent from Tianjin, 26 per cent from Chifeng and 15 per cent from Shenyang. Fifty-one per cent of the respondents were male and 49 per cent were female. About 60 per cent of the participants were 40-years-old and older and 11.5 per cent were younger than 30. More than 60 per cent of respondents had been educated beyond high school. The monthly income of the respondents was mostly between 500 and 3,000 yuan.[11]

Dialogue Design and Implementation

The survey feedback revealed that most participants thought the roundtable dialogues were well prepared on aspects such as pre-announcement, provision of background material, location choice, selection of representatives and moderators, and definition of rights and responsibilities. Less than 10 per cent rated the preparation work as poor. Most participants regarded the community public announcement board as the best channel to pre-announce the dialogue meetings. There is no convergence on the best way to select resident representatives. The popular way is self-nomination plus striking a balance between districts or sectors.

All meetings were completed within three hours, with 24 per cent less than an hour. More than 60 per cent of the respondents thought the time allocation for different activities, such as introduction of background information and viewing exchanges and negotiations, during the dialogue was reasonable. More than 80 per cent thought that representatives of each type of stakeholders should be less than ten. Forty-two per cent thought choosing dialogue moderators from community leaders was the

[11] As of October 2016, the exchange rate of Renminbi yuan to the US dollar is about 6.7 to 1.

best but 26 per cent thought it should be independent NGO staff. About 80 per cent thought the dialogue meetings had given the representatives sufficient time to discuss the issues raised. Nineteen per cent of respondents did not say anything in the meetings in which they participated.

Impacts

The survey statistics show that more than 80 per cent of government officials who participated in the meetings felt that after the dialogue process they had better understandings of the issues raised, including the enterprises' measures on the issues, residents' attitudes and impacts of pollution. About 80 per cent of those government officials felt that the trust between the government and the residents/enterprises had increased. More than 85 per cent felt that the dialogue meetings helped to promote cooperation between the government and the citizens and/or enterprises.

More than 95 per cent of business representatives who participated in the meetings felt that they had better understanding of the issues involved, the relevant government policies, residents' attitudes and impacts of pollution. About 90 per cent believed that the trust of the business community in the government and the residents increased and that their companies could have better cooperation with the government, residents and the mass media. Fifty-three per cent of the enterprises fully fulfilled their promises made at the meetings and 47 per cent partially fulfilled.

More than 80 per cent of the residents who participated in the meetings had better understanding of the issues involved as well as the relevant government policies. About 75 per cent of the residents felt they had better understanding about the impact of pollution as well as the measures taken by the enterprises. Sixty-two per cent of the residents and 49 per cent of enterprises felt that their trust in the government had increased. About 85 per cent of residents felt that the dialogues improved their awareness for participating in social management and they would pay more attention to the work of the government. About 60 per cent thought that the dialogue would improve their cooperation with the government and the business community. In summary, participants felt that after the dialogue process, their overall understanding of the issues had improved, and that mutual understanding and trust between the different stakeholders were enhanced, with some of the problems resolved either fully or in some cases, partially.

DISCUSSION

Necessity and Importance

It is clear that the sustainability and resilience of the socio-ecological system in China cannot be solved by traditional legal, administrative or economic approaches on their own. It would take a long time to improve the legal system in China. Added to that, law enforcement is still uncertain, given the unique culture in China towards it. The administrative approach can be designed and implemented quickly, but the government itself is part of the challenge given the citizens' lack of trust in their government, and that companies know better how to negotiate with the government. Economic instruments can be improved but are far from being able to be applied to solving even some simple issues. Stakeholder dialogue can be an important alternative and a complement to the traditional approaches. As traditional legal, administrative and economic approaches are usually reflected in the dialogues, the dialogue approach can help better implement or enforce the traditional approaches and may even assist the development of the traditional approaches.

Despite some common characteristics, the social and environmental issues are location- and sector specific. A problem-solving mechanism should be so developed that it can flexibly fit into the local- and sector-specific situations, for the mechanism to be effective and efficient. Stakeholder dialogue is such a mechanism. While it may be less effective when applied to higher levels of constituency in China,[12] the dialogue approach has proven successful at the community level, where the issues discussed are closely related to the direct benefits of the stakeholders.

Feasibility

While there is room for improvement, the dialogue strategy as currently practised at the community level in China has proven to be feasible in design and implementation, and to be potentially cost-effective in resolving social and environmental problems. The feasibility issue is one of the first concerns that the researchers have had in China. Politically, the community workers can request government leaders, company

[12] There has been no serious effort in applying the stakeholder dialogue approach at higher levels of constituency in China yet. Some other benefits may be observed if the dialogue approach is applied at higher levels and more research on this issue is warranted.

managers and citizen representatives to participate in such meetings, but in reality, the community workers may not be able to involve them, especially government officials. In past decades, government officials in China have developed a top-down culture of giving instructions to citizens and some of these officials may be uncomfortable at having to be equal participants at the same table as ordinary citizens to discuss issues exercising the public. For almost all public meetings in China, government officials are honourably presiding on a stage facing the audience. With a roundtable setting, all participants are equal, at least in style. The experiments show that this tradition can be changed, even though it is still a challenge for the community workers to get government officials into the dialogues before the strategy is institutionalised in China. To sustain community stakeholder dialogue work, it is necessary as reinforcement to have the approach integrated into the community management procedures with higher echelons of the Chinese Communist Party (CCP) leaders supervising and monitoring the dialogue work, and the mass media as observers.

Technically, community workers in China have not been trained to organise such forms of dialogue. Skills are needed for preparing and facilitating dialogues, and conducting summaries and follow-ups. Although it has not been a serious issue, participant selection is not a trivial task, as it could affect the fairness or balance of a dialogue, and therefore the trust of the public and the final success of the work. There are also concerns about the veracity of pollution reports from company managers and unreasonable demands of some pollution victims. If not handled well, a dialogue can end in generating more conflicts than settling them. However, the pilots so far demonstrate that with adequate training, community workers are able to properly deal with those issues raised and facilitate dialogues constructively.

The financial issue was also of concern initially. If organising a dialogue is too costly, a dialogue programme would be unable to sustain itself in the future. The major costs may include labour costs of community workers, conference facilities and meals of participants, which are expected to be provided by a conference organiser according to tradition. However, it was found that in almost all communities, community workers were able to use the conference facilities owned by organisations within the jurisdiction of a community for free for community meetings. No complaints were received from participants of dialogues when food was not provided during the meetings. The only major cost associated with the dialogue strategy would be the labour cost of community workers organising dialogue activities, which was paid from the government budget.

Impact

While feasibility is no longer a major concern for the dialogue strategy to be institutionalised, the impacts of the strategy have not been well studied due to limited research resources. However, the following conclusions can be drawn from preliminary observations of case studies and the survey of dialogue participants:

1. The roundtable dialogue can help improve mutual understanding among different stakeholders. As discussed before, communication between the citizens and the government and between the citizens and the polluters is inadequate in China, especially in the rural areas. The parties involved generally do not really have a good understanding of each other's role, even though most of them thought they did.
2. The roundtable dialogue provides a platform for all stakeholders to speak for themselves. Almost all resident representatives and some of the company managers appreciated the opportunity to present their case. It is rare that ordinary citizens have a window to speak publicly on issues which affect the quality of their daily lives, health or economic activities. For those companies that have a good environmental record, it is also an occasion for them to publicise to their neighbours their efforts or actions on controlling pollution. And for those companies that have not brought about pollution control to a desired level, it gives them an opportunity to explain the reasons why they have fallen short. Environmental authorities in China have few forums to communicate their work to the public, especially to citizens who do not read newspapers or have no access to television.
3. The roundtable dialogue provides a channel for different stakeholders to negotiate on terms of actions in the future. During the dialogues, many community representatives and company managers requested that government officials as well as company managers take action on some specific issues. For some of the requests, promises are given and for some others, reasons are provided for not being able to achieve the desired goals. Of course, there are some requests which hit a blank wall. There is evidence that most promises are kept at least partially and actions are taken. There is also evidence that different stakeholders work collaboratively after the dialogues to solve some issues.
4. The roundtable dialogue generates pressure on the poor performers and gives appreciation to good performers. Polluters need to participate from time to time in the roundtable dialogues and report to their neighbours what they have done in the past to improve on pollution control. The poor performers felt the social pressure as they were

shamed and scrutinised even outside of the dialogue meetings. One of the common practices of companies seriously deficient in pollution control in China's rural areas is to shut down the pollution treatment facilities while the environmental inspectors are not present. The likelihood of being caught by the environmental authorities is very low, because the monitoring and inspection capacity of the local environmental authorities is limited. However, after the dialogue meetings, the local residents, who live nearby, are able to keep watch to notify the environmental authorities.

5. The roundtable dialogue raises the environmental awareness of the ordinary citizens and encourages public participation in environmental management. It is also an educational process about the relevant laws, government policies and administrative procedures, etc.
6. It is thought that during the dialogues, the social and cultural forces are at work, much more than the forces of legal threat, administrative penalty and economic incentives.
7. The stakeholder roundtable dialogue approach is more than a simple participatory approach. It is a mechanism or tool for community management and service, which functions at picking up signals of the issues involved, balancing interests of various parties and facilitating execution of the decisions or agreements made.
8. In general, the dialogue approach helps not only to improve environmental and social sustainability, but enhances the resilience of a socio-ecological system. It can affect the outcomes of the socio-ecological system in various positive ways as discussed above, which in turn helps to ensure that the system is sustainable for the future. The dialogue approach itself is also a dynamic socio-ecological process that facilitates continuous feedback and therefore strengthens the resilience of the system.

Challenge

There are potential obstacles, however, that can prevent such a dialogue approach from being institutionalised. Among the challenges is that of local government's political will, or the lack of it, as local governments are relatively unfamiliar with a participatory approach. The capacity at the implementation level is also a concern although it can be readily improved as long as there is a serious commitment to building that capacity.

While the overall situation with the community environmental dialogue programmes in China is moving in the right direction, a number of conceptual questions remain to be answered. These should ideally be dealt with before the dialogue approach becomes institutionalised. The first question is how, and in what capacity community leaders can facilitate such a dialogue? As stakeholders may not be obligated to participate in such a dialogue and some even do not want to be engaged in it, community workers will need to work out a strategy to bring all relevant parties to the table. The second question is: how do the organisers incentivise the responsible parties into making promises to improve their performance at the dialogue and to keep their word after the dialogue? Here, moral and social forces are at play although legal penalties, economic benefits as well as political pressure may also need to be generated in preparing and organising the dialogues. The third question is: how can the practice of community environmental roundtables facilitate democratic governance in China at the local level while simultaneously promoting rule-by-law instead of rule-by-man in the society?

The community stakeholder roundtable dialogue should also be a feasible and effective tool for solving other public governance issues in China, such as public security, health services, education and transportation, among others. Stakeholder dialogue would also be useful for solving social and environmental issues beyond the community level in China. More research in these areas is warranted.

CONCLUDING REMARKS

Environmental stakeholder dialogue, as practised in Chinese communities, can help prevent, manage and resolve environmental problems and the associated social conflicts, if well designed and executed. It could therefore help enhance socio-ecological sustainability and resilience. It is essentially a dynamic mechanism for building good governance. Stakeholder dialogue can help lead public governance to a more efficient level, both economically and socially. The dialogue approach may not replace the existing regulatory instruments in practice, but can be an important supplement or complement to the current institutions.

The rapid economic growth in China in the past three decades has significantly improved the living standards of the Chinese populace and contributed to its economic development worldwide. However, it has also generated serious social and environmental issues. Traditional legal, economic and administrative instruments have limitations in solving those socio-environmental issues in China and thus, stakeholder dialogue may be a solution. The programmes experimented in dozens of Chinese municipalities have shown that the community roundtable dialogue strategy is feasible for adoption in China, if the CCP and regional government leaders in a region or the higher echelon government agencies decide to do so. There are no serious technical difficulties because the dialogue operation can be very simple at the community level. The major financial item would be the labour cost of the community workers who organise roundtable dialogues, but this issue is considered to be minor in China as wages are not prohibitive.

The immediate and short-term benefits of the community roundtable dialogue programmes in China include: better communication and understanding between different stakeholders – government agencies, business entities and local citizens; reducing social conflicts that are fuelled by problems; and improving performance of all stakeholders in the area of public good provision and sharing. The long-term benefits may include: raising community awareness and knowledge about the economic, social and environmental issues that a community needs to resolve; building a sense of community, trust and collaboration among the different stakeholders; educating people about the legal provisions, government policies, rights of different stakeholders and moral standards in various areas; practising at the community level, people's rights to know, participate, monitor or be compensated, as defined by Chinese laws; training people to live in a society with participatory democracy; and building a harmonious society with good governance from the grassroots level to the top. The major challenges to institutionalising such community stakeholder roundtable dialogue programmes in China are the government leaders' willingness to adopt this strategy at different levels and the capacity of local community workers to facilitate the dialogues. Substantial training for both government officials and community workers on the dialogue approach is necessary.

10. Environmental risks and authoritarian resilience in China

Thomas Johnson

INTRODUCTION

On the evening of 12 August 2015, two massive explosions, the second of which was equivalent to the force of 21 tons of TNT, ripped through a warehouse storing hazardous chemicals in the northern Chinese port city of Tianjin. Hundreds of people, many of whom lived in residential buildings less than one kilometre from the blast, were hospitalised. The official death toll from the tragedy was later confirmed at 173 people, including 104 firefighters. Domestic and international media published footage of utter devastation at the scene of one of China's worst, and highest profile, industrial accidents, and alarms were raised about potential serious long-term environmental and health consequences (Chan et al, 2015). Reports claimed that levels of some toxic chemicals in the vicinity of the blast were hundreds of times in excess of national standards (Hanna and Hunt, 2015). They included 700 tons of highly toxic sodium cyanide, which was stored by the warehouse at a level 70 times in excess of its approved limit, and was later discovered at levels up to 27 times above national standards at several local wastewater monitoring stations (Phillips, 2015). An official investigation into the disaster also identified the existence of local air and soil pollution, although it found no permanent damage to the Bohai Sea (Hernández, 2016).

In many ways, the Tianjin tragedy was a microcosm of the shortcomings associated with China's system of regulating environmental risks, many of which have been documented in the literature (Suttmeier, 2008). Chinese political scientist Zhang Ming called it 'a man-made disaster that could have been prevented, and [which] has exposed a range of systemic problems, from the lack of regulation for handling hazardous chemicals to the collusion of business and corrupt officials' (Jacobs et al, 2015). The warehouse from which the blast originated was owned by the Ruihai International Logistics Company. Founded in 2011 by two local elites, the company had started business without obtaining the necessary permits. These were later acquired illegally through personal connections (Jacobs et al, 2015). Although the project's environmental impact assessment (EIA) passed without a hitch, suspicions were raised when it transpired that 100 per cent of the 128 local residents allegedly surveyed about the warehouse had supported its construction: public participation is required for EIAs in China, yet NGOs claim surveys are often manipulated and results are routinely falsified).[1] The warehouse stored a staggering quantity – as much as 3,000 tons – of highly toxic chemicals including the aforementioned sodium cyanide and 1,300 tons of fertiliser nitrates (Jacobs et al, 2015). Chemicals were stored haphazardly with disregard for regulations, and the warehouse location violated official guidelines that require a minimum of one kilometre between facilities storing hazardous chemicals and residential areas and major roads (Jacobs et al, 2015). With hindsight, the Ruihai warehouse was a disaster waiting to happen, yet the explosions did not occur without prior warning. Since 2008, local academics had publicly expressed concern about environmental risks in the Binhai New Area, where the Ruihai warehouse was located, but they were ignored (Jacobs et al, 2015). And although the fire department had written a risk-management plan identifying the port's most dangerous sites in 2015, Ruihai was omitted (Jacobs et al, 2015).

Remedial action only occurred after the blasts had caused devastation. The aftermath of the explosions was also indicative of the Chinese Communist Party's (CCP) desire to uphold control, and prevent any political repercussions from such a high-profile tragedy. The authorities moved to control the agenda through tight censorship of media reporting (Levin, 2015). This included limited disclosure of information related to the environmental impact of the disaster (Xu and Webb, 2015). This did not prevent dozens of citizens who had suffered from the blasts to converge at a media briefing to protest, although they mainly did so in order to demand compensation from the government. They reportedly held banners stating 'We want the truth!' and 'We love the party and the government, please buy back our homes' (Phillips, 2015). Recriminations soon followed. A subsequent central government investigation found 123 people, including five ministerial-level officials, responsible for the blasts.

Worryingly, regulatory violations related to the Ruihai warehouse are not unusual. A *New York Times* investigation based on satellite imagery and public records revealed numerous other examples around the country of potentially hazardous facilities being sited excessively close to civilian areas (Boehler et al, 2015). Serious industrial accidents have become

---

[1] See, for example, http://ipen.org/sites/default/files/documents/EIA_Guidebook_press_release_final.pdf

relatively commonplace in China, albeit rarely on the scale of the Tianjin blasts. They include a recent spate of industrial disasters in Chinese cities – a fire and blast in Changchun, an oil spill and blast in Qingdao, and a blast in Kunshan each resulted in more than 100 casualties (Chan et al., 2015). Yet most environmental risk is manifested in less dramatic, but equally serious forms of industrial pollution. For example, many rural areas suffer from severe pollution, and numerous 'cancer villages' have been documented (Lora-Wainwright, 2013). In contrast to 'suddenly imposed grievances' (Snow et al, 1998) akin to the Tianjin example, most communities are victims of risks that gradually accrue over extended time periods, something that Rob Nixon (2011) appositely labels 'slow violence'. The origin of both can, to a large extent, be traced to regulatory failings, which affect a range of areas including food safety, occupational safety and environmental protection (van Rooij, 2012).

While some praised the authorities' immediate response to the Tianjin blasts for its speed (Chan et al, 2015), tackling the underlying causes of the problem would require reforms that represent a much more complex undertaking. Richard Suttmeier (2008, p. 130) argued that management of environmental and technological risk in China has failed, and that it needs to establish a 'sixth modernisation', namely 'the development of institutions and values that can manage environmental and technological risks'. Creating decentralised mechanisms for identifying risks and promoting accountability are crucial elements of this approach (Suttmeier, 2008), and there is official support for the notion of 'public supervision' over local officials and enterprises. Yet so far the CCP has been reluctant to undertake significant reforms in this area (van Rooij, 2012). This highlights the tension that lies at the heart of risk management work in China between a more 'responsive' or 'adaptable' form of authoritarianism that promotes greater accountability, transparency and adherence to rules, on the one hand, and the reluctance to empower actors and institutions in such a way that could undermine the CCP's monopoly on political power, on the other.

This chapter presents an overview of environmental risk regulation in China. Macrae (2010, p. 141) defines risk regulation as 'all organisational activities that aim to control the threat of harmful, adverse or unintended outcomes'. This includes formal risk management systems designed to reduce, or eliminate risk *before* it occurs, while also encompassing regulatory actions performed by 'street level' actors such as local officials, frontline workers and community groups. This broad approach to risk regulation blurs the conceptual boundaries between 'traditional' pre-emptive risk regulation and the more flexible, decentralised work that comprises resilience (Hutter, 2010; Macrae, 2010). It therefore offers a more holistic approach to analysing the regulation of risk.

CHINA'S ENVIRONMENTAL RISK REGIME: COMMAND WITHOUT CONTROL?

Although the concept of risk management (*fengxian guanli*) is well established, risk and resilience strategies do not resonate with current Chinese approaches to environmental regulation. Instead, China's approach to environmental protection remains dominated by command and control instruments (Kostka, 2015). For example, China has constructed an impressive legal framework for environmental protection during the past three decades. Shapiro (2016, p. 59) calls it 'a sophisticated and credible framework for achieving resource protection and pollution prevention'. However, significant tension exists between this approach and the key Chinese governance tool of bureaucratic performance goals whereby government officials are evaluated against a range of specific targets. This tension has contributed to weak enforcement of environmental regulations. As Wang (2013) argues, environmental laws and regulations have played a secondary role to bureaucratic performance goals. He writes that 'despite years of official rhetoric on the development of Chinese rule of law, laws and regulations remain secondary . . . bureaucratic cadre mandates, not laws and regulations, are at the core of Chinese governance' (Wang, 2013, pp. 372, 440). In one example, Ran (2013) showed how officials in Nantong, Jiangsu, were incentivised *not* to implement environmental regulations due to the belief that doing so would jeopardise their achievement of what they perceived as more important economic performance goals. Since 2006, however, growing central government concern has resulted in environmental targets becoming increasingly stringent, and they now form a central part of local officials' performance evaluations (Wang, 2013; Kostka, 2015). Problems remain, however, and some have characterised China's top-down approach to environmental regulation as 'command without control' (Kostka, 2015; Lo, 2015). China's approach to managing environmental risk was predominantly reactive as opposed to proactive as the country pursued a path of 'pollute now, clean up later' (Zusman, 2004). The shift to a target-based approach to some extent represents a more proactive stance, although pollution remains a severe problem in many localities.

ENVIRONMENTAL LEGISLATION AND THE IMPLEMENTATION GAP

After the start of the Reform and Opening-Up era in 1978, China began to develop a comprehensive bureaucratic and legal framework for addressing environmental issues, which was consistent with the party-state's newly stated commitment to 'rule of law' and desire to ameliorate environmental degradation stemming from rapid economic growth.[2] This included the promulgation of the Environmental Protection Law (Trial Version) in 1979, which was amended in 1989. The establishment of China's 'environmental state' (Mol and Carter, 2006) significantly deepened in the 1990s as environmental problems intensified (van Rooij, 2006). One manifestation of this was the promulgation of more specific legislation to govern the environment. China has more than 20 laws and hundreds of regulations related to the environment, addressing all of the major sectors including pollution control, energy conservation and endangered species protection (Mol and Carter, 2006). This legal framework is still a work in progress, and in 2014, after several years of intense internal deliberation, the central government passed a revised and updated Environmental Protection Law that stiffened polluter penalties and provided extra power to environmental protection departments (Zhang et al, 2013). Environmental laws and regulations are implemented by Environmental Protection Bureaus (EPBs) at the provincial, municipality and county levels. At the central level, the State Environmental Protection Administration (SEPA) was promoted to full ministerial status in 2008, becoming the Ministry of Environmental Protection (MEP), in a further sign that environmental issues were gaining importance.

Despite having made considerable progress in establishing a regulatory system, environmental degradation remains a severe problem (Wong, 2013). It is widely known that weak enforcement seriously undermines environmental regulation in China, resulting in a serious implementation gap (Jahiel, 1998; Ma and Ortolano, 2000; van Rooij, 2006; Ran, 2013). According to one explanation, the problem of weak enforcement is symptomatic of a gap between central government aspirations and local government realities. EPBs come under the direct influence of local government officials who, since the early stages of the reform period, have been given powerful economic and career incentives to maximise economic growth (Whiting, 2006; Landry, 2008). This has long been viewed as a major factor contributing to lax enforcement of environmental legislation (Lieberthal, 1997; Oshita and Ortolano, 2006; van Rooij, 2006). In some cases, local governments ignore polluters and prevent EPBs from carrying out their enforcement duties, especially when these polluting companies are important for the local economy (Ma and Ortolano, 2000; van Rooij, 2006; Economy, 2005). Poor enforcement is further exacerbated by

[2] China's constitution was amended in 1999 to explicitly endorse establishment of a 'socialist rule-of-law state' (Peerenboom, 2002, p. 1).

'local protectionism' (*difang baohu zhuyi*), whereby local officials ignore environmental legislation in order to protect their own industries from external competition, thereby maximising local economic growth (van Rooij, 2006; Lo, 2015). It has also been shown that EPBs lack resources, including financial and human resources, to effectively carry out their enforcement duties (Economy, 2005). Another problem with China's environmental protection regulatory system concerns vague and ambiguous environmental legislation that is also frequently out of touch with local realities and therefore difficult to enforce (Alford and Shen, 1997; Lo and Fryxell, 2005; Beyer, 2006; van Rooij, 2006). Although EPBs can fine polluters, these fines are often lower than the cost of installing or running pollution control equipment (Lotspeich and Chen, 1997; Economy, 2005). While the updated Environmental Protection Law (2014) raises the ceiling on fines, local officials are unlikely to favour harsh punishments for companies that contribute to the local economy. In addition, the high turnover rates of local officials, who typically serve between three and four years in one jurisdiction before moving on, has also been found to hinder the implementation of environmental regulations (Eaton and Kostka, 2014).

A closer look, however, reveals a more complicated picture. China's size and diversity ensure significant regional variation in pollution generation and control. Although van Rooij and Lo's (2010) longitudinal study suggests that enforcement of environmental legislation has become more formalistic and coercive over the past decade, they also note significant regional variation, with punishments in poorer areas lagging behind those in richer ones. In addition, there has been significant relocation of industry within the country during the past decade, from the relatively wealthy eastern seaboard to poorer inland areas, which Zheng et al (2014) claim has increased the latter communities' pollution burden and disrupted quality of life. At the same time, they argue that this trend may produce a net social benefit assuming newer inland factories adopt green technology, and due to the fact that the eastern seaboard is more densely populated (Zheng et al, 2014). Some industrial location has occurred within cities. Liu (2013, p. 140) found that 41 per cent of China's 84 'environmental Model Cities' were 'spatially related to cancer villages', suggesting that some attempts to clean up the environment were simply resulting in the relocation of pollution to more disadvantaged communities on the urban fringes.

TARGET-BASED APPROACHES

Performance targets have been an important governance tool in China since imperial times (Minzner, 2009). They are a mechanism through which higher levels can monitor subordinates and ensure that their priorities align. Each administrative level is given a set of specific targets, which are prioritised into soft (least important), hard and veto (*yi piao foujue*, most important). Failure to achieve veto targets, which typically include issues of fundamental importance to the CCP such as family planning and social stability maintenance, may incur serious consequences for officials, including precluding them from promotion. Officials are evaluated each year through the cadre responsibility system (*mubiao zeren zhi*). There is often friction between performance targets and law, particularly when (as is often the case) the two contradict each other (Minzner, 2009). In such cases, adherence to the former tends to trump the law (Minzner, 2009).

The low priority afforded to environmental issues in the target-based cadre responsibility system before 2006 significantly contributed to the lax enforcement of environmental legislation (Wang, 2013). This changed in 2006 with the advent of the 11th Five-Year Plan (FYP) (2006–10), which introduced compulsory environmental targets for the first time. Five binding targets were incorporated into the 11th FYP, increasing to nine in the 12th FYP (2011–15) (Kostka, 2015). Local officials became responsible for meeting pollution and energy intensity reduction targets as part of their assessment criteria, with Premier Wen Jiabao calling on local officials to use an 'iron hand' to ensure targets were met (*China Daily*, 2010). The plan mandated a 20 per cent reduction in energy consumption per unit of GDP and a reduction in the total volume of chemical oxygen demand (COD) and sulphur dioxide (SO_2) by 10 per cent. Specific targets were formulated for each administrative level by the jurisdiction one level up in the hierarchy, which enabled a degree of flexibility to account for regional differences (Kostka, 2015). For example, in order to minimise the economic impact, poorer inland provinces were generally given lower targets compared with wealthy eastern seaboard jurisdictions. Under the 11th FYP, provincial energy intensity reduction targets ranged from 22 per cent to 12 per cent. One official, quoted by Wang (2013, p. 402), called this a 'common, but differentiated, responsibilities' approach.

In response to strict energy intensity and pollution control targets, many local governments have overseen industrial restructuring and consolidation, investment in environmental and energy sectors, and improved resource efficiency (Wang, 2013). For example, in order to achieve its 11th FYP targets the Shanghai Municipal Government formulated a work plan to speed up the elimination of 'backward' (or inefficient) production, replace small units with large ones in the electric power sector, limit proposed energy-intensive and heavily polluting projects 'at source' by refusing to grant permission for their operation, promote the restructuring of the energy sector away from coal and towards cleaner forms of energy, and promote the Municipality's service sector (Shanghai Municipal Government, 2007). This work plan also incorporated specific targets such as improving or renovating 3,000 coal boilers and kilns to make them more energy-efficient, thus saving 200,000 tons of standard coal equivalent.

As Kostka (2015) points out, a key difference between targets in Western countries and China is that, in the former, standards are enforced by law whereas Chinese officials are sanctioned via the cadre evaluation system. The driving force behind the growing prioritisation of environmental protection is another difference between China and liberal democracies. Wang (2013, p. 370) argues that environmental targets were introduced 'as part of a broader political strategy to limit risks to the party-state's hold on power'. Energy efficiency and pollution reduction targets became tools to bolster declining performance legitimacy, through promoting more efficient economic growth and energy security, and by preventing social instability associated with public concern over industrial pollution (Wang, 2013). The introduction of stringent targets was seen as a much less risky approach to achieving this end compared with reforming the legal system, which would have strengthened the courts and therefore potentially undercut CCP control (Wang, 2013).

Binding targets are credited with stimulating considerable investment in pollution control infrastructure and the shutdown of numerous polluting facilities (Wang, 2013). But they have also resulted in numerous unintended consequences (Kostka and Hobbs, 2012; Wang, 2013; Kostka, 2015). For example, environmental targets are sometimes mutually exclusive, meaning officials must choose which to prioritise (Kostka, 2015). Pressure to meet target deadlines has resulted in extreme short-term energy-saving measures including hospital and enterprise closures (Kostka and Hobbs, 2012). Furthermore, not all environmental issues are given targets – for example, PM2.5 control was neglected for many years because it was not included as a target (Kostka, 2015).[3] There are also serious monitoring problems. Government officials acknowledge that statistical data is inaccurate – China's climate change envoy Xie Zhenhua claimed that, 'at every level of statistics there are exaggerations added to the data. Everyone knows that, and everyone is anxious [to fix it]' (Li and Gan, 2016). Moreover, some jurisdictions lack sufficient resources to monitor compliance (Kostka, 2015). This lack of monitoring and

---

[3] PM2.5 refers to atmospheric particulate matter with a diameter measuring no more than 2.5 micrometres.

verification undermines China's top-down approach to environmental protection, and alongside weak enforcement of legislation, is another reason why Kostka (2015) finds a system based on 'command without control'. While Lo (2015) suggests that one possible solution is to make China's environmental governance system more authoritarian in order to overcome local intransigence, other commentators have advocated 'decentred' forms of regulation (van Rooij, 2012).

DECENTRING ENVIRONMENTAL REGULATION IN CHINA

Regulatory scholars have long called for a more flexible and diverse decentred approach to regulation (Black, 2002). Whereas command-and-control approaches centre regulation on the state and its formal legal apparatus, decentred approaches view regulation as a hybrid process involving a complex mix of governmental and non-governmental actors and a wide variety of strategies (Black, 2002). As well as bringing the role of non-state actors into focus, decentred approaches incorporate a wider range of activities into what constitutes 'regulation' (Black, 2002). Decentred regulation is therefore seen to overlap significantly with resilience strategies (Hutter, 2010), and is playing an increasing role in regulating risk.

Some actors within the Chinese central government believe that empowering the public to hold polluters, and the officials that shield them, accountable can help improve environmental outcomes (Johnson, 2014a). This approach was partly embodied in the party-state's official adoption of depoliticised 'good governance' principles such as transparency, public participation and rule of law (Johnson, 2014a). For example, the updated Environmental Impact Assessment (EIA) Law (2002) included a clause that allowed for public consultation in the EIA process. And the MEP introduced regulations in 2008 that required greater disclosure of environmental information and which enabled citizens to file environmental information disclosure requests (Johnson, 2014a). These principles were written into the updated 2014 Environmental Protection Law under a new chapter entitled 'information disclosure and public participation'.

These developments should be understood in the context of a broader 'deliberative turn' that has taken place in Chinese politics, whereby authoritarian control is augmented by 'authoritarian deliberation', thus resulting in a more 'consultative' or 'responsive' form of authoritarian governance (He and Warren, 2011; see also Nathan, 2003; Weller, 2008; Tsang, 2009). Rather than dominate society through direct repression alone, the CCP has attempted to incorporate public opinion into its policies and focus on improving its governance capacity. This has enabled environmental regulation in China to become increasingly decentred, or 'pluralised', albeit this decentring is governed by an 'authoritarian logic' (van Rooij et al, 2014).

The emergence of responsive authoritarianism (Weller, 2008) has potentially important implications for managing environmental risk. New actors, including environmental NGOs, lawyers, judges, journalists and contentious citizens have emerged and begun to play regulatory roles (van Rooij et al, 2014; see also Stern, 2013; Johnson, 2014a; Shi and van Rooij, 2014). Urban middle class protestors often frame grievances in terms of regulatory shortcomings. For example, Zhang (2014) showed how anti-incinerator protestors in Guangzhou relied upon 'rational resistance' that drew upon expert knowledge to counter the state's assertion that a proposed incinerator would be safely regulated. Other studies have shown how protestors have become increasingly assertive in demanding that their public participation and transparency 'rights' be respected by the state (Johnson, 2014a). In several cases, unpopular projects have been halted by local officials ostensibly to enable a more thorough round of public participation (Johnson, 2013). In practice, however, environmental disputes are usually resolved in an ad hoc manner with considerations such as potential for social instability and concerns over regime legitimacy at the forefront (Cai, 2010; Liu et al, 2016). If anything, allowing projects to be halted to allow for greater public participation is just a means for local officials to defuse tension and reinstate social order before deciding how to react. In some cases such as the 2007 protest in Xiamen against a planned chemical plant manufacturing paraxylene (PX), resistance has resulted in the relocation of potentially polluting projects to poorer areas with fewer opportunities for resistance. Although this does not amount to the democratisation of regulation in a traditional sense, it shows how citizens can influence outcomes in cases where they distrust the ability of experts and officials to anticipate and respond to risk (Hutter, 2010). And even though official channels for public participation function poorly (Li et al, 2012), the growing prominence of discourses concerning transparency, participation and adherence to law in environmental disputes is important because it helps embed these concepts in the public consciousness.

Citizens can also adopt regulatory roles through litigation, and it is clear that some actors within the Chinese central government want to make greater use of the law in fighting pollution (Stern, 2014; Carpenter-Gold, 2015). China has expanded standing,[4] and in 2012 amended the Civil

---

[4] Standing refers to the right of an individual or organisation to initiate a lawsuit.

Procedure Law to allow public interest litigation by 'lawful authorities' and 'relevant organizations' (Stern, 2014, p. 64).[5] However, Stern concludes that litigation is still a largely unsatisfactory means for resolving environmental disputes (Stern, 2013). Obstacles include prohibitive cost, difficulties associated with gathering sound evidence and effective legal representation and, perhaps most significantly, local government control of the courts (Stern, 2013). As well as influencing outcomes, local officials can prevent cases from entering the courts at all. For example, the All-China Environment Federation (ACEF), which is a government-organised NGO (GONGO) closely affiliated with the MEP, filed eight public interest lawsuits in 2013, which were all rejected due to 'lack of standing' (Carpenter-Gold, 2015, p. 264).

China opened more than 130 specialist environmental courts between 2007 and 2013 (Stern 2014). Stern (2014) found that these courts play several important political roles. First, they potentially help resolve disputes, thus contributing to social stability. Second, they represent a continuation of a tradition whereby 'the masses' help the party-state achieve its objectives (here, environmental protection) when it lacks resources to do so. And third, environmental courts contribute to good governance, which is tied to CCP legitimacy and, ultimately, longevity. Rather than being a new way to hold powerful polluters accountable, however, Stern finds that the majority of defendants have been ordinary people who represent 'some of China's least-educated, most-disadvantaged citizens' (Stern, 2014, p. 69). For example, in 2010 in Guiyang, Guizhou, illegal fire starting by negligence and illegal logging accounted for more than 90 per cent of environmental crimes (Stern, 2014). Shi and van Rooij (2014) found a similar situation regarding the use of civil litigation in relation to environmental issues by Chinese prosecutors, whereby the majority of cases they examined targeted 'relatively small and weak defendants' (Shi and van Rooij, 2014, p. 8). Stern (2014, p. 54) concludes that, 'China's new environmental courts are not a step toward judicial empowerment, as international observers might be tempted to conclude, but an effort to enlist courts to serve alongside government bureaus in a multi-pronged environmental campaign.' Indeed, some view the courts as just another piece of China's social stability maintenance system (Chen, 2013).

It would be wrong to view China's system of risk regulation in purely top-down terms. China has a long history of local level policy experimentation. Some of these policies have been adopted by the central

---

[5] As Stern (2014) notes, the law does not specify what constitutes 'lawful authorities' or 'relevant organizations'.

government and rolled out across the country. Initiatives such as public interest litigation (Carpenter-Gold, 2015) and the establishment of specialised environmental courts (Stern, 2014) began at the municipal and provincial levels before becoming much more widespread. Yet when innovation is pursued for its own sake, it can result in limited change. This appears to have been the case in relation to the use of public prosecutors to tackle polluters, an approach that has proved particularly successful in Brazil (McAllister, 2008). As Shi and van Rooij (2014, p. 14) note, 'spurred by innovation incentive structures, the Chinese prosecutors have gone after the lowest hanging fruit, fulfilling limited regulatory need and having almost no regulatory effect'. There is reluctance to empower public prosecutors as a relatively independent check against local officials.

When compared with decentred regulation in Western countries, China's attempts to extend regulatory roles to new actors appear seriously circumscribed. However, as other scholars have emphasised, political initiatives in authoritarian states are designed to serve authoritarian ends (Svolik, 2012). When viewed this way, China's limited success in decentring regulation takes on a different sheen – the ultimate goal is not to improve environmental governance per se, but to shore up the regime and ensure that environmental risk does not become a threat to the CCP. Regulatory work exists first and foremost to serve party-state interests. It is strongly affected by the context whereby goals including regime survival and the maintenance of social stability are viewed as paramount.

A more optimistic view might be the development of a decentred regulation with Chinese characteristics. To an extent, this is already apparent, albeit in a relatively unintended way. For example, as van Rooij and others have noted, the authorities' desire to limit social unrest by incentivising local officials to resolve disputes quickly – often by handing out financial compensation to protestors – paradoxically encourages citizens to protest in response to realised or potential environmental risks (Cai, 2010; Su and He, 2010; van Rooij, 2012).

SOCIAL STABILITY AND COMPENSATION AS RISK MITIGATION

As Stockmann (2012) notes, liberalisation and control are two sides of the same coin. Hence, while actors within the central government have encouraged regulatory pluralisation as a means to improve oversight of local officials, this process has been checked by the belief that increasingly influential non-state actors need to be controlled. This tension encapsulates the 'authoritarian logic' that characterises regulatory pluralism in China (van Rooij et al, 2014). Thus courts, for example, have a dual purpose: resolving disputes according to law on the one hand, and upholding social stability on the other. These purposes are often in direct conflict with each other, with the latter invariably prevailing (Su and He, 2010).

The rule of law is threatened by a counter-trend in Chinese politics, namely the rise since the early 1990s of China's 'security state' (Wang and Minzner, 2015). The CCP has identified the maintenance of social stability (*weiwen*) as its paramount goal, and has dedicated a huge amount of resources to this task to the extent that the domestic security budget exceeds that of the military (Blanchard and Ruwitch, 2013). Government spending on domestic security increased from 27.78 billion yuan in 1995 to 314 billion yuan in 2008 (Xie, 2012, pp. 23–4), and officials are set targets under the cadre evaluation system that stipulate the maximum allowed number of protests (Minzner, 2009).

Since the start of the 21st century the CCP has emphasised 'comprehensive management of public security' over rule of law as the main means to achieve social stability maintenance (Xie, 2012). Under this approach, upholding stability (which equated with upholding CCP control) is carried out by a plethora of actors and institutions, including officials, enterprises, police, courts and petition-receiving offices (Su and He, 2010; Chen, 2013). For example, officials are required to appear on the scene of protests and try to resolve them (Su and He, 2010). As one local official recounted:

> At 11:15 p.m., about 500 workers blocked the main road leading to the hotel hosting leaders from Beijing. By 11.35 p.m., we had assembled on the scene officials from the street, the district, the trade union, the police together with 200 of our hired security officers. By 11.45 p.m., we cleared the road. Only 30 minutes. Then we started working and negotiating. (Lee and Zhang, 2013, p. 1,487)

Social stability maintenance funds are a recent and important tool for officials to restore public order during such negotiations (Xie, 2012). 'Buying stability' has origins in the run-up to the 2008 Olympics (Lee and Zhang, 2013). It includes cash payments to protestors, and government payment for services such as water supply and the construction of new schools when these are demanded in such a way that threatens stability. Victims of the Tianjin blasts, for example, protested to demand compensation payments from the government. According to Lee and Zhang (2013, p. 1,486), 'the grassroots state has turned into a marketplace where gamesmanship (or *boyi*, meaning strategic game playing) between officials and citizens determines the price tag of stability'.

The existence of 'compensation culture' in the West is strongly disputed due to a lack of empirical evidence (Lloyd-Bostock, 2010). Few studies have examined this phenomenon in China. However, we do know that there is growing willingness to spend public money on maintaining social stability. In one sense, this helps depoliticise issues by shifting the focus onto money. Yet ironically, the government's willingness to give concessions when faced with forceful protest may encourage aggrieved citizens to take to the streets. Protestors are aware that, to cite a commonly used phrase, 'a small disturbance results in a small settlement, a big disturbance results in a big settlement, no disturbance results in no settlement' (Cai, 2010). As a result, this focus on compensation is potentially seriously at odds with a decentred regulatory approach, one aspect of which involves members of the public calling out regulatory infractions. Van Rooij et al (2012) showed how the 'compensation trap' undermines regulatory enforcement. Their study showed how poor rural dwellers became dependent on handouts from polluting factories whose environmental despoliation had undermined farming as a source of livelihood. Although villagers initially demanded that the factories cease their polluting activities, they were placated by compensation and became locked into a cycle of dependency. This, in turn, undermined the potential regulatory role that local people could play through, for example, alerting higher levels about regulatory infractions. At the same time, research shows that wealthier middle class communities may be relatively less willing to be placated through compensation. This is partly because the cost of placating relatively well-off homeowners is potentially huge compared with paying off poor villagers. In addition, most documented urban environmental protests have been against projects still in the planning stages, meaning that pollution has not yet occurred (Steinhardt and Wu, 2016). With officials often vehemently insisting on the safety of these projects, compensation for pollution is not a feasible option. However, as Johnson (2013) shows in relation to waste incinerators, middle class opposition to polluting facilities sometimes results in their relocation to poor areas. Hence, middle class opposition results in the pollution problem being shifted onto lower-income communities instead of being resolved. The root causes of the problem are not addressed (Lee and Zhang, 2013).

CONCLUSION

As McElwee et al (2001, p. 301) concluded, the environmental law system 'hangs on China like an ill-fitting suit . . . Some of the problems can be fixed easily. Others will require changes in the structure of governance in China. These changes will require fundamental shifts in the distribution of power and significant political will to implement.' China's environmental risk regime (Hood et al, 2001) must be understood in the context of its authoritarian political system. In China, the political threat of 'harmful, adverse or unintended outcomes' is heightened by the country's one-party system and the fear that societal unrest (including that caused by environmental risks) might spiral out of control and undermine CCP rule. This is partly manifested in significant (and growing) tension between the rule of law and social stability maintenance, including in the realm of environmental protection. The predictability and rules-bound nature of the former is at odds with a flexible approach to handling problems whereby outcomes (upholding stability) trump processes. For example, Su and He (2010, p. 175) showed how, when faced with a large labour protest against a company's refusal to compensate workers for overtime, a District court in Guangdong Province 'stepped in long before the formal litigation process began, and it took assertive action by freezing the company's assets and bank accounts'. They conclude that '"legal" decisions are based not only on their own merits, but also on the threat of associated community disruption' (Su and He, 2010, p. 179). Maintaining social stability is seen as a vital element of CCP resilience. This leads to several unintended consequences, including the apparently growing trend of some pollution victims prioritising financial recompense and gain over procedural justice, and 'regulation by escalation', whereby citizens who protest regulatory infractions are more likely to receive recompense due to the need to restore public order (van Rooij, 2012).

The tension between social stability maintenance (and, by extension, CCP resilience) and rule of law is one of the defining features of China's environmental risk regime. Ironically, the same prioritisation of outcomes over processes that gives officials flexibility in handling disruptive events exacerbates risk and undermines public trust in the government. The Tianjin explosions may have been avoided had Ruihai been governed by a predictable rules-based system. Instead, it was able to cut corners – in stark violation of regulations – that exposed the vulnerability of China's system for regulating environmental risk. This example also shows how the target responsibility system is not a panacea for mitigating all environmental risks, and needs to be supplemented by greater supervision both within the system and from non-state actors.

The very issues that make risk management and regulation difficult in China also undermine resilience. Chan et al. (2015, pp. 1,421–22) optimistically stated that:

> The Tianjin incident provides an important opportunity for China to improve its resilience by upgrading the training of emergency responders in handling specific disaster hazards, and educating the public about environmental health risks of chemical incidents. If the Chinese Government shows zero tolerance of illegal industrial practices and holds the relevant stakeholders accountable

for such practices, the Tianjin incident could become a historical milestone for improvement of disaster risk reduction in China.

However, narrowly defining resilience in terms of authorities' immediate responses to industrial disasters ignores the root cause of the problem. Resilience in this sense is more usefully seen as one aspect of a broader approach to regulation – it does not make sense to detach it from other elements of the regulatory process. China's problems with risk regulation are deep and systemic, and the elimination of risk through a 'zero tolerance' approach is unlikely to succeed. Although improving stakeholder accountability is a crucial aspect of enhancing China's environmental risk regime, doing so through empowering the public is perceived as being in conflict with CCP resilience that is increasingly associated with maintaining social stability. As long as social stability is equated with direct CCP control, the prospects for public involvement in environmental risk regulation will likely remain limited.

As this chapter has noted, there is a good deal of inequality in China with regards to environmental governance, mirroring broader trends in economic and developmental inequality throughout the country. This is partly manifested in stricter enforcement of environmental regulations in richer eastern seaboard areas, and the relocation of inefficient and polluting enterprises to poorer inland areas. In addition, there is evidence to suggest that poorer communities may be more easily placated with compensation payments to the extent that some become dependent on pollution as an alternative source of livelihood (van Rooij et al, 2012).

Finally, external pressure has influenced environmental protection in China to some extent. China's first steps towards establishing an 'environmental state' in the early 1970s were partly influenced by international pressure (Mol and Carter, 2006). And since officially becoming the world's biggest carbon emitter in 2007, China has come under external pressure to take stronger action on climate change (Cao, 2010). However, recent moves towards setting pollution reduction, and energy- and carbon-intensity targets, align strongly with China's own domestic priorities, namely the need to uphold CCP legitimacy through maintaining social stability and sustaining economic growth (Wang, 2013), and thus cannot be attributed to international pressure alone.

PART V

Conclusion

11. Risk, resilience, inequality and environmental law: prospects and obstacles

Bridget M. Hutter

Contributors to this collection have analysed issues associated with the role of law in managing the environment in the 21st century. In particular, they have considered two major approaches for environmental control which have gained traction over the past decades, namely risk and more recently resilience approaches. An important focus of the collection has been to examine whether environmental law is compatible with resilience approaches and whether such approaches can facilitate improvements in the environment without exacerbating existing inequalities, and indeed whether they can help to expedite greater equality. The perspectives taken have varied across legal, sociological, political science, policy and development views, while the substantive cases discussed have been drawn from varying regions of the world.

This final chapter pulls together what we have learned from the collection. It draws out the main theoretical and analytical themes identified and considers which themes demand greater examination and which help us to expand our theoretical understanding of risk, resilience and inequality as it relates to environmental law. This chapter also reflects on what can we say about more pragmatic policy concerns, the experiments discussed in different chapters and their applicability to different social and economic contexts of environmental regulation.

RISK, UNCERTAINTY AND RESILIENCE

Risk and Uncertainty Remain Central

Issues of risk and uncertainty have emerged as intractably central to many of the debates about environmental control. The contestation of the risks associated with the environment remains a major issue. It is generally accepted that humans contribute to environmental risks, but the particulars are disputed. As we saw in Chapter 1, the distinction between risk and uncertainty is fundamental to understanding the differences between risk and resilience approaches. Risk approaches are portrayed as based on science and presenting a rational, objective basis for decision-making, while resilience approaches are seen as more appropriate in circumstances of uncertainty. A greater appreciation of the uncertainties surrounding the environmental problems we face has resulted in resilience approaches becoming more dominant in many environmental discourses across the world. Their popularity hinges on a number of features which have been drawn out through the collection.

The Attractions of Resilience

The first reason resilience strategies are regarded as helpful is because they are premised on uncertainty: coping with uncertainty in risk frameworks can be a major challenge for policy makers. In the environmental area this is especially important as discussions of environmental risks particularly challenge risk approaches, given the changing nature of the threats posed by climate change and their global generation. In managing the environment, we need more than ever to balance learning from the past against imagining the novel and unexpected (Hutter, 2010). Moreover, an important lesson from the disaster literature is the temptation to translate uncertainties into risks through contingency planning (Clarke, 1999). This can be a dangerous practice if the foundational thinking is falsely premised and one which can undermine risk-based approaches. A resilience approach which assumes uncertainty is an important counterpoint in these situations.

The second important advantage of resilience strategies is that they should be adaptable, flexible and open to modification in the event of unexpected change. This means having in place social and political systems and institutions which can cope with change and adapt to changing circumstances (Ebbesson, 2010). This is also an important message in the disaster literature, where authors advocate resilience approaches and caution that much contingency planning is focused on the last disaster when two disasters are rarely the same (Boin, 2010).

A third and major attraction of resilience approaches is that they tend to be bottom-up rather than top-down (which risk approaches are often thought to be because of their emphasis on expertise). This resonates with calls for greater democratisation and a belief that participation should be equally open to local communities, households and individuals as to elite participants in business, civil society and government. The inclusion of wider 'publics' in environmental decision-making has been a growing trend worldwide (Richardson and Razzeque, 2006). It is the subject of transnational conventions, notably the Aarhus Convention, and has become encoded in law, for example European Union environmental legislation (Lee, 2014).

Wide-ranging challenges to expertise and top-down decision-making, especially following some spectacular failures, have forced governments and regulatory agencies to be more inclusive in their decision-making and to recognise that alternative epistemologies and local knowledge need to be incorporated into risk governance (Jasanoff, 2010; Wynne, 1996). There is a growing recognition that there are advantages to being more inclusive of local populations and their knowledge and buy-in. Disaster planning has increasingly acknowledged the need to involve broader communities in planning, evaluating and implementing disaster plans (Tierney, 2012). The advantages are seen to include the deployment of a greater variety and range of knowledge of environmental risks and uncertainties and a wider range of resources for their management, mitigation and resolution (Lee, 2006). Arguments in favour of resilience approaches make normative claims about shared rights, responsibilities and decentralisation having 'the potential of enhanced efficiency of decision making, increased trust in government, and increased capacity at the local scale to undertake, for example, monitoring and enforcement' (Nelson et al, 2007; pp. 93–96).

A fourth attraction and aspiration of resilience approaches is the hope that they might foster greater equality, not just of participation in decision-making but also more equal outcomes. There is anticipation that these approaches will give 'a voice to vulnerable and marginalized stakeholders' (Nelson et al, 2007; pp. 93–96) and effect greater equality of outcome. A major aspiration for many commentators is that the current disparities in exposure to environmental risks are reduced for the benefit of future generations.

The reasons which have given rise to the popularity of resilience approaches resonate to some extent with the conditions for their success. Articulating further the conditions which facilitate resilience and risk approaches is important, as is identifying the factors and conditions which might undermine them. Let us, in turn, consider what the contributors to this collection have to say about these debates and more specifically what we can learn about risk and law by focusing on resilience and inequality.

Resilience Strategies Are Still Largely Ideational but the Aspirations Remain Vague

We saw in Chapter 1 that perspectives on the notion of resilience vary widely. The subject is still bedevilled by definitional issues including debates about the status of the term resilience, for example, whether it is an approach, a way of thinking, or a basis for action. Perspectives range from those which see resilience as a way of thinking to those who discuss issues about its evaluation and measurement (Agur, 2006: 274; Jones and Tanner, 2015). In this collection there is broad agreement about the contours of resilience involving notions of flexibility, bouncing back and the inclusion of broad populations in decision-making. But there are different emphases on the subject of resilience – ranging from considerations of ecology, biodiversity and socio-ecology through to considerations of more specific groups of people such as those living in urban settings, classes and individuals.

Resilience discussions can, compared to risk approaches, provoke debate about what types of society and ecosystems we are aspiring to. But there is little agreement about what these are. Often the society and ecosystems that resilience strategies aspire to 'bounce back' to are unspecified, perhaps implying that it is a bounce back to the same or a similar society or ecosystem that previously or already exists. Some discussions imply that the aspiration is to bounce back to a more inclusive and equal society through resilience processes that are more inclusive and participatory. Is the ambition stasis or system change? One view is that this might not even be part of the equation, and that resilience is an approach rather than a basis for action (see Chapter 1). Others see resilience as offering opportunities for change rather than mere survival or stationarity (McDonald, this volume). This in part depends upon how issues are framed and how narrowly problems are defined, for example, as long-term or short-term problems (Adger et al, 2011; p. 765).

The aspirations underlying resilience approaches also depend on how much appetite there is for system change. This is of course an issue that has major implications for issues of inequality and for this reason some authors believe that a radical transformation of existing social and economic institutions and practices are demanded (Curran, this volume; Tierney, 2014). But several contributors have identified obstacles to system changes. Their arguments are varied. One argument is that because sustainability agendas are underpinned by economic stationarity their aims are inherently conservative and limited (McDonald, this volume). Moreover, there may be no political will for change, for example because climate change is slow burn (McDonald, this volume). Related to this there are also economic interests in stasis (see Chapter 1) and vested interests in the present rather than intergenerational equality.[1]

[1] This argument was made by the Governor of the Bank of England in 2015 when addressing the insurance industry about the costs and challenges of climate

These issues have enormous ethical implications, which lead some to argue that resilience is an inherently normative concept, tied up with issues of power, justice and the rule of law (Duit et al, 2010; p. 367). As Ebbesson (2010; p. 365) cautions, there are distributional and moral consequences to resilience policies. This is of course also true of risk approaches, the difference being that resilience approaches seem to offer more hope for, and discussion of, greater equality. Indeed, one of the main distinctions between the two strategies seems to be aspirational – risk approaches are apparently very pragmatic in relation to the use of state resources, how to make decisions about what the risks are, and how to prioritise their management in tandem with other beyond the state actors (Black, 2005; Hutter, 2005). Resilience approaches are much more flexible and apparently inclusive. But as we can already begin to see when we start to analyse the approaches more deeply there is much that is assumed and demands greater interrogation. Indeed, some argue that risk approaches are ideational to the extent that they may imply that risks can be anticipated and managed (Haines, 2011; Hutter, 2010). Resilience strategies by contrast acknowledge that risks may not be anticipated, the unexpected may happen and the consequences may be difficult to manage. So in different ways both risk and resilience approaches are aspirational and both have elements of pragmatism. Let us now consider how this resonates with the role of the law and its ability to facilitate these approaches to environmental control.

DIFFERENT PERSPECTIVES ON THE ROLE OF LAW

Differences have emerged throughout this collection about the role of existing legal systems and their ability to facilitate risk and especially resilience approaches. In part these issues depend upon which country, legal system and laws one is referring to. It is important to keep in mind that the laws affecting environmental management are not simply those designated as environmental laws but also embrace a wide range of branches of law. This is well illustrated by the UK where environmental risks cut across multiple areas of fragmented legislation which are informed by diverse interests and values (Scotford and Robinson, 2013; p. 388).

Ituarte-Lima (this volume) considers the relationship between biodiversity law, livelihoods, equity and changes for sustainability and their

---

change. He observed that this generation has little incentive to avert future problems http://www.bbc.com/news/business-34396961

connections with property, which she takes to be the social organisation of rights and duties over physical resources, such as land forms, and intellectual resources, such as traditional knowledge about biodiversity. Also important in the transnational context is the role of soft law and the recognition that increasingly these laws are cross-cut by the diverging pressures of globalisation and localism and a blurring of the boundaries with hard law (Ituarte-Lima, this volume).

Some see the existing legal system as working for stationarity. McDonald (this volume) argues this, but she is also optimistic that law can play an important role in promoting resilience and pushing for greater change than would be achieved incrementally. She maintains that climate change offers an opportunity to rethink legal rights and responsibilities to the natural world. In particular McDonald (this volume) sees the role of law as offering stability and the foundation for reform in nation states and in international law.

In part the opportunities available depend upon which legal system one is referring to. McDonald's chapter (this volume) includes discussion of Australia. In addressing questions about the type of society and future the law envisages and can facilitate Pedersen (this volume) writes exclusively about the UK. He argues that some legal systems such as the UK's already incorporate some of the features necessary for facilitating resilience.

The importance of national legal systems in influencing the ability of the law to play a role in environmental control is clear in the discussion of China. Johnson (this volume) explains that while China has developed an 'impressive legal framework' over the past 30 years its impact has been limited partly because the rule of law in China is secondary to social stability (ibid). So while China has undoubted environmental problems the role of environmental law is primarily to manage the public unrest and social conflicts these generate, with managing the environment being a secondary consideration.

Ituarte-Lima (this volume) focuses on Latin America, where the extractive industries pose particularly serious risks to biodiversity and the livelihoods of indigenous peoples. She selects the region because of innovative local and regional developments which have to some extent incorporated biodiversity and equity, for example with laws protecting indigenous peoples' collective knowledge about biological resources. However, she also discusses the risks of conflict attaching to these issues in areas with powerful economic interests and weak and corrupt governance institutions.

An important issue regarding the role that law can play is its ability to reconcile the flexibility and adaptation of resilience with the certainty and predictability of law. Ebbesson (2010; p. 356) argues that it is possible to reconcile these differences, but Pedersen (this volume) is less optimistic. He discusses the epistemological, legal and practical limitations on explicitly designing resilience into legal systems. One of these is the tension between legal uncertainty and coping with the flexibility and uncertainty which are at the core of resilience strategies. This is a more extreme tension than exists between the law and risk strategies, where risk strategies provide greater certainty to the extent that they assign a probability to the risk. This is a subject at the core of Patton and Barnes' (this volume) consideration of the role of science in resolving or perhaps exacerbating these debates. They discuss how the gaps between science and the law make it especially difficult for them to co-operatively handle uncertainty and change. The frames science and the law use and the evidence they require differ (Wynne, 1989).

Climate change poses difficulties for science and the law, particularly in attributing cause and liability. At a very general level scientific agreement that human activity contributes to climate change is a step forward, but the particulars are still disputed and compounded by natural variability (Patton and Barnes, this volume). Nevertheless, improvements in the science are discernible, leading potentially to enhanced resilience, a greater moral responsibility to act and a greater role for the law to play.

Holley and Sofronova, (this volume) believe that the law can best play a role in facilitating resilience approaches as part of a broader portfolio of governance techniques. Crucially it is part of more deliberative, collaborative and flexible approaches than traditional legal approaches.

GOVERNANCE APPROACHES TO MANAGING THE ENVIRONMENT: EXPLOITING THE SYNERGIES BETWEEN GOVERNANCE AND RESILIENCE

It has long been recognised that the law is but one tool among many in efforts to manage risks in modern societies. This is underlined by the move from government to governance, and the incorporation of a broader range of actors into the management of the environment. This does not mean that the law is redundant, but it does highlight the need to think about the role of law in different ways and particularly its role in broader environmental governance structures.

Contributors argued that there is a degree of affiliation between resilience approaches and governance. This is particularly so around issues of democratisation and the inclusion of NGOs, businesses and the citizenry (McDonald, this volume). Holley and Sofronova, (this volume) discuss how the new environmental governance can give voice to marginalised and indigenous peoples and build resilience through understanding and incorporating their needs better. Resilience needs participation and buy-in from groups within and beyond the state in recognition of the scale of environmental risks and it also needs to command broader support for environmental governance. This contrasts with risk approaches which are often regarded as more expert- and government-led, although in fairness it should be recognised that greater participation has increasingly been a feature of some risk-based systems, in particular through taking into account a greater range of public or social risk perceptions (Hutter, 2005). This said, resilience approaches are to a much greater extent premised on the need for broader inclusion. Indeed, the introduction of resilience approaches may present new opportunities for renewing and reviewing governance agendas, in particular in helping to identify strengths and weaknesses in current governance arrangements (Duit et al, 2010; p. 367).

There are implementation challenges to the participatory and inclusive ambitions attaching to governance and resilience. Numerous studies have examined the difficulties associated with who participates, in what capacity and with what effect (see Irwin and Jones, 2010 for a good summary). The very definition of participation is problematic and covers a broad range of possible mechanisms and procedures, from access to information through to full seats at decision-making tables (see Arnstein, 1969; Dryzek, 1997; Richardson and Razzaque, 2006 for good discussions on this). Often the participatory base is not as broad or as empowered as many discussions of resilience would lead us to expect. The law can facilitate or prove an obstacle to participation, for example much depends on its framing and implementation (see below). There may be financial obstacles to implementation, and participation can be lengthy and costly.

An important theme running through this collection is that the opportunities offered to non-state actors, organisations and individuals to participate very much depends upon the political systems and social structures within which they operate. Two chapters consider the case of China which has an authoritarian political regime. This means that responsiveness to environmental risks can come into tension with a reluctance to empower beyond the state actors who could undermine the ruling party (Johnson, this volume). China has given greater rights to its citizens to consult and participate, for example rights to more information about the environment, and greater voice to NGOs, citizens, the media and lawyers (Johnson, this volume; Wang, this volume). This has met with limited success but it is quite circumscribed relative to participation in more democratic political systems. The processes and channels for participation are not working well (Johnson, this volume), and typically the government is still heavily involved in the process. For example, NGOs in China are weak, and lack legal, financial and political support (Wang, this volume).

Operationalising multi-governance and polycentric governance systems to work in the furtherance of environmental improvements is a challenge. Although governance has become more important as environmental risks have come to be defined as global rather than local risks, we can see that the role of governments can still be crucial. They can play a key role in facilitating local, wider participation (Comfort et al, 2010; p. 281; Richardson and Razzaque, 2006; p. 177ff). Governments define the legal rights and responsibilities to participation, but they may also be silent on the issue or contain rights which are not implemented. Some authors believe that broadening participation can be mandated (as reflected in the Aarhus Convention) and that polycentric governance can be encouraged by inclusive legal arrangements (McDonald, this volume).

Pedersen (this volume) however is less optimistic. In his discussion of how the law can facilitate governance Pedersen focuses on public participation and the challenges the law faces in terms of balancing competing views about participation, risk perceptions and the tensions that may exist between local and central governments. He finds that at some level the law already provides for participation in terms of soft law provisions, and in harder law provision for public participation and consultation. But in examining the operation of such provision in the UK courts he found less than full support for public participation in legal decision-making. Moreover, he also discerned a division between decision-making through public participation and high-level decision-making (this volume).[2]

Ituarte-Lima (this volume) reminds us that there may be varying perspectives of the rights accorded by law. She explains how some indigenous people in Latin America regard the intellectual property rights they have been accorded with suspicion, as a commodification of their knowledge by Western conceptualisations of property. However, aspects of the law concerning participation, representation and fair distribution accord well with Amazonian views of their collective rights and biocultural heritage (Ituarte-Lima, this volume).

The law is not disconnected from other governance structures. Patton and Barnes (this volume) discuss the role of insurance, which they argue is in many respects dependent on the law. Insurance is described by some as a major emerging form of governance in its own right (Erikson and

---

[2] See also Lee and Abbot, 2003, who critically examine the Aarhus Convention's implementation in the UK and find it wanting in its ambitions and focus on NGOs rather than broader public participation.

Doyle, 2003). Patton and Barnes (this volume) similarly believe that insurance has a major role to play alongside governments, in helping to increase resilience and mitigate the risks associated with climate change. They argue that the roles of government and insurance are very different but can be complementary. Government regulations can facilitate *ex ante* resilience and mitigation through, for example, zoning and building codes (Patton and Barnes, this volume; see also Hutter, 2009). Insurance can insist on compliance with these being a precondition of insurance (Kunreuther, 1996). Insurance can also help through post-loss recovery payments and here some new insurance products, facilitated by improved attrition science, can help to 'fill governance gaps' (Patton and Barnes, this volume). An example Patton and Barnes draw on is that of parametric insurance which agrees *ex ante* to pay out upon the occurrence of a trigger, such as an extreme weather event, arguably helping to improve the capacity to 'bounce back'. Insurance can also be an important part of public–private partnerships to increase resilience, for example where governments partially underwrite insurance provision (Patton and Barnes, this volume).

An important feature of governance systems is that they can operate within, and also across, national boundaries. Holley and Sofronova, (this volume) explain how examples of the new environmental governance can be found in different regions of the world. Indeed, they can enable organisations from the business and civil society sectors to work together with more formal global governance organisations. Moreover, they can facilitate the management of different magnitudes of problem from those occurring locally to those regarded as global risks. This is captured in such terms as multi-level or polycentric governance, the different terms denoting the various levels of formality that may be involved between different states, organisations and individuals (Ostrom, 2012). And it is at the transnational level that the multi-level collaborative approaches that can be facilitated by environmental governance may be most valuable.

Multi-Level Governance: Managing the Environment Across Borders

Notions of governance, multi-level governance and polycentric governance encourage a more holistic conceptualisation of the transnational effort that is demanded to mitigate and control damage to the environment. This does not just refer to consideration of the transnational stage (although this is of course crucial) but also means incorporating local micro levels of governance. Satterthwaite (2011) details how this must involve co-operation between countries and between central and local governments and international organisations. The interdependencies and interconnectivity between regions and cities is further discussed by Sattherthwaite (this volume) where he examines how cities are reliant on the broader ecosystems, rural areas and supply chains for their own resilience. Of course, resilience planning in cities also requires capacity at local level. Sattherthwaite (this volume) examined the influence of local governments on health outcomes and found that cities with well-functioning local governments had greater adaptive capacity with respect to climate change. They were most able to adapt infrastructures and services to climate change risks and most able to reduce emissions. But they also needed the capacity to work with those at risk from these adaptations. Sattherwaite (this volume) observes that this level of government has been overlooked in many discussions on climate change, reinforcing Duit et al's (2010; p. 367) claim that 'rethinking problems of governance and law in a resilience perspective can often prove very helpful in identifying strengths and weaknesses of contemporary governance systems'.

Implementation is of course crucial to the impact of the law. This includes consideration of whether an adequate implementation regime is in place, in terms of resources and capacity. It involves information gathering which could encourage citizens to report environmental incidents and allow for civil society organisations and individuals to use the law in the absence of state regimes doing so (McDonald, this volume). Also relevant is that much environmental legislation has been subject to the dual influence of globalisation and localism. In the UK for instance environmental law has been influenced by the European Union but also the growing localism attaching to devolution and localised implementation (Scotford and Robinson, 2013). Such dual tensions can have a profound effect on the ability to implement.

Transnational and national frameworks need to be translated into local more detailed laws (Ituarte-Lima, this volume; Holley and Sofronova, this volume). Failure to implement environmental laws at local level is another major obstacle to the impact of environmental laws, for example in China where enforcement of the law is a local responsibility and at this level it comes into conflict with pressures for economic growth (Wang, this volume) and local protectionism (Johnson, this volume). Those responsible for economic growth and the enforcement of environmental laws may lack the political will to protect the environment as it threatens the local economy, especially as their economic performance is the main measure of their performance by central government (Johnson, this volume).

It is partly for these reasons that Wang (this volume) proposes new workable forms of financially viable participation at community level. He advocates stakeholder dialogues as a possible way forward at community level. His chapter discusses their experimental introduction in China in

2000 with reference to environmental pollution and their roll-out to incorporate a wider range of neighbourhood environmental issues thereafter. The stakeholders involved were community leaders, NGOs, government representatives, business representatives and the media. Wang's evaluation of these experiments identified some positive effects such as greater participation and in some cases environmental improvements. Most encouraging with respect to environmental management was the greater awareness of environmental matters that the forums generated and the creation of greater pressure on businesses to come to the table and contemplate accounting for their environmental difficulties and even negotiating around them. Wang (this volume) found that the forums also increased levels of trust between stakeholders, although he acknowledges that such processes are not the norm in China and that if the forums are to become more common they will demand a preparedness for greater participation and finance to train facilitators and organise meetings, and above all they will demand political backing. Holley and Sofronova, (this volume) also remark on the need for financing to facilitate the cost and capacity to experiment with new forms of governance.

THE CHALLENGES POSED BY INEQUALITY

Issues of inequality are at the core of the challenge posed by resilience approaches (Nelson et al, 2007). Resilience, multi-governance and participatory governance do not by themselves ensure equality. We have already seen that it can be difficult for less powerful groups and individuals to participate and those who do participate do not necessarily promote or facilitate equality, indeed they may amplify existing inequalities.

If we consider some of the other organisations involved in governance, then the difficulties become clearer. There are, for example, strong arguments that insurance is a form of governmentality which privatises risk (see Chapter 1 this volume; Joseph, 2013). Where this occurs, insurance may well come into tension with one of the main attractions of resilience approaches for many authors, namely democratisation.[3] Insurance can have unequal effects in terms of its accessibility and impact, and exacerbate the inequalities attaching to the protection it can offer from the effects of environmental risks. For example, social and state protections may be displaced by private insurance which is available only to those who

[3] Some scholars also see resilience strategies as a form of governmentality. See Chapter 1.

can afford insurance premiums. There may be forms of public–private partnership co-operation which can be designed for the public good, but the distributional effects of these need careful consideration.

Other actors beyond the state encounter similar difficulties. In the economic sector there are differential commitments to environmental issues and also serious inequalities between different business sectors and between multinational companies and medium, small and micro businesses. NGOs vary greatly in their commitment to environmental and equality issues. They do not always work in the public interest (Hutter and O'Mahony, 2004; Lee, 2014), indeed it is important to remember there are NGOs operating on pro- and anti-climate change agendas (Doherty, 2014; p. 282).

Inequalities occur at all levels – between regions, nations, urban and rural areas, communities, households and between individuals. Curran's chapter focuses on the considerable inequalities in resilience to the economic, physical and social impacts of climate change between individuals. He argues that these inequalities are relational and herein lies a major dilemma for resilience strategies, namely that the greater resilience of some individuals is at the expense of the weakened resilience of others. Indeed, this is a major problem at all levels from the individual to different transnational regions. As Curran (this volume) discusses, this generates major moral difficulties as 'sacrificing individuals for the sake of the species' is an aspect of resilience as a concept relating to collective groups and systems that has to be overcome.

Curran (this volume) uses the concept of risk classes to analyse the systemic and collective dimensions of the risk inequalities which exist at local, national and transnational levels. Like others in the collection, he argues that understanding existing power relations is essential to understanding and tackling inequalities, in this case the relational aspects of risk and resilience. Curran explains this through the concept of organised irresponsibility, the fact that no-one is held accountable for the risks they generate and the damage they cause. In the case of the environment an accumulation of individual acts can systematically cause massive damage. These are 'ordinary acts' but the ability to engage in these acts is, he argues, linked to inequality. Individuals with greater resources generate more risks through their higher levels of consumption and energy use and command of food supplies. In this respect most of us living in the developed world may be implicated in this, thus underlining the need for greater participation in contributing to the effort to control the environment (see below). Curran (this volume) believes that resilience thinking might play a role in any radical transformation if focusing on the resilience of individuals can transform social rationality, away from the maximising logics of production, consumption, profit and risks.

The possibility of transformative change would also demand legal changes. At the moment, many harms tend to be regarded at the level of individuals rather than construed as something that can affect wider groups or classes of people (Curran, this volume). It is precisely this that Ituarte-Lima (this volume) examines in her consideration of collective property rights in Latin America and her broader concern with transnational soft laws which seek to foster social equity. She found that despite these rights there was often discrimination, for example the way in which indigenous land not being worked in Peru could be deemed to have been abandoned. Also, property rights do not extend to sub-soil, thus permitting the extractive industries access. Ituarte-Lima concludes that while property laws are a step in the right direction there is a need to focus on their operation and to sort out legal obstacles to achieving the ideals underlying the spirit of the law. She advocates connecting property and human rights approaches to effect greater consideration and privileging of justice and equity in the design of biodiversity and livelihoods. The major challenge is to affect this at multiple levels of governance.

Inequalities in wider society are reflected in the legal system. McDonald, (this volume) explains that legal systems can be very narrowly focused on single issues and weighted in favour of political and economic goals rather than ecological sustainability. The cost–benefit analyses which often underlie implementation of environmental laws tend to be weighted to the economic costs and benefits rather than environmental gains and impacts (McDonald, this volume). Litigation can be very expensive for ordinary citizens. Indeed, they may not have the right to litigate – this is why regulation can be so important. Johnson's chapter identifies inequalities in China's environmental legal system. At one level legal representation can be very costly and difficult to secure. There are also inequalities between state and non-state actors, with the courts in which environmental cases are heard being controlled by local government and able to refuse court hearings (Johnson, this volume). One consequence of this is a very unequal distribution of defendants, with the majority of cases being taken against small, weak ordinary citizens not powerful polluters. Another rather perverse effect of inequalities is that compensation schemes for environmental harms can become a source of finance for poor communities as they are bought off, or use the system to trade tolerance of the harm for the compensation (Johnson, this volume; Van Rooij et al, 2012). There may also be unequal effects attaching to protest as richer protesters successfully lever relocation decisions of proposed polluting plants to poorer areas (Johnson, this volume).

Sattherthwaite's chapter does offer some possibility of dealing with the relational dilemmas of resilience. He considers urban populations in low- and middle-income countries with a focus on inequalities in environmental health. These relate, for example, to living and working conditions across the life cycle, including access to services such as clean water, sanitation and health care. The resilience perspective adds consideration of how cities cope with extreme weather events, including how urban areas address the inequalities generated by enhancing the resilience of the city. He examined cities which had successfully achieved this, such as Rosario in Argentina and found that success partly depended on the capacity of local government to work with those at risk and to ensure that the resilience of the vulnerable was not compromised by, for example, rehousing them. This required resources and sensitivity to the distribution of power and it depended upon the ability of local government to work with neighbouring and central governments. Also important was good local knowledge to enable equity and fairness in the distribution of resources, for example through the involvement of local civil society groups that could facilitate local participation.

RISK, RESILIENCE, INEQUALITY AND ENVIRONMENTAL LAW

What can we learn from the collection about the relationship between law, risk and resilience, and their implications for inequality? Clearly there are very wide variations in environmental regimes worldwide. The chapters on China show that it is still very much in command and control mode compared to other countries where risk approaches are more firmly embedded. But risk-based approaches to environmental control are themselves highly variable, both conceptually and in their implementation (Black, 2005; Fisher, 2013; Hutter, 2005; Rothstein et al, 2013). The same is true of resilience approaches where there is a conceptual minefield (Tierney, 2014), a lot of rhetoric and less evidence of implementation.

One of the attractions of resilience approaches is that they can deal with uncertainty, whereas risk approaches are more appropriate for issues involving certainty (or some level of probability). This distinction seems to struggle to be sustained in practice. We know that the distinctions between risk and uncertainty are often not used in routine regulatory enforcement (Hutter and Lloyd-Bostock, 1992). We also know that risk approaches are susceptible to treat uncertainties as if they are risks (Clarke, 1999). Some of the authors in this collection reveal how this can also happen in the case of resilience approaches. For example, insurance transforms uncertainties to risks – losing the premise of uncertainty upon which resilience is based but enabling insurance to contribute to managing the environment and the damage caused by climate change (Patton and Barnes, this volume). This echoes the view that insurance can transform obstacles into possibilities (Ewald, 1991; p. 200; Joseph, 2013; p. 260).

Framing is crucial to both approaches. Risk is a lens for making sense of the world, but the frameworks under which risk approaches inform policy are multiple and are often not interrogated (Fisher, 2013). Indeed, they may be inappropriate for dealing with the environmental problems climate change confronts us with (Heyvaert, 2011). Resilience approaches are similarly subject to framing and the ways in which resilience is socially constructed clearly has a profound effect on its implementation and impact (Leach et al, 2010).

The chapters in this collection consider different aspects of resilience and what ends are envisaged. What emerges strongly is that resilience and risk approaches both involve difficult compromises. For example, both risk and resilience approaches encounter tensions between the demands of globalisation and localism, and the relational inequalities that exist at all levels in between. An explicit recognition of the trade-offs between economic and environmental costs and benefits are built into risk approaches which are theoretically at least premised on harder data than resilience approaches. These data lead to the prioritisation of risks but they do this in a social context which is value-laden and this infuses political decision-making about how to set priorities. What is not clear is whether resilience approaches involve systematic ways of assessing these trade-offs: there is no clear evidence emerging from this collection that they do. Cost is relevant in facilitating resilience approaches as they require training, new skills and organisational costs (Holley and Sofronova, this volume; Wang, this volume) but there is no suggestion that this cost is being weighed against the potential environmental benefits. Nor is there is evidence of resilience approaches involving systematic prioritisation although, as Nelson (2011; p. 117) observes, it may not be possible to make systems resilient to all types of change so we have to decide what to prioritise.

Risk and resilience approaches are meant to be flexible to changing circumstances but, as with other aspects of the distinction between risk and resilience, there is a difference between the two approaches in the degree to which this is emphasised. Risk approaches are intended to be sensitive to changes in the state of knowledge or risk appetites in assessing and prioritising activities. Resilience approaches stress flexibility and adaptation. One means by which this flexibility is seen to be achieved is through the third attraction of resilience approaches, namely their empowerment and inclusion of a much wider range of participants. This is why governance approaches are seen to resonate with resilience approaches.

Research by Adger et al (2011; pp. 764–5) found that it is the application of adaptive capacities by governance structures that is most significant in achieving flexibility and better adaptation. Especially important is their sensitivity to feedbacks and the way they framed issues. Vertical top-down governance structures which narrowly defined problems were least facilitative of resilience, flexibility and adaptation. This is echoed by Sattherthwaite (this volume), who found that local governments able to work vertically with those at risk and horizontally with neighbouring jurisdictions were most able to help with the relational aspects of enhancing resilience. Holley and Sofronova (this volume), regard one of the advantages of the new environmental governance over traditional law to be its ability to facilitate the capacity of local communities to accept and manage change. This includes enabling local capacity among developing nations and communities rather than their being the recipients of top-down approaches from developed nations.

The openness of governance structures to broad participation is clearly vital in facilitating resilience strategies. We have seen that governments can still play an important role in this but they need to have the political will to support such participation and facilitate it. Our chapters have shown that this is not always forthcoming and even where governments do see greater openness as desirable, implementation can pose major difficulties. This is partly because of difficulties in achieving procedural justice whereby participation in the framing of problems and decision-making about their resolution is open to non-elite and disadvantaged groups. In short, our chapters and the broader literature suggest that participation does not always mean inclusion.

The fourth attraction of resilience represents the most difficult challenge, namely enabling greater equality. Consideration of inequalities throws into sharp relief the differences and similarities of risk and resilience strategies. Reducing inequalities is not an integral part of risk approaches, but it is much more closely associated with resilience. The concern here is distributive justice, so the focus is on the harm caused and efforts to rebalance the relational inequalities that Curran (this volume) discusses in his chapter. Nelson et al (2007; pp. 408–9) argue that a failure to recognise power imbalances between stakeholders can reinforce existing inequalities. As we have seen, there are disincentives among some powerful players to change the status quo and partly for this reason effecting greater equality may be a major challenge for resilience strategies. And as Ituarte-Lima (this volume) reminds us, even where laws have been introduced to protect the rights of less powerful peoples the operation of these laws can nevertheless undermine their effectiveness.

THE PROSPECTS FOR RESILIENCE ARE CHALLENGING

Overall the prospects for resilience are quite challenging with the conditions conducive for the success of these strategies demanding major changes to our economy, polity and individuals' behaviour. Indeed, we need to understand much better what the conditions for facilitating or undermining resilience are. It is important to look for examples of achievements in this respect and our contributions in this collection did offer some.

Sattherthwaite (this volume) identified some success stories with respect to cities which have managed to improve their resilience and he maps out some of the conditions of these accomplishments. China is one of our toughest cases and while the prospects for resilience are not very encouraging so far some of the fundamental groundwork is emerging. Notwithstanding the limits to the expanding environmental law framework in China, it has facilitated greater participation and an increase in awareness of environmental problems (Wang, this volume) and there does seem to be some embedding of environmental issues and notions of participation in the public consciousness (Johnson, this volume). But there is much more to do – for instance there needs to be a greater preparedness of government to tolerate a flexible participative system. The law could facilitate greater dialogue but of paramount importance is the political prioritisation of environmental issues and a strengthening of the legal apparatus to facilitate this.

There is clearly a multi-governance challenge ranging from transnational arenas through to the individual level (Ituarte-Lima, this volume). There are difficulties of collective and individual action that need to be surmounted and a need for greater joined up or mutually facilitative actions. These are themes in our chapters and also in the wider literature. Research has found limited evidence across countries of individual understandings of climate change (Renn, 2011; p. 154). Many find climate change intangible and there is inconclusive evidence that educational levels motivate behavioural change (Wolf and Moser, 2011). Moral, ethical and value judgements do seem to affect individual environmental behaviour (Lorenzoni et al, 2006), but a counterweight can be free-riding by other individuals and countries who do not change: their inaction can become a rationale for others not changing (Doherty, 2014; Renn, 2011). Factors such as these also explain community responses to environmental initiatives. This is the level at which resilience strategies are often pitched.

There is some evidence that community activities can educate, sensitise and help change social norms about the environment (Centre for

Sustainable Energy, 2007; p. 4). This echoes the findings in our chapters relating to China (Johnson; Wang). But more is needed, working with community-based NGOs and local authorities (ibid). In these contexts, cultural preferences, and responsible and trusted leadership can make a difference (Lorenzoni, 2006; p. 90). Incentives are also important, for example demonstrations of tangible benefits for individuals and communities (Whitmarsh, 2008). In all of these the long term nature of change and the levels of uncertainties can be obstacles to change. But governments can facilitate action including through their use of law. They can facilitate co-operation between administrative areas and the private, public and charitable sectors (Holley and Sofronova, this volume; Reynolds et al, 2007; Sattherthwaite, this volume).

Regulation could also be much more interventionist with regard to, for instance, limiting choices to lower carbon products, through support for labelling and certification schemes, and through generally supporting green consumption (Centre for Sustainable Energy, 2007; pp. 6–7). And environmental performance could be much more commonly used as a measure of performance, for example at local government and corporate levels (cf Johnson, this volume). Conversely, we need to appreciate the ways in which the silences in the law can play a role in supporting the status quo and how the implementation of the law can also be an obstacle to risk and resilience approaches. Pedersen (this volume) reminds us that the law in action can have consequences that are unexpected and unintended.

TRANSFORMATIVE AND INCREMENTAL CHANGE: THE IMPORTANCE OF EXPERIMENTATION

The spectacular rise in the popularity of resilience has not made it a replacement for risk approaches. At the moment, there is too much noise and confusion over its definition and implementation (Tierney, 2014). It does however in some respects complement risk strategies and to some extent support Macrae's (2010) caution that we should not draw too stark a contrast between anticipation and resilience as there may be very important ways in which they overlap and can work together. Resilience also helps to temper the high expectations risk strategies can generate, namely that it is possible to anticipate and manage all risks. Resilience approaches try to facilitate systems which can absorb disruption and respond quickly to disaster, since they are premised on the belief that zero tolerance of risk is unachievable. This may raise the objection that in the case of the environment this is unacceptable, but resilience approaches also represent a more radical perspective on risk reduction. However, this perspective demands transformative changes to thinking and practice, namely changes to a system which privileges economic interests over environmental ones, the present over the future and the rich over the poor. The changes demanded are massive across space, domains and all levels from the individual to the global. But while resilience at one level demands radical transformation it can also encourage ground level incremental change. The chapters in this volume have demonstrated that there are some signs of change at the level of cities and some national and regional regimes. This suggests the possibilities for change and for a developing a basis for longer-term transformative change.

It is clear throughout the collection that the law still has an important role to play in environmental control and the capacity to work with both risk and resilience approaches. But this is a part of a broader governance framework where the law has the potential to facilitate some of the conditions that will make resilience strategies a reality. Holley and Sofronova (this volume), explain that there is a continuum of possible relationships between the law and the new environmental governance. The most appropriate role for law in part depends upon features of the particular legal system. Some legal systems already have features that encourage resilience (Pedersen, this volume), but there can nevertheless be obstacles, notably around issues of implementation and enforcement (Wang, this volume). Issues of governance and implementation are also important for risk strategies and the crucial role played by enforcement is one of the strong messages of socio-legal research across all domains. Accountability is also important, especially in polycentric government systems oriented to resilience approaches. Again, the law can play a role here, for example, by setting baselines to ensure that new approaches do not result in deregulation (Holley and Sofronova, this volume). This is not just a matter of legal tools and frameworks but of the social and political systems which constitute the legal system and within which legal systems operate.

Where the rule of law is not respected and where the political will to act is absent no amount of law will make a major difference. Patton and Barnes (this volume) make it very clear that this is an important consideration in facilitating the conditions under which insurance can play a central role in environmental control and in closing the climate-resilience gap. Co-operation between different parts of society is crucial in managing the fundamental tensions in all risk governance between equity, economics and risk. Holley and Sofronova (this volume), note that the capacity and willingness of governmental and non-governmental actors to work together are crucial to effecting change. Similarly, as explained by McDonald (this volume), politicians may be uncomfortable with the distributive justice implications of controlling climate change. This, in turn, will influence the ways in which the law is framed and used to facilitate action. Moreover, such considerations come to constitute cultural understandings of risk and resilience.

A final theme to emerge from this volume has been the importance of experimentation. Holley and Sofronova (this volume), regard the new environmental governance as experimental. The same is true in many respects of resilience approaches. We need to assess carefully the results of particular experiments, such as those discussed by Wang (this volume), to give us insights into what may and may not work. We also need to embrace 'natural experiments' enabled by comparing the experiences of different locations and examples across the world. This can give us a greater understanding of where the law and risk and resilience strategies can best work together to protect our environment and promote greater equality.

Bibliography

Abbot, C. and Lee, M. (2015) 'Economic actors in EU environmental law' in *Yearbook of European Law* 34: 26–59.

Abbott, A. (2015) 'Inequality and process' in Makrinus, L., Otremba, K., Rennert, C. and Stoeck, J. (eds.) *(De)Standardisierung von Bildungsverläufen und strukturen*. Springer Fachmedien Wiesbaden.

Abuodha, J. (2002) 'Environmental impact assessment of the proposed titanium mining project in Kwale District, Kenya' in *Marine Georesources & Geotechnology* 20(3): 199–207.

Ackerman, F. (2007) *Debating Climate Economics: The Stern Review vs. Its Critics. Report to Friends of the Earth England, Wales and Northern Ireland*. Tufts University, Medford MA.

Adaptation Fund (2016) 'Projects & Programmes' [Online]. [Accessed 2 June 2016]. Available from: https://www.adaptation-fund.org

Adger, N., Brown, K. and Tomkins, E. (2005) 'The political economy of cross-scale networks in resource co-management' in *Ecology and Society* 10(2): 9. [Online]. Available from: http://www.ecologyandsociety.org/vol10/iss2/art9/

Adger, W. (2006) 'Vulnerability' in *Global Environmental Change* 16: 268–281.

Adger, W., Brown, K., Nelson, D., Berkes, F., Eakin, H., Folke, C., Galvin, K., Gunderson, L., Goulden, M., O'Brien, K., Ruitenbeek, J. and Tompkins, E. (2011) 'Resilience implications of policy responses to climate change' in *Wiley Interdisciplinary Reviews: Climate Change* 2: 757–766.

Adger, W., Brown, K. and Waters, J. (2011) 'Resilience' in Dryzek, J., Norgaard, R. and Schlossberg, D. (eds.) *Oxford Handbook of Climate and Society*. Oxford: Oxford University Press.

Adler, M. (2011) *Well-being and Fair Distribution Beyond Cost-Benefit Analysis*. New York; Oxford: Oxford University Press.

Agnew, R. (2013) 'The ordinary acts that contribute to ecocide: a criminological analysis' in South, N. and Brisman, A. (eds.) *Routledge International Handbook of Green Criminology*. Abingdon: Routledge.

Agrawal, A., Wollenberg, E. and Persha, L. (2014) 'Governing agriculture

– forest landscapes to achieve climate change mitigation' in *Global Environmental Change* 29: 270–280.

Alabama Center for Insurance Information and Research (2015) BuildStrong Coalition report calls for national mitigation strategy to protect from natural disasters. [Online]. 23 October 2015 [Accessed 4 December 2016]. Available from: http://aciir.culverhouse.ua.edu/buildstrong-coalition-report-calls-for-national-mitigation-strategy-to-protect-from-natural-disasters/

Albuquerque, A. (2012) 'Land inequality and deforestation in the Brazilian Amazon'. Munich Personal RePEc Archive.

Alcalde, M., Ponce, C. and Curonisy, Y. (2009) 'Peace Parks in the Cordillera del Cóndor Mountain Range and Biodiversity Conservation Corridor' [Online] [Accessed 18 August 2016]. Available from: https://www.wilsoncenter.org/sites/default/files/ponce.pdf

Alderman, H. and Haque, T. (2007) Insurance Against Covariate Shocks: The Role of Index-Based Insurance in Social Protection in Low-Income Countries of Africa. World Bank Working Papers [Online]. [Accessed 2 June 2016]. Available from: https://agriskmanagementforum.org/sites/agriskmanagementforum.org/files/Documents/SP_Insurance_covariate_shocks_index%20based%20insurance%20in%20social%20protection%20Africa.pdf

Aldunce, P., Beilin, R., Howden, M. and Handmer, J. (2015) 'Resilience for disaster risk management in a changing climate: Practitioners' frames and practices' in *Global Environmental Change* 30: 1–11.

Alexander, L. (2009) 'Stakeholder participation in new governance: lessons from Chicago's public housing reform experiment' in *Georgetown Journal of Poverty Law and Policy* 16: 117–185.

Alexander, M., Chamundeeswari, A., Kambu, A., Ruiz, M. and Tobin, B. (2004) *The role of registers and databases in the protection of traditional knowledge: A comparative analysis*. Vienna: UNU-IAS.

Alford, W. and Shen, Y. (1997) 'Limits of the law in addressing China's environmental dilemma' in *Stanford Environmental Law Journal* 16: 125–148.

Aligica, P. and Tarko, V. (2012) 'Polycentricity: from Polanyi to Ostrom, and beyond' in *Governance: An International Journal of Policy, Administration and Institutions* 25: 237–262.

Allison, E., Perry, A., Badjeck, M., Adger, W., Brown, K., Conway, D., Halls, A., Pilling, G., Reynolds, J., Andrew, N. and Dulvy, N. (2009) 'Vulnerability of national economies to the impacts of climate change on fisheries' in *Fish and Fisheries* 10(2): 173–196.

André, F., Sokri, A. and Zaccour, G. (2011) 'Public disclosure programs vs. traditional approaches for environmental regulation: green goodwill and the policies of the firm' in *European Journal of Operational Research* 212(1): 199–212.

APEEL (Australian Panel of Experts on Environmental Law) (2017) Terrestrial Biodiversity Conservation and Natural Resources Management, Australian Panel of Experts in Environmental Law, 2017. [Online]. (forthcoming).

APHRC (African Population and Health Research Center) (2002) 'Population and Health Dynamics in Nairobi's Informal Settlements'.

Arnold, C. and Gunderson, L. (2013) 'Adaptive law and resilience' in *Environmental Law Reporter* 43: 10436–10443.

Arnold, C. and Gunderson, L. (2014) 'Adaptive law and resilience' in *Legal Studies Research Paper Series* Paper No. 2014-04.

Arnold, C. and Gunderson, L. (2014) 'Adaptive law' in Garmestani, A.S. and Allen, C. (eds.) (2014) *Social-Ecological Resilience and Law*. New York: Columbia University Press.

Arnstein, S. (1969) 'Eight rungs on the ladder of citizen participation' in *Journal of the American Institute of Planners* 35(4): 216–224.

Arnstein, S. (1969) 'A Ladder of citizen participation' in *Journal of American Planning Association* 35(4): 216–224.

Arsel, M. and Büscher, B. (2012) 'Nature™ Inc.: changes and continuities in neoliberal conservation and market-based environmental policy' in *Development and Change* 43: 53–78.

Ashford, N. and Rest, K. (1999) *Public Participation in Contaminated Communities*. The Technology and Law Program at MIT. Cambridge, MA: MIT.

ASOCASAN, PNUMA, IIAP and NJ (2012) 'Protocolo Comunitario Biocultural para El Territorio del Consejo Comunitario Mayor del Alto San Juan' in Instituto de Investigaciones Ambientales del Pacifico, PNUD, Natural Justice [Online] [Accessed 21 May 2016] Available from: www.pnuma.org/publicaciones/PCB%20ASOCASAN_espanol_2012.pdf

Australian State of the Environment 2011 Committee (2011) Australia State of the Environment 2011. Independent report to the Australian Government Minister for Sustainability, Environment, Water, Population and Communities. Canberra: DSEWPaC.

Bahadur, A. and Tanner, T. (2014) 'Transformational resilience thinking: putting people, power and politics at the heart of urban climate resilience' in *Environment and Urbanization* 26(1): 200–214.

Baker, J. (2012) *Climate Change, Disaster Risk, and the Urban Poor: Cities Building Resilience for a Changing World*. Washington DC: World Bank.

Banaszak, I., Shkaruba, A. and Kireyeu, V. (2010) The emergence of multi-level governance in Belarusian biodiversity protection policies.

The Leviathan's collapse? Paper presented at the Governance of Natural Resources in a Multi-Level Context. Leipzig, Germany.

Bandura, A. (1997) *Self-efficacy: The Exercise of Control*. New York: WH Freeman and Company.

Bardsley, D. and Hugo G. (2013) 'Migration and climate change: examining thresholds of change to guide effective adaptation decision-making' in Hugo G. (ed.) *Climate Change and Migration*. Cheltenham, UK: Edward Elgar.

Barié, C. (2003) *Pueblos indígenas y derechos constitucionales en América Latina: un panorama*. Mexico and Ecuador: Ediciones Abya-Yala.

Bartlett, S. and Satterthwaite, D. (eds.) (2016) *Cities on a Finite Planet: Towards Transformative Responses to Climate Change*. London: Routledge.

Batabyal, A. (1998) 'The concept of resilience: retrospect and prospect' in *Environment and Development Economics* 3: 221–262.

Bavikatte, K. and Jonas, H. (2010) 'How bio-cultural community protocols can empower local communities' in *Endogenous Development Magazine* 6: 4–6.

Beck, U. (1992a) *Risk Society: Towards a New Modernity*. London: Sage.

Beck, U. (1992b) 'From industrial society to the risk society: questions of survival, social structure and ecological enlightenment' in *Theory, Culture & Society* 9(1): 97−123.

Beck, U. (1995) *Ecological Politics in an Age of Risk*. Cambridge: Polity.

Beck, U. (1999) *World Risk Society*. Cambridge: Polity.

Beck, U. (2013) 'Why "class" is too soft a category to capture the explosiveness of social inequality at the beginning of the 21st century' in *British Journal of Sociology* 64(1): 63–74.

Begg, C., Walker, G. and Kuhlicke, C. (2015) 'Localism and flood risk management in England: the creation of new inequalities?' in *Environment and Planning C: Government and Policy* 33(4): 685–702.

Bene, C., Wood, G. and Davies, N. (2012) 'Resilience: new Utopia or New Tyranny? Reflection about the potentials and limits of the concept of resilience in relation to vulnerability reduction programs', Working Paper 405, Brighton: Institute for Development Studies.

Benson, M. (2015) 'Reconceptualising environmental challenges – is resilience the new narrative?' in *Journal of Environmental and Sustainability Law* 21(1): 99–126.

Benson, M. and Craig, R. (2014) 'The end of sustainability' in *Society & Natural Resources*, 27(7): 777–782.

Berkes, F. and Folke, C. (eds.) (1998) *Linking Social and Ecological Systems: Management Practices and Social Mechanisms for Building Resilience*. Cambridge: Cambridge University Press.

Berkes, F. and Jolly, D. (2001) 'Adapting to climate change: social-ecological resilience in a Canadian western Arctic community' in *Conservation Ecology* 5(2): 18. [Online]. Available from: http://www.consecol.org/vol5/iss2/art18/

Berkes, F., Colding, J. and Folke, C. (eds.) (2003) *Navigating Social Ecological Systems: Building Resilience for Complexity and Change*. Cambridge: Cambridge University Press.

Beyer, S. (2006) 'Environmental law and policy in the People's Republic of China' in *Chinese Journal of International Law* 5(1): 185–211.

Bhan, G. (2009) 'This is no longer the city I once knew; Evictions, the urban poor and the right to the city in Millennial Delhi' in *Environment and Urbanization* 21(1): 127–142.

Bhat, G., Karanth, A., Dashora, L. and Rajasekar, U. (2013) 'Addressing flooding in the city of Surat beyond its boundaries' in *Environment and Urbanization* 25(2): 429–441.

Biermann, F. (2014) 'The Anthropocene: a governance perspective' in *The Anthropocene Review* 1(1): 57–61.

Bingham, B. and Noon, B.R. (1997) 'Mitigation of habitat "take": Application to habitat conservation planning' in *Conservation Biology* 11(1): 127–139.

Black, J. (2002) 'Critical reflections on regulation' in *Australian Journal of Legal Philosophy* 27: 1–27.

Black, J. (2005) 'The emergence of risk based regulation and the new public management in the UK' in *Public Law* Autumn: 512–549.

Blackburn, R. (2012) *Age Shock: How Finance is Failing Us*. London: Verso.

Blaikie, P., Cannon, T., Davis, I. and Wisner, B. (1994) *At Risk: Natural Hazards, People's Vulnerability and Disasters*. London: Routledge.

Blanchard, B. and Ruwitch, J. (2013) China Hikes Defense Budget, To Spend More On Internal Security. [Online] 5 March. [Accessed 28 July 2016]. Available from: http://www.reuters.com/article/us-china-parliament-defence-idUSBRE92403620130305

Blowers, A. and Leroy, P. (1994) 'Power, politics and environmental inequality: A theoretical and empirical analysis of the process of "peripheralisation"' in *Environmental Politics* 3: 197–228.

Bodansky, D. (2010) 'Climate change and human rights: unpacking the issues' in *Georgia Journal of International and Comparative Law* 38: 514–524.

Bodansky, D., Brunnée, J. and Hey, E. (2007) 'Introduction' in Bodansky, D., Brunnée, J. and Hey, E. (eds.) *The Oxford Handbook of International Environmental Law*. Oxford; New York: Oxford University Press.

Bodansky, D., Brunnée, J. and Hey, E. (2007) 'International environmental law mapping the field' in Bodansky, D., Brunnée, J. and Hey, E. (eds.)

The Oxford Handbook of International Environmental Law. Oxford; New York: Oxford University Press.

Bodenhorn, B. (2000) 'It's good to know who your relatives are but we were taught to share with everybody: shares and sharing among Inupiaq households' in Wenzel, G.W., Hovelsrud-Broda, G. and Kishigami, N. (eds.) *The Social Economy of Sharing: Resource Allocation and Modern Hunter-Gatherers*. Osaka: Senri Ethnological Series 53.

Boehler, P., Keller, J., Lai, K., Piao, V. and Tse, C. (2015) Tianjin Blasts Expose the Dangerous Proximity of Toxic Chemicals in China. *The New York Times*, [Online] 21 August. [Accessed 28 July 2016]. Available from: http://www.nytimes.com/interactive/2015/08/21/world/asia/tianjin-china-explosion-hazardous-chemical-sites.html?_r=0

Bolte, G., Tamburlini, G. and Kohlhuber, M. (2010) 'Environmental inequalities among children in Europe – evaluation of scientific evidence and policy implications' in *European Journal of Public Health* 20: 14–20.

Bord, R.J. and O'Connor, R. (1997) 'The gender gap in environmental attitudes: the case of perceived vulnerability to risk' in *Social Science Quarterly* 78(4): 830–840.

Botes, L. and van Rensburg, D. (2000) 'Community participation in development: nine plagues and twelve commandments' in *Community Development Journal* 35(1): 41–58.

Botts, H., Jeffery, T., Du, W. and Suhr, L. (2014) 2014 CoreLogic Storm Surge Report.

Bourdieu, P. (1984) *Distinction: a Social Critique of the Judgement of Taste.* Cambridge, MA: Harvard University Press.

Bourdieu, P. (2001) 'The forms of capital' in M. Granovetter and R. Swedberg (eds.), *The Sociology of Economic Life*, 2nd Edition, Boulder, CO: Westview Press.

Boyce, J. (2007) 'Is inequality bad for the environment?' in Wilkinson, R. and Freudenburg, W. (eds.) *Equity and the Environment* (Research in Social Problems and Public Policy). Bingley, UK: Emerald Group.

Bradley, S. (2011) *Scientific Uncertainty: A User's Guide*. Grantham Research Institute on Climate Change and the Environment, London: LSE.

Bradshaw, C. and Brook, B. (2014) 'Human population reduction is not a quick fix for environmental problems' in *Proceedings of the National Academy of Sciences of the United States of America* 111(46): 16610–16615.

Braithwaite, J. and Drahos, P. (2000) *Global Business Regulation*. Cambridge: Cambridge University Press.

Brand, F. and Jax, K. (2007) 'Focusing the meaning(s) of resilience: resilience as a descriptive concept and a boundary object' in *Ecology and Society* 12(1): 23. [Online]. Available from: http://www.ecologyandsociety.org/vol12/iss1/art23/

Brisbois, M. and de Loë, R. (2016) 'Natural resource industry involvement in collaboration for water governance: influence on processes and outcomes in Canada' in *Journal of Environmental Planning and Management* 60: 1–18.

Brody, C. (1984) 'Differences by sex in support for nuclear power' in *Social Forces* 63(1): 209–228.

Brown, M. (2005) 'Heritage trouble: recent work on the protection of intangible cultural property' in *International Journal of Cultural Property* 12(1): 40–61.

Brown, W. (2015) *Undoing the Demos: Neoliberalism's Stealth Revolution*. Cambridge, MA: Zone Books.

Bull, J., Blake Suttle, K., Gordon, A. and Singh, N. (2013) 'Biodiversity offsets in theory and practice' in *Oryx* 47(3): 369–380.

Búrca, G. de. (2010) 'New governance and experimentalism: an introduction' in *Wisconsin Law Review* 2: 227–38.

Búrca, G. de., Keohane, R. and Sabel, C. (2013) 'New modes of pluralist global governance' in *New York University Journal of International Law & Politics* 45: 723–86.

Búrca, G. de. and Scott, J. (eds.) (2006) *Law and New Governance in the EU and the US*. Oxford: Hart Publishing.

Burrows, M., Schoeman, D., Buckley, L., Moore, P., Poloczanska, E., Brander, K., Brown, C., Bruno, J., Duarte, C., Halpern, B., Holding, J., Kappel, C., Kiessling, W., O'Conner, M., Pandolfi, J., Parmesan, C., Schwing, F., Sydeman, W. and Richardson, A. (2011) 'The pace of shifting climate in marine and terrestrial ecosystems' in *Science* 334(6056): 652–655.

Cai, Y. (2010) *Collective Resistance in China: Why Popular Protests Succeed or Fail*. Stanford, CA: Stanford University Press.

Cairncross, S., Hardoy, J. and Satterthwaite, D. (1990) 'The urban context' in Hardoy, J., Cairncross, S. and Satterthwaite, D. (eds.) *The Poor Die Young: Housing and Health in Third World Cities*. London: Earthscan Publications.

Campanella, R. (2006) *Geographies of New Orleans: Urban Fabrics Before the Storm*. University of Louisiana at Lafayette.

Cançado T., Gómez, P. and Burelli, A. (2001) 'Joint separate opinion in the judgment on the merits and reparations in the "Mayagna (sumo) Awas Tingni community case"' in I/A Court H.R., Case of the *Mayagna (Sumo) Awas Tingni Community v. Nicaragua*. Merits, Reparations and Costs. Judgment of 31 August 2001. Series C No. 79.

Cao, J. (2010) 'Reconciling economic growth and carbon mitigation: challenges and policy options in China' in *Asian Economic Policy Review* 5: 110–129.

The Caribbean Catastrophe Risk Insurance Facility (2015) *Annual Report 2014–2015*.

Carpenter, S., Walker, B., Anderies, J. and Abel, N. (2001) 'From metaphor to measurement: resilience of what to what?' in *Ecosystems* 4(8): 765–781.

Carpenter-Gold, D. (2015) 'Castles made of sand: public-interest litigation and China's new environmental protection law' in *Harvard Environmental Law Review* 39: 241–274.

Carr, D. (2009) 'Population and deforestation: why rural migration matters' in *Progress in Human Geography* 33(3): 355–378.

Carr, D. and Halvorsen, K. (2001) 'An evaluation of three democratic, community-based approaches to citizen participation: surveys, conversations with community groups and community dinners' in *Society and Natural Resources* 14: 107–126.

Carruthers, D. (2008) *Environmental Justice in Latin America: Problems, Promise, and Practice*. Cambridge, MA: MIT Press.

CEBR (2012) Lloyd's Global Underinsurance Report.

Center for Environmental Communication and Education (CECE), China's Ministry of Environmental Protection (2009) *Exploring New Ways to Solve Environmental Problems at the Community Level: Guidance for Conducting Community Environmental Roundtable Dialogues*. Beijing: China Environmental Science Press.

Centre for Sustainable Energy (2007) Mobilising individual behavioural change through community initiatives: lessons for tackling climate change. The Energy Review Study. Summary Report to Government.

Centro Nacional de Planeamiento Estratégico (2011) 'Plan Bicentenario: el Perú hacia el 2021' [Online] [Accessed 22 July 2016] Available from: https://www.mef.gob.pe/contenidos/acerc_mins/doc_gestion/Plan Bicentenarioversionfinal.pdf

Chaffin, B. and Gunderson, L. (2016) 'Emergence, institutionalisation and renewal: rhythms of adaptive governance in complex socio-ecological systems' in *Journal of Environmental Management* 165: 81–87.

Chaffin, B., Gosnell, H. and Cosens, B. (2014) 'A decade of adaptive governance scholarship: synthesis and future directions' in *Ecology and Society* 19(3): 56. [Online]. Available from: http://dx.doi.org/10.5751/ES-06824-190356

Chakrabarty, D. (2009) 'The climate of history: four theses' in *Critical Inquiry* 35(2): 197–222.

Challinor, A., Watson, J., Lobell, D., Howden, S., Smith, D. and Chhetri, N. (2014) 'A meta-analysis of crop yield under climate change and adaptation' in *Nature Climate Change* 4: 287–291.

Chalmers, H. (2005) 'Policy profile: addressing environmental inequalities through UK research and policy' in *European Environment* 15(6): 374–390.

Chambers, L., Barnard, P., Poloczanska, E., Hobday, A., Keatley, M., Allsop, N. and Underhill, L. (2017) 'Southern hemisphere biodiversity and global change: data gaps and strategies' in *Austral Ecology* 42: 20–30.

Chan, E., Wang, Z., Mark, C., and Da Liu, S. (2015) 'Industrial accidents in China: risk reduction and response' in *The Lancet* 386(10002): 1421–1422.

Chandler, D. (2014) 'Beyond neoliberalism: resilience, the new art of governing complexity' in *Resilience* 2(1): 47–63.

Chen, X. (2013) 'The rising cost of stability' in *Journal of Democracy* 24(1): 57–64.

Chess, C. and Purcell, K. (1999) 'Public participation and the environment: do we know what works? in *Environmental Science and Technology* 33(16): 2685–2692.

Chicaiza, G. (2010) 'The mining enclave of the "Cordillera del Cóndor"' in *Civil Society Engagement with ECological EConomics (CEECEC)* [Online] [Accessed 17 August 2016] Available from: http://www.ceecec.net/wp-content/uploads/2008/10/CORDILLERA_CONDOR_ECUADOR_V2.pdf

China Daily. (2010) '"Iron hand" to realise green goals' [Online] 6 May [Accessed 28 July 2016] Available from: http://www.chinadaily.com.cn/china/2010-05/06/content_9814122.htm

Chirif, A. (2006) 'La Lucha del pueblo Achuar del Corrientes' in Semanario Kanatari [Online]. [Accessed 25 October 2016]. Available from: http://www.oilwatchsudamerica.org/petroleo-en-sudamerica/peru/1724-peru-lucha-del-pueblo-achuar-del-rio-corrientes.html

Clark, L., Millet, D. and Marshall, J. (2014) 'National patterns in environmental injustice and inequality: outdoor NO_2 air pollution in the United States' in *PLoS ONE* 9(4). [Online]. Available from: http://journals.plos.org/plosone/article?id=10.1371/journal.pone.0094431

Clarke, L. (1989) *Acceptable Risk?: Making Decisions in a Toxic Environment*. Berkeley, CA: University of California Press.

Clarke, L. (1999) *Mission Improbable: Using Fantasy Documents to Tame Disaster*. Chicago, IL: University of Chicago Press.

Clarvis, M., Allan, A. and Hannah, D. (2014) 'Water, resilience and the law: from general concepts and governance design principles to actionable mechanisms' in *Environmental Science and Policy* 43: 98–110.

Clement, S., Moore, S.A. and Lockwood, M. (2015b) 'Using insights from pragmatism to develop reforms that strengthen institutional competence for conserving biodiversity' in *Policy Science* 48: 463–489.

Clement, S., Moore, S., Lockwood, M. and Morrison, T. (2015a) 'A diag-

nostic framework for biodiversity conservation institutions' in *Pacific Conservation Biology* 21: 277–290.
Clermont, K. (2012) 'Death of paradox: the killer logic beneath the standards of proof' in *Notre Dame Law Review* 88(3): 1061–1138.
Clermont, K. and Sherwin, E. (2002) 'A comparative view of standards of proof' in *The American Journal of Comparative Law* 50(2): 243–275.
Coates, D. (2000) *Models of Capitalism: Growth and Stagnation in the Modern Era*. Malden, MA: Polity.
Cohen, A. (2008) 'Negotiation, meet new governance: interests, skills, and selves' in *Law & Social Inquiry* 33(2): 501–562.
Coleman, J. (2013) 'Unilateral climate regulation' in *Harvard Environmental Law Review* 38: 88–126.
Collier, B. and Skees, J. (2012) 'Increasing the resilience of financial intermediaries through portfolio-level insurance against natural disasters' in *Natural Hazards* 64: 55–72.
Collins, J. (1986) 'Smallholder settlement of tropical South America: the social causes of ecological destruction' in *Human Organization* 45: 1–10.
Comfort, L., Boin, A. and Demchak, C. (2010) *Designing Resilience: Preparing For Extreme Events*. Pittsburgh, PA: University of Pittsburgh Press.
Congreso de la República de Perú (2002) Ley que establece el régimen de protección de los conocimientos colectivos de los pueblos indígenas vinculados a los recursos naturales Ley 27811 / Law introducing a protection regime for indigenous peoples' collective knowledge associated with biological resources Law 27811 [Online] [Accessed 27 October 2016] Available from: https://www.indecopi.gob.pe/documents/20791/199826/Ley27811-spanish.pdf/ebf10223-52ba-4a15-b790-90caf0a059a1
Congressional-Executive Commission on China (2015) Annual Report 2015 [Online] [Accessed 28 July 2016] Available from: http://www.cecc.gov/sites/chinacommission.house.gov/files/2015%20Annual%20Report.pdf
Constitution of Nicaragua (1995) [Online] [Accessed 18 August 2016] Available from: https://www.constituteproject.org/constitution/Nicaragua_2005.pdf
Constitutión Política del Perú/Peruvian Constitution (1993) [Online] [Accessed 22 July 2016] Available from: http://www.oas.org/dil/esp/Constitucion_Peru.pdf
Convention on Biological Diversity (1993) 'Convention on Biological Diversity (with annexes). Concluded at Rio de Janeiro on 5 June 1992' in *United Nations – Treaty Series* 1760(30619): 142–382.
Convention on Biological Diversity (2004) 'Akwé:Kon Voluntary guidelines for the conduct of cultural, environmental and social impact assessments regarding developments proposed to take place on, or which

are likely to impact on, sacred sites and on lands and waters traditionally occupied or used by indigenous and local communities' [Online] [Accessed 18 August 2016] Available from: https://www.cbd.int/doc/publications/akwe-brochure-en.pdf

Convention on Biological Diversity (2014) 'Multi-year programme of work of the Conference of the Parties up to 2020' [Online] 19 December 2014 [Accessed 26 October 2016] Available from: https://www.cbd.int/doc/decisions/cop-12/cop-12-dec-31-en.pdf

Convention on Biological Diversity (2015) Note by the Executive Secretary: Mainstreaming and the Integration of Biodiversity within and across Sectors [Online] 10 November 2015 [Accessed 25 October 2016] Available from: https://www.cbd.int/doc/meetings/biodiv/impws-2015-01/other/impws-2015-01-background-en.pdf

Coombe, R. (1998) 'Intellectual property, human rights & sovereignty: new dilemmas in international law posed by the recognition of indigenous knowledge and the conservation of biodiversity' in *Indiana Journal of Global Legal Studies* 6(1): 59–115.

Coombe, R. (2003) 'Works in progress: traditional knowledge, biological diversity and intellectual property in a neoliberal era' in Perry R.W. and Maurer, B. (eds.) *Globalization and Governmentalities*. Minnesota: University of Minnesota Press.

COPWASH (2003) Funding proposal prepared for Deutsche Gesellshaft für Technische Zusammenarbeit GTZ, Consejo de Pueblos Wampis, Awajun and Shuar COPWASH, Quito.

Cornwall, W. (2015) 'Inside the Paris climate deal' in *Science* 350(6267): 1451.

Cosens, B., Gunderson, L. and Chaffin, B. (2014) 'The adaptive water governance project: assessing law, resilience and governance in regional socio-ecological water systems facing a changing climate' in *Idaho Law Review* 1: 1–27.

Cosens, B. (2013) 'Legitimacy, adaptation and resilience in ecosystem management' in *Ecology and Society* 18(1): 3–12.

Cosens, B. and Stow, C. (2014) 'Resilience and water governance', in Garmestani. A. and Allen, C. (eds.) (2014) *Social-Ecological Resilience and Law*. New York: Columbia University Press.

Costello, A., Abbas, M., Allen, A., Ball, S., Bell, S., Bellamy, R., Friel, S., Groce, N., Johnson, A., Kett, M., Lee, M., Levy, C., Maslin, M., McCoy, D., McGuire, B., Montgomery, H., Napier, D., Pagel, C., Patel, J., Puppim de Oliveira, J., Redclift, N., Rees, H., Rogger, D., Scott, J., Stephenson, J., Twigg, J., Wolff, J.and Patterson, C. (2009) 'Managing the health effects of climate change' in *The Lancet* 373(9676): 1693–1733.

Cottrell, M. and Trubek, D. (2012) 'Law as problem solving: stand-

ards, networks, experimentation and deliberation in global space' in *Transnational Law and Contemporary Problems* 21: 359–393.
Coumou, D. and Rahmstorf, S. (2012) 'A decade of weather extremes' in *Nature Climate Change* 2: 491–496.
Council of Australian Governments (COAG) (1992) National Strategy for Ecologically Sustainable Development. Prepared by the Ecologically Sustainable Development Steering Committee for the Council of Australian Governments. December 1992. Canberra: Australian Government.
Cox, J. (2012) 'Community resilience and decision theory challenges for catastrophic events' in *Risk Analysis* 32: 1919–1934.
Craig, R. (2010) 'Stationarity is dead – long live transformation: five principles for climate change adaptation law' in *Harvard Environmental Law Journal* 34: 9–75.
Craig, R. (2016) 'Learning to live with the trickster: narrating climate change and the value of resilience thinking' in *Pace Environmental Law Review* 33: 351.
Craig, R. and Benson, H. (2013) 'Replacing sustainability' in *Akron Law Review* 46: 841–880.
Craig, R. and Ruhl, J. (2014) 'Designing administrative law for adaptive management' in *Vanderbilt Law Review* 67(1): 1–87.
Croat, T., Swart, A. and Yates, E. (2005) 'New species of Araceae from the Río Cenepa region, Amazonas Department, Peru' in *Rodriguésia* 56(88): 65–126.
Crutzen, P. and Stoermer, E. (2000) 'The Anthropocene' in *IGBP Newsletter* 41(17): 17–18.
Cumming, G., Olsson, P., Chapin III, F. and Holling, C. (2013) 'Resilience, experimentation, and scale mismatches in socio-ecological landscapes' in *Landscape Ecology* 28(6): 1139–1150.
Curran, D. (2013a) 'Risk society and the distribution of bads: theorizing class in the risk society' in *British Journal of Sociology* 64(1): 44–62.
Curran, D. (2013b) 'What is a critical theory of the risk society? A reply to Beck' in *British Journal of Sociology* 64(1): 75–80.
Curran, D. (2015) 'Risk illusion and organized irresponsibility in contemporary finance: rethinking class and risk society' in *Economy and Society* 44(3): 392–417.
Curran, D. (2016) *Risk, Power, and Inequality in the 21st Century*. Basingstoke: Palgrave Macmillan.
Cvitanovic, C., Hobday, A.J., van Kerkoff, L., Wilson, S., Dobbs, K. and Marshall, N. (2015) 'Improving knowledge exchange among scientists and decision-makers to facilitate the adaptive governance of marine

resources: a review of knowledge and research needs' in *Ocean and Coastal Management* 112: 25–35.
David, E. and Enarson, E. (2012) *The Women of Katrina: How Gender, Race, and Class Matter in an American Disaster.* Nashville, TN: Vanderbilt University Press.
Davidson, J., Jacobson, C., Lyth, A., Baldwin, C., Dedekorkut-Owes, A., Ellison, J., Holbrook, N., Howes, M., Serrao-Neumann, S., Singh-Peterson, L. and Smith, T. (2016) 'Interrogating resilience: towards a typology to improve its operationalization' in *Ecology and Society* 21(2): 27. [Online]. Available from: http://dx.doi.org/10.5751/ES-08450-210227
Department for Environment Food and Rural Affairs (2015) '2010 to 2015 government policy: biodiversity and ecosystems'.
Descola, P. (1996) *La Selva Culta. Simbolismo y Praxis en la Ecología de los Achuar*. Cayambe: Ediciones Abya-Yala.
Dewey, J. (1946) *The Problems of Men*. New York: Philosophical Library.
Dietz, T., Ostrom, E. and Stern, P. (2003) 'The struggle to govern the commons' in *Science* 302(5652): 1907–1912.
Diprose, K. (2015) 'Resilience is futile' in *Soundings* 58(58): 44–56.
Djalante, R., Holley, C. and Thomalla, F. (2011) 'Adaptive governance and managing resilience to natural hazards' in *International Journal of Disaster Risk Science* 2: 1–14.
Djelic, M. and Bothello, J. (2013) 'Limited liability and its moral hazard implications: the systemic inscription of instability in contemporary capitalism' in *Theory and Society* 42(6): 589–615
Dobbin, F. and Jung, J. (2010) 'The misapplication of Mr Michael Jensen: how agency theory brought down the economy and why it might again' in *Markets on Trial: The Economic Sociology of the U.S. Financial Crisis (Research in the Sociology of Organizations)* 30B: 29–64.
Dobbs, D. (2008) *The Law of Torts.* St. Paul, MN: West Academic Publishing.
Doelle, M. and Lahey, W. (2015) 'Putting the train of environmental protection on track: Nova Scotia's experiment in using legislation to strengthen environmental governance' in Martin, P. and Kennedy, A. (eds.) *Implementing Environmental Law*. Cheltenham: Edward Elgar.
Doherty, K. (2014) 'From alarm to action: closing the gap between belief and behavior in response to climate change' in *Dissertations & Theses* 146. PhD dissertation, Antioch University. [Online]. Available from: http://aura.antioch.edu/etds/146/
Dombrowsky, I., Hagemann, N. and Houdret, A. (2014) 'The river basin as a new scale for water governance in transition countries? A comparative study of Mongolia and Ukraine' in *Environmental Earth Sciences* 72(12): 4705–4726.

Doremus, H. (2010) 'Adapting to climate change with law that bends without breaking' in *San Diego Journal of Climate & Energy Law* 2: 45–83.

Doremus, H. (2011) 'Adaptive management as an information problem' in *North Carolina Law Review* 89: 1455–1498.

Dorf, M. and Sabel, C. (1998) 'A constitution of democratic experimentalism' in *Columbia Law Review* 98(2): 267–473.

Downey, L. (2005) 'Assessing environmental inequality: how the conclusions we draw vary according to the definitions we employ' in *Sociological Spectrum* 25: 349–369.

Downey, L. and Hawkins, B. (2008) 'Single-mother families and air pollution: a national study' in *Social Science Quarterly* 89(2): 523–536.

Drèze, J. and Sen, A. (1989) *Hunger and Public Action*. Oxford: Clarendon Press.

Driesen D. (ed.) (2003) *The Economic Dynamics of Environmental Law*. Cambridge, MA.: MIT Press.

Driessen, P., Dieperink, C., van Laerhoven, F., Runhaar, H. and Vermeulen, W. (2012) 'Towards a conceptual framework for the study of shifts in modes of environmental governance: experiences from the Netherlands' in *Environmental Policy and Governance* 22(3): 143–160.

Dryzek, J. (1997) *The Politics of the Earth*. Oxford: Oxford University Press.

Duit, A., Galaz, V., Eckerberg, K. and Ebbesson, J. (2010) 'Governance, complexity, and resilience' in *Global Environmental Change* 20(3): 363–368.

Dunlop, M. and Brown, P. (2008) 'Implications of climate change for the Australian National Reserve system: a preliminary assessment. A report to the Department of Climate Change'. Canberra: DCC.

Dunlop, M., Parris, H., Ryan, P., and Kroon, F. (2013) 'Climate-ready conservation objectives: a scoping study'. National Climate Change Adaptation Research Facility.

Dutfield, G. (2001) 'TRIPS-related aspects of traditional knowledge' in *Case Western Reserve Journal of International Law* 33(2): 233–275.

Dwight, J. and Russell, T. (2013) 'The welfare economics of catastrophe losses and insurance' in *The Geneva Papers on Risk and Insurance* 38: 469–494.

Dworkin, R. ([1977] 2013) *Taking Rights Seriously*. London: Bloomsbury.

Dyson, L. (2011) 'Time to call it a day: some reflections on finality and the law'. Speech to Edinburgh University, Edinburgh.

Eaton, S., and Kostka, G. (2014) 'Authoritarian environmentalism undermined? Local leaders' time horizons and environmental policy implementation in China' in *The China Quarterly* 218: 359–380.

Ebbesson J. (2009) 'Piercing the state veil in the pursuit of environmental justice' in Ebbesson J. and Okowa, P. (eds.) *Environmental Law and Justice in Context*. Cambridge: Cambridge University Press.

Ebbesson, J. (2010) 'The rule of law in governance of complex socio-ecological changes' in *Global Environmental Change* 20: 414–422.

Ebbesson, J. and Folke, C. (2014) 'Matching scales of law with social-ecological contexts to promote resilience' in Garmestani, A. and Allen, C. (eds) *Social-ecological Resilience and Law*. New York: Columbia University Press.

Economy, E. (2005) 'Environmental enforcement in China' in K. D. Day (ed) *China's Environment and the Challenge of Sustainable Development*. Armonk, NY and London: M.E. Sharpe.

Elliot, L. (2014) 'Climate change will "lead to battles for food", says head of World Bank'. *The Guardian*. [Online]. 3 April 2014 [Accessed 28 July 2016]. Available from: https://www.theguardian.com/environment/2014/apr/03/climate-change-battle-food-head-world-bank

Elliott, J. and Pais, J. (2010) 'When nature pushes back: environmental impact and the spatial redistribution of socially vulnerable populations' in *Social Science Quarterly* 91: 1187–1202.

Emerson, K. and Gerlak, A. (2014) 'Adaptation in collaborative governance regimes' in *Environmental Management* 54(4): 768–781.

Engel, C. (2009) 'Preponderance of the evidence versus in time conviction: a behavioral perspective on a conflict between American and Continental European law' in *Vermont Law Review* 33: 435–467.

Engel, K. (2016) 'Policy innovation under dynamic, adaptive federalism and democratic experimentalism compared: lessons for federalism and climate change adaptation policy' in *Arizona Legal Studies* Discussion Paper No. 16(1): 1–24.

Engelen, E., Ertürk, I., Froud, J., Johal, S., Leaver, A., Moran, M., Nilsson, A. and Williams, K. (2011) *After the Great Complacence: Financial Crisis and the Politics of Reform*. Oxford: Oxford University Press.

The Environment Council (2002) 'Stakeholder dialogue: actively brokering solutions'. London: The Environment Council.

Ericson, R., Doyle, A. and Barry, D. (2003) *Insurance as Governance*. Toronto: University of Toronto Press.

Erturk, I., Froud, J., Johal, S., Leaver, A. and Williams, K. (2007) 'Against agency: a positional critique' in *Economy and Society* 36(1): 51−77.

European Commission (2013) Green paper on the insurance of natural and man-made disasters. [Online] 14 April 2013. [Accessed 4 December 2016]. Available from: http://eur-lex.europa.eu/legal-content/EN/TXT/PDF/?uri=CELEX:52013DC0213&from=EN

European Environment Agency (2012) 'Climate Change, Impacts and Vulnerability in Europe'.

Everson, M. and Vos, E. I. L. (2008) 'European Risk Governance in a Global Context. European Risk Governance: Its Science, Its

Inclusiveness And Its Effectiveness'. Connex Report Series.

Falkner, R. (2003) 'Private environmental governance and international relations: exploring the links' in *Global Environmental Politics* 3(2): 72–87.

Fallding, M. (2014) 'Biodiversity offsets: practice and promise' in *Environmental and Planning Law Journal* 31(1): 11–33.

FECONACO (2006) 'Perú: 'Victoria de los Pueblos Indígenas Achuar, Quichua y Urarina del Río Corrientes!' [Online] [Accessed 26 October 2016] Available from: https://www.servindi.org/node/41314

Field, C., Barros, V., Dokken, D., Mach, K., Mastrandrea, M., Bilir, T., Chatterjee, M., Ebi, K., Estrada, Y., Genova, R., Girma, B., Kissel, E., Levy, A., MacCracken, S., Mastrandrea, P. and White, L. (eds.) (2014) 'Climate Change 2014 Impacts, Adaptation and Vulnerability', Working Group II Contribution to the Fifth Assessment Report of the Intergovernmental Panel on Climate Change. New York: Cambridge University Press.

Finer, M., Jenkins, C.N., Pimm, S.L., Keane, B. and Ross, C. (2008) 'Oil and Gas Projects in the Western Amazon: Threats to Wilderness, Biodiversity, and Indigenous Peoples' in *PLoS ONE* 3(8): e2932. [Online]. Available from: http://doi.10.1371/journal.pone.0002932

Finucane, M., Slovic, P., Mertz, C.K., Flynn, J. and Satterfield, T. (2000) 'Gender, race, and perceived risk: the "white male" effect' in *Health, Risk & Society* 2(2): 159–172.

Fiorino, D. (1990) 'Citizen participation and environment risk: a survey of institutional mechanisms' in *Science, Technology and Human Values* 15(2): 226–243.

Fish, S. (1994) 'Being interdisciplinary is so very hard to do' in Fish, S. *There is no Such Thing as Free Speech: And it's a Good Thing Too.* Oxford: Oxford University Press.

Fisher, D. (2010) *Australian Environmental Law: Norms, Principles and Rules.* Sydney: Lawbook Co.

Fisher, E. (2010) *Risk Regulation and Administrative Constitutionalism.* Oxford: Hart.

Fisher, E. (2013) 'Environmental law as "hot" law' in *Journal of Environmental Law* 25: 347–358.

Fisher, E. (2013) 'Framing risk regulation: a critical reflection transnational risks and multilevel regulation: a cross-comparative perspective' in *European Journal of Risk Regulation* 4: 125–132.

Fisher, E., Jones, J. and Schomberg, R. (2006) *Implementing the Precautionary Principle: Perspectives and Prospects.* Cheltenham, UK; Northampton, MA: Edward Elgar.

Fisher, E., Lange, B. and Scotford, E. (2013) *Environmental Law Text, Cases and Materials.* Oxford: Oxford University Press.

Flynn, J., Slovic, P. and Mertz, C. (1984) 'Gender, race, and perception of environmental health risks' in *Risk Analysis* 14(6): 1101–1108.
Folke, C. (2006) 'Resilience: The emergence of a perspective for social-ecological systems' in *Global Environmental Change* 16(3): 2253–2267.
Folke, C., Carpenter, S., Walker, B., Scheffer, M., Elmqvist, T., Gunderson, L. and Holling, C. (2004) 'Regime shifts, resilience, and biodiversity in ecosystem management' in *Annual Review of Ecology and Systematics* 35: 557–581.
Folke, C., Hahn, T., Olsson, P. and Norberg, J. (2005), 'Adaptive governance of social-ecological systems' in *Annual Review of Environment and Resources* 30: 441–473.
Folke, C., Jansson, Å., Rockström, J. et al. (2001) 'Reconnecting to the Biosphere' in *AMBIO* 40(7): 719–738.
Forsyth, T. (2014) 'Climate justice is not just ice' in *Geoforum* 54: 230–232.
Foucault, M. ([1971] 1984) 'Nietzsche, genealogy, history' in P. Rabinow (ed.), *The Foucault Reader.* New York: Pantheon Books
Fox, D. (2007) 'Back to the no-analog future' in *Science* 316(5826): 823–825.
Fraser, A., Pelling, M. and Solecki, W. (2016) 'Understanding risk in the context of urban development: definitions, concepts and pathways' in Bartlett, S. and Satterthwaite, D. (eds.) *Cities on a Finite Planet; Towards Transformative Responses To Climate Change*. London: Routledge.
Fraser, N. (2005) 'Mapping the feminist imagination: from redistribution to recognition to representation' in *Constellations* 12(3): 295–307.
Freeman, J and Farber, D. (2005) 'Modular environmental regulation' in *Duke Law Journal* 54: 795–912.
Friedman, M. (1970) 'The social responsibility of business is to increase its profits' in *New York Times Magazine*, 13 September 1970.
Friend, R. and Moench, M. (2013) 'What is the purpose of urban climate resilience? Implications for addressing poverty and vulnerability' in *Urban Climate* 6: 98–113.
Fyfe, J., Meehl, G., England, M., Mann, M., Santer, B., Flato, G., Hawkins, E., Gillett, N., Xie, S., Kosaka, Y. and Swart, N. (2016) 'Making sense of the early-2000s warming slowdown' in *Nature Climate Change* 6: 224–228.
Gaba, J. (1999) 'Environmental ethics and our moral relationship to future generations: future rights and present virtue' in *Columbia Journal of Environmental Law* 24(2): 249–288.
Gage, A. and Byers, M. (2014) 'Payback time? What the internationalization of climate litigation could mean for Canadian oil and gas companies'. West Coast Environmental Law and Canadian Centre for Policy Alternatives.

Gallopín, G. (2006) 'Linkages between vulnerability, resilience, and adaptive capacity' in *Global Environmental Change* 16: 293–303.
Gamble, A. (2014) *Crisis without End? The Unravelling of Western Prosperity*. Basingstoke: Palgrave Macmillan.
García Ramírez, S. (2001) Concurring opinion in the judgment on the merits and reparations in the 'Mayagna (sumo) Awas Tingni community case' in I/A Court H.R., Case of the *Mayagna (Sumo) Awas Tingni Community v. Nicaragua*. Merits, Reparations and Costs. Judgment of 31 August 2001. Series C No. 79.
Garmestani, A. and Allen, C. (eds.) (2014) *Social-Ecological Resilience and Law*. New York: Columbia University Press.
Garmestani, A., Allen, C. and Benson, M. (2013) 'Can law foster social-ecological resilience?' in *Ecology and Society* 18(2): 37.
Garmestani, A., Allen, C. and Cabezas, H. (2008), 'Panarchy, adaptive management and governance: policy options for building resilience' in *Nebraska Law Review* 87: 1036–1054.
Giddens, A. (1999) 'Risk and responsibility' in *The Modern Law Review*, 62(1): 1–10.
Giddens, A. (2009) *The Politics of Climate Change*. Cambridge: Polity.
Gittell, J., Kim, C., Lim, S. and Rivas, V. (2006) 'Relationships, layoffs, and organizational resilience: airline industry responses to September 11' in *The Journal of Applied Behavioral Science* 42(3): 300–329.
Glicksman, R. (2009) 'Ecosystem resilience to disruptions linked to global climate change: an adaptive approach to Federal land management' in *Nebraska Law Review* 87(4): 834–892.
Godden, L. and Peel, J. (2010) *Environmental Law: Scientific, Policy and Regulatory Dimensions*. South Melbourne: Oxford University Press.
Godden, L., Rochford, F., Peel, J., Caripis, L. and Carter, R. (2013) 'Law, governance and risk: deconstructing the public–private divide in climate change adaptation' in *UNSW Law Journal* 36(1): 224–255.
Grabosky, P. (1994) 'Green markets: environmental regulation by the private sector' in *Law & Policy* 16: 419–448.
Grabosky, P. (2013) 'Beyond responsive regulation: the expanding role of non-state actors in the regulatory process' in *Regulation & Governance* 7: 114–123.
Grannis, J. (2011) 'Adaptation tool kit: sea-level rise and coastal land use'. Georgetown Climate Center.
Green, M. and Hulme, D. (2005) 'From correlates and characteristics to causes: thinking about poverty from a chronic poverty perspective' in *World Development* 33(6): 867–879.
Green, O., Garmestani, A., Allen, C., Gunderson, L., Ruhl, J.B., Arnold, C., Graham, N., Cosens, B., Angeler, D., Chaffin, B., Holling, C. (2015)

'Barriers and bridges to the integration of social-ecological resilience and law' in *Frontiers in Ecology and Environment* 13(6): 332–337.

Gunderson, L. and Holling, C. (eds.) (2002) *Panarchy: Understanding Transformations in Human and Natural Systems*. Washington, DC: Island Press.

Gunningham, N. (2009) 'Environment law, regulation and governance: shifting architectures' in *Journal of Environmental Law* 21: 179–212.

Gunningham, N. and Holley, C. (2016) 'Next-generation environmental regulation: law, regulation, and governance' in *Annual Review of Law and Social Science* 12: 273–293.

Gutteling, J. and Wiegman, O. (1993) 'Gender-specific reactions to environmental hazards in the Netherlands' in *Sex Roles* 28(7): 433–447.

Hacker, J. (2006) *The Great Risk Shift: The Assault on American Jobs, Families, Health Care, and Retirement and How you can Fight Back*. New York: Oxford University Press.

Hanna, J. and Hunt, K. (2015) China: Sodium cyanide levels well past limit at Tianjin explosion site. CNN [Online] 21 August [Accessed 28 July 2016] Available from: http://edition.cnn.com/2015/08/20/asia/china-tianjin-explosions/

Hardoy, J., Herrera, V. and Mastrangelo, D. (2016) 'Rosario, Argentina' in Bartlett, S. and Satterthwaite, D. (eds.) *Cities on a Finite Planet; Towards Transformative Responses to Climate Change*. London: Routledge.

Harlow, C. (2005) 'Deconstructing government?' in Ginsburg, T. and Kagan, R. (eds) *Institutions and Public Law, Comparative Approaches*. New York: Peter Lang Publishing.

Harremoës, P. and European Environment Agency. (2002) *The Precautionary Principle in the 20th Century: Late Lessons from Early Warnings*. London: Earthscan Publications.

Haughton, G. (1999) 'Environmental justice and the sustainable city' in *Journal of Planning Education and Research* 18(3): 233–243.

Hawkins, K. (1984) *Environment and Enforcement: Regulation and Social Definition of Pollution*. Oxford: Oxford University Press.

Hayek, F. (1998) *Law, Legislation and Liberty*. Oxford, Routledge.

Hayward, T. (2007) 'Human rights versus emissions rights: climate justice and the equitable distribution of ecological space' in *Ethics & International Affairs* 21: 431–450.

He, B. and Warren, M. (2011) 'Authoritarian deliberation: the deliberative turn in Chinese political development' in *Perspectives on Politics* 9(2): 269–289.

Heazle, M., Tangney, P., Burton, P., Howes, M., Grant-Smith, D., Reis, K. and Bosomworth, K. (2013) 'Mainstreaming climate change adaptation:

an incremental approach to disaster risk management in Australia' in *Environmental Science & Policy* 33: 162–170.
Heede, R. (2014) 'Tracing anthropogenic carbon dioxide and methane emissions to fossil fuel and cement producers' in *Climatic Change* 122: 229–241.
Heerink, N., Mulatu, A. and Bulte, E. (2001) 'Income inequality and the environment: aggregation bias in environmental Kuznets curves' in *Ecological Economics* 38: 359–367.
Heijden, J. van der. (2011) 'Friends, enemies, or strangers? On relationships between public and private sector service providers in hybrid forms of governance' in *Law & Policy* 33: 367–390.
Heijden, J. van der. (2012) 'Voluntary environmental governance arrangements' in *Environmental Politics* 21: 486–509.
Heijden, J. van der. (2013) 'Is new governance the silver bullet? Insights from the Australian buildings sector' in *Urban Policy and Resilience* 31(4): 453–471.
Heijden, J. van der. (2014) *Governance for Urban Sustainability and Resilience: Responding to Climate Change and the Relevance of the Built Environment*. Cheltenham: Edward Elgar.
Heijden, J. van der. (2015) 'Regulatory failures, split-incentives, conflicting interests and a vicious circle of blame: the New Environmental Governance to the rescue?' in *Journal of Environmental Planning and Management* 58(6): 1034–1057.
Hernández, J. (2016) Tianjin explosions were result of mismanagement, China finds. *The New York Times* [Online] 5 February [Accessed 28 July 2016] Available from: http://www.nytimes.com/2016/02/06/world/asia/tianjin-explosions-were-result-of-mismanagement-china-finds.html?_r=0
Herring, S., Hoell, A., Hoerling, M., Kossin, J., Schreck, C. and Stott, P. (2016) 'Explaining extreme events of 2015 from a climate perspective' in *Bulletin of the American Meteorological Society* 97(12): S1–S145. [Online]. Available from: http://www.ametsoc.net/eee/2015/2015_bams_eee_low_res.pdf
Hess, D. (2008) 'The three pillars of corporate social reporting as New Governance Regulation: disclosure, dialogue, and development' in *Business Ethics Quarterly* 18(4): 447–482.
Heyvaert, V. (2011) 'Governing climate change: towards a new paradigm for risk regulation' in *The Modern Law Review* 74(6): 817–844.
Hill Clarvis, M., Allan, A. and Hannah, D. (2014) 'Water, resilience and the law: from general concepts and governance design principles to actionable mechanisms' in *Environmental Science and Policy* 43: 98–110.
Hilson, C. (2015) 'Framing fracking: which frames are heard in English

planning and environmental policy and practice?' in *Journal of Environmental Law* 27(2): 177–202.

Hirschman, A. (1970) 'The search for paradigms as a hindrance to understanding' in *World Politics* 22(3): 329–343.

Hirschman, A. (1991) *The Rhetoric of Reaction*. Cambridge, MA: Harvard University Press.

Hobbes, T. (1985[1651]) *Leviathan*. CB Macpherson (ed) [1985], London: Penguin.

Hobday, A. and McDonald, J. (2014) 'Environmental issues in Australia' in *Annual Review of Environment and Resources* 39: 1–28.

Hobday, A., Alexander, L., Perkins, S., Smale, D., Straub, S., Oliver, E., Benthuysen, J., Burrows, M., Donat, M., Feng, M., Holbrook, N., Moore, P., Scannell, H., Gupta, A. and Wernberg, T. (2016) 'A hierarchical approach to defining marine heatwaves' in *Progress in Oceanography* 141: 227–238.

Holder, J. and Lee, M. (2007) *Environmental Law*. Cambridge: Cambridge University Press.

Holley, C. (2008) *New Environmental Governance*. Doctor of Philosophy, The Australian National University.

Holley, C. (2010) 'Facilitating monitoring, subverting self-interest and limiting discretion: learning from "new" forms of accountability in practice' in *Columbia Journal of Environmental Law* 35(1): 128–211.

Holley, C. (2015) 'Crafting collaborative governance: water resources, California's delta plan, and audited self-management in New Zealand' in *Environmental Law Reporter* 45(4): 10324–10337.

Holley, C. (2016) 'Linking law and new governance: examining gaps, hybrids and integration in water policy' in *Law & Policy* 38(1): 24–53.

Holley, C. (2017a) 'Environmental regulation and governance' in Drahos, P. (ed.), *Regulatory Theory: Foundations and Applications*. Canberra: ANU E Press.

Holley, C. (2017b) 'National water reforms and pragmatism' in Sabel, C. and Marsh, I. (eds.) *Learning from Discretion* (forthcoming).

Holley, C. and Lawson, A. (2015) 'Implementing law and collaborative governance: water and natural resource management' in Martin, P. and Kennedy, A. (eds.) *Implementing Environmental Law*. Cheltenham: Edward Elgar.

Holley, C. and Gunningham, N. (2011), 'Natural resources, new governance and legal regulation: when does collaboration work?' in *New Zealand Universities Law Review* 24: 309–336.

Holley, C. and Shearing, C. (2016) 'Environmental policing: harms, enforcement and collaboration' in Bradford, B., Jauregui, B., Loader,

I. and Steinberg, J. (eds.) *SAGE Handbook of Global Policing*. London: SAGE Publications.

Holley, C. and Sinclair, D. (2011) 'Collaborative governance and adaptive management: (mis)applications to groundwater, salinity and run-off' in *The Australasian Journal of Natural Resources Law and Policy* 14(1): 37–69.

Holley, C., Gunningham, N. and Shearing, C. (2012) *New Environmental Governance*. Abingdon: Earthscan.

Holling, C. (1973) 'Resilience and the stability of ecological systems' in *Annual Review of Ecology and Systematics* 4: 1–23.

Holling, C. (2012) 'Response to "panarchy and the law"' in *Ecology and Society* 17(4): 37. [Online]. Available from: http://dx.doi.org/10.5751/ES-05402-170437

Holling, C. (ed.) (1978). *Adaptive Environmental Assessment and Management*. Chichester: Wiley.

Hollnagel, E., Woods, D.D. and Leveson, N. (eds.) (2006) *Resilience Engineering: Concepts and Precepts*. Aldershot: Ashgate.

Hood, C., Rothstein, H. and Baldwin, R. (2001) *The Government of Risk: Understanding Risk Regulation Regimes*. Oxford: Oxford University Press.

House of Lords – In Re B (Children) (Fc) Appellate Committee Lord Hoffmann Lord Scott of Foscote Lord R (2008).

Howlett, M. (2014) 'From the "old" to the "new" policy design: design thinking beyond markets and collaborative governance' in *Policy Science* 47: 187–207.

Humby, T. (2014) 'Law and resilience: mapping the literature' in *Seattle Journal of Environmental Law* 4: 85–130.

Humphreys, S. and Robinson, M. (2010) *Human Rights and Climate Change*. Cambridge; New York: Cambridge University Press.

Hunt, R. (2000) 'Forager food sharing economy: transfers and exchanges' in Wenzel, G.W., Hovelsrud-Broda, G. and Kishigami, N. (eds.) *The Social Economy of Sharing: Resource Allocation and Modern Hunter-Gatherers*. Osaka: Senri Ethnological Series 53.

Hutter, B.M. (2005) 'Risk management and governance' in Eliadis, F.P., Hill, M.M. and Howlett, M. (eds.) *Designing Government: from Instruments to Governance*. Montreal: McGill-Queen's University Press.

Hutter, B.M. (2010) 'Anticipating risk and organising risk regulation: current dilemmas' in B.M. Hutter (ed) *Anticipating Risks and Organising Risk Regulation*. Cambridge: Cambridge University Press.

Hutter, B.M. (2011) 'Understanding the New Regulatory Governance: business perspectives' in *Law & Policy* 33(4): 459–476.

Hutter, B.M. (2006) 'Risk, regulation, and management' in Taylor-Gooby,

P. and Zinn, J. (eds.) *Risk in Social Science*. Oxford: Oxford University Press.
Hutter, B.M. (2009) 'The role of regulation in mitigating the risks of natural disasters' in Kunreuther, H. and Useem, M. (eds.) *Learning From Catastrophes: Strategies for Reaction and Response*. Upper Saddle River, NJ: Wharton School Publishing.
Hutter, B.M. and Lloyd-Bostock, S. (1993) 'Field level perceptions of risk in regulatory agencies' in Short, J. and Clarke, L. (eds.) *Organisations, Uncertainty and Risk*. Boulder, CO: Westview Press.
Hutter, B.M. and O'Mahony, J. (2004) 'Business regulation: reviewing the regulatory potential of civil society organisations' CARR discussion paper, 26. Centre for Analysis of Risk and Regulation. London: London School of Economics and Political Science.
IDLO (2014) 'Doing justice to sustainable development: integrating the rule of law into the post-2015 development agenda' [Online] [Accessed 26 October 2016] Available from: http://www.idlo.int/sites/default/files/pdfs / Doing % 20Justice % 20to % 20Sustainable % 20Development % 20report.pdf
IDLO (2016) 'Connecting the dots across the SDGs: environment, justice and people: what can we learn from biodiversity mainstreaming', framing paper for workshop organized by the International Development Law Organisation, The Hague, 11 June 2016.
IGBP (2000) *Global Change Newsletter* No. 41.
Interamerican Court of Human Rights (2001) I/A Court H.R., Case of the *Mayagna (Sumo) Awas Tingni Community v. Nicaragua*. Merits, Reparations and Costs. Judgment of 31 August 2001. Series C No. 79.
Intergovernmental Panel on Climate Change (2007) Climate Change 2007: Synthesis Report. Geneva, Switzerland.
Intergovernmental Panel on Climate Change (2014a) Climate Change 2014: Impacts, Adaptation, and Vulnerability, Annex II, Glossary.
Intergovernmental Panel on Climate Change (2014b) Report of the Conference of the Parties on its twentieth session, held in Lima from 1 to 14 December 2014.
The Intergovernmental Panel on Climate Change (2015) Climate Change 2014: Synthesis Report. Contributions of Working Groups I, II and III to the Fifth Assessment Report of the Intergovernmental Panel on Climate Change. Geneva: IPCC.
International Labour Organization (1989) Geneva Convention No. 169 Concerning Indigenous and Tribal Peoples in Independent Countries.
International Union for Conservation of Nature (2015) Annual Report 2014. Gland, Switzerland.
Isunju, B., Christopher, J., Orach, G. and Kempa, J. (2016) 'Community-

level adaptation to minimise vulnerability and exploit opportunities in Kampala's wetlands' in *Environment and Urbanization* 29(1): 1–20.

Ituarte-Lima, C. (2004) 'Desarrollo progresivo de los derechos humanos en el Sistema Interamericano, pueblos indígenas y medio ambiente' in Rodríguez-Pinzón, M. and Guevara-Bermudez, J. (eds) *Derecho International de los Derechos Humanos*. Washington College of Law: Universidad Iberoamericana, Fontamara.

Ituarte-Lima, C. (2009) 'Categories of intellectual property rights and biodiversity in Western inspired legal cultures' in Freeman, M. and Napier, D. (eds.) *Law and Anthropology: Current Legal Issues*. Oxford and New York: Oxford University Press.

Ituarte-Lima, C. (2011) 'Legal mechanisms for environmental justice and intellectual property rights' in Ishida, S. (eds.) *Alternative Justice*. Osaka: Osaka University Press.

Ituarte-Lima, C. and Subramanian, S. (2011), 'Environment-related property laws: a means to achieve equity or inequity?' UNU-IAS Working Paper No. 164 [Online] [Accessed 18 August 2016] Available from: http://archive.ias.unu.edu/resource_centre/Working%20Paper%20164_Claudia%20Ituarte%20Lima_Suneetha%20Subramanian.pdf

Ituarte-Lima, C. and Subramanian, S. (2013) 'Retreading negotiations on equity in environmental governance: case studies contrasting the evolution of ABS and REDD+' in Maes, F., Cliquet, A., du Plessis, W. and McLeod-Kilmurray, H. (eds.) *Climate Change and Biodiversity: Linkages at International, National and Local Levels*. Cheltenham, UK and Northampton, MA: Edward Elgar Publishing.

Jabeen, H., Allen, A. and Johnson, C. (2010) 'Built-in resilience: learning from grassroots coping strategies to climate variability' in *Environment and Urbanization* 22(2): 415–431.

Jackson, S., Pollino, C., Maclean, K., Bark, R. and Moggridge, B. (2015) 'Meeting indigenous peoples' objectives in environmental flow assessments: case studies from an Australian multi-jurisdictional water sharing initiative' in *Journal of Hydrology* 522: 141–151.

Jacobs, A., Hernández, J.C., and Buckley, C. (2015) Behind deadly Tianjin blast, shortcuts and lax rules. *The New York Times* [Online] 30 August [Accessed 28 July 2016] Available from: http://www.nytimes.com/2015/08/31/world/asia/behind-tianjin-tragedy-a-company-that-flouted-regulations-and-reaped-profits.html

Jaffee, D. and Russell, T. (2013) 'The welfare economics of catastrophe losses and insurance' in *The Geneva Papers on Risk and Insurance* 38(3): 469–494.

Jahiel, A.R. (1998) 'The organization of environmental protection in China' in *The China Quarterly* 156: 757–785.

Janssen, M. and Ostrom, A. (2006) 'Resilience, vulnerability, and adaptation: a cross-cutting theme of the International Human Dimensions Programme on Global Environmental Change' in *Global Environmental Change* 16(3): 237–239.

Jasanoff, S. (2004) *States of Knowledge: the Co-Production of Science and Social Order.* London: Routledge.

Jerneck A. and Olsson, L. (2008) 'Adaptation and the poor: development, resilience, transition' in *Climate Policy* 8(2): 170–182.

Johns, F. (2013) *Non-legality in International Law: Unruly Law*. Cambridge; New York: Cambridge University Press.

Johnson, B. (2002) 'Gender and race in beliefs about outdoor pollution' in *Risk Analysis* 22(4): 725–738.

Johnson, T. (2013) 'The politics of waste incineration in Beijing: the limits of a top-down approach?' in *Journal of Environmental Policy & Planning* 15(1): 109–128.

Johnson, T. (2014a) 'Good governance for environmental protection in China: instrumentation, strategic interactions and unintended consequences' in *Journal of Contemporary Asia* 44(2): 241–258.

Johnson, T. (2014b) 'Regulatory dynamism of environmental mobilization in urban China' in *Regulation & Governance* 10(1): 14–28.

Jonas, H., Kothari, A. and Shrumm, H. (2012) Legal and institutional aspects of recognizing and supporting conservation by indigenous peoples and local communities. Indigenous Peoples and Local Communities' Conserved Territories and Areas (ICCAs) [Online] [Accessed 26 October 2016] Available from: http://naturaljustice.org/resources-and-research/icca-legal-reviews/

Jones, L. and Tanner, T. (2015) 'Measuring "subjective resilience": using peoples' perceptions to quantify household resilience'. ODI Working Paper 423.

Jones, R. (1998) 'Black concern for the environment: myth versus reality' in *Society and Natural Resources* 11(3): 209–228.

Joseph, J. (2013) 'Resilience in UK and French security strategy: an Anglo-Saxon bias?' in *Politics* 33(4): 253–264.

Joseph, J. (2016) 'Governing through failure and denial: the new resilience agenda' in *Millennium: Journal of International Studies* 44(3): 370–390.

Kant, I. ([1785] 2012) *Groundwork of the Metaphysics of Morals.* Cambridge: Cambridge University Press.

Karkkainen, B. (2002) 'Collaborative ecosystem governance: scale, complexity, and dynamism' in *Virginia Environmental Law Journal* 21: 189–243.

Karkkainen, B. (2003) 'Adaptive ecosystem management and regulatory penalty defaults: toward a bounded pragmatism' in *Minnesota Law Review* 87: 943–998.

Karkkainen, B. (2004a) 'Reply, new governance in legal thought and in the world: Some splitting as antidote to overzealous lumping' in *Minnesota Law Review* 89: 471–497.

Karkkainen, B. (2004b) 'Post-sovereign environmental governance' in *Global Environmental Politics* 4(1): 72–96.

Karkkainen, B. (2006) 'Managing transboundary aquatic ecosystems: lessons from the Great Lakes' in *Pacific McGeorge Global Business & Development Law Journal* 19: 209–240.

Karkkainen, B., Fung, A. and Sabel, C. (2000) 'After backyard environmentalism: toward a performance-based regime of environmental regulation' in *American Behavioral Scientist* 44(4): 690–709.

Karpouzoglou, T., Dewulf, A. and Clark, J. (2016) 'Advancing adaptive governance of social-ecological systems through theoretical multiplicity' in *Environmental Science & Policy* 57: 1–9.

Kathlene, L. and Martin, J.A. (1991) 'Enhancing citizen participation: panel designs, perspectives, and policy formation' in *Journal of Policy Analysis and Management* 10(1): 46–63.

Kendra, J. and Wachtendorf. T. (2003) 'Elements of resilience after the World Trade Center disaster: reconstituting New York City's Emergency Operations Centre' in *Disasters* 27(1): 37–53.

Kettunen, M., Terry, A., Tucker, G. and Jones, A. (2007) 'Guidance on the maintenance of landscape features of major importance for wild flora and fauna – Guidance on the implementation of Article 3 of the Birds Directive (79/409/EEC) and Article 10 of the Habitats Directive (92/43/EEC)'. Brussels: Institute for European Environmental Policy (IEEP).

Kim, R. and Bosselmann, K. (2013) 'International environmental law in the Anthropocene: towards a purposive system of multilateral environmental agreements' in *Transnational Environmental Law* 2(2): 285–309.

Kimani, N. (2010) 'A collaborative approach to environmental governance in East Africa′ in *Journal of Environmental Law* 22(1): 27–57.

Kirton, J. and Trebilcock, M. (2004) *Hard Choices, Soft Law: Voluntary Standards in Global Trade, Environment and Social Governance*. Oxford: Routledge.

Kiunsi, R. (2016) 'Dar es Salaam, Tanzania' in Bartlett, S. and Satterthwaite, D. (eds.) *Cities on a Finite Planet; Towards Transformative Responses to Climate Change*. London: Routledge.

Kjellstrom, T. and Mercado, S. (2008) 'Towards action on social determinants for health equity in urban settings' in *Environment and Urbanization* 20(2): 551–574.

Klinke, A. and Renn, O. (2012) 'Adaptive and integrative governance on risk and uncertainty' in *Journal of Risk Research* 15(3): 273–292.

Knight, F. (1921) *Risk, Uncertainty and Profit*. Boston, MA: Houghton Mifflin.

Knoisky, D. and Beierle, T. (2001) 'Innovations in public participation and environmental decision making: examples from the Great Lakes region' in *Society and Natural Resources* 14: 815–826.

Knox, J. (2009) 'Linking human rights and climate change at the United Nations' in *Harvard Environmental Law Review* 33: 477–498.

Koehn, P. (2010) 'Climate policy and action "underneath" Kyoto and Copenhagen: China and the United States' in *Wiley Interdisciplinary Reviews: Climate Change* 1: 405–417.

Koivurova, T., Kankaanpää, P. and Stępień, A. (2015) 'Innovative environmental protection: lessons from the Arctic' in *Journal of Environmental Law* 27: 285–311.

Koontz, T., Gupta, D., Mudliar, P. and Ranjan, P. (2015) 'Adaptive institutions in social-ecological systems governance: a synthesis framework' in *Environmental Science and Policy* 53(B): 139–151.

Koop, G. and Tole, L. (2001) 'Deforestation, distribution and development' in *Global Environmental Change* 11: 193–202.

Kostka, G. (2015) 'Command without control: the case of China's environmental target system' in *Regulation & Governance* 10(1): 58–74.

Kostka, G. and Hobbs, W. (2012) 'Local energy efficiency policy implementation in China: bridging the gap between national priorities and local interests' in *The China Quarterly* 211: 765–785.

KPMG International (2012) Expect the Unexpected: Building Business Value in a Changing World.

Kramarz, T. and Park, S. (2016) 'Accountability in global environmental governance: a meaningful tool for action?' in *Global Environmental Politics* 16(2): 1–21.

Landry, P.F. (2008) *Decentralized Authoritarianism in China*. New York: Cambridge University Press.

Lane, M. and Williams, L. (2008) 'Colour blind: indigenous participation in regional environmental governance in Australia' in *Journal of Planning Education and Research* 28: 38–49.

Lange, B. (2008) *Implementing EU Pollution Control*. Cambridge: Cambridge University Press.

Latour, B. (2005) *Reassembling the Social: an Introduction to Actor-Network Theory*. Oxford: Oxford University Press.

Lausche, B., Farrier, D., Verschuuren, J., La Viña, A., Trouwborst, A., Born, C. and Aug, L. (2013) 'The legal aspects of connectivity conservation. a concept paper'. Gland, Switzerland: IUCN.

Lawrence, J., Sullivan, F., Lash, A., Ide, G., Cameron, C. and McGlinchey, L. (2015) 'Adapting to changing climate risk by local government in New Zealand: institutional practice barriers and enablers' in *Local Environment* 20(3): 298–320.

Layzer, J. (2002) 'Citizen participation and government choice in local environmental controversies' in *Policy Studies Journal* 30(2): 193–207.

Leach, M., Scoones, I. and Stirling, A. (2010) 'Governing epidemics in an age of complexity: narratives, politics and pathways to sustainability' in *Global Environmental Change* 20: 369–377.

Lebel, L., Anderies, J., Campbell, B., Folke, C., Hatfield-Dodds, S., Hughes, T. and Wilson, J. (2006) 'Governance and the capacity to manage resilience in regional social-ecological systems' in *Ecology and Society* 11(1): 19. [Online]. Available from: http://www.ecologyandsociety.org/vol11/iss1/art19/

Lee, C. and Zhang, Y. (2013) 'The power of instability: unraveling the microfoundations of bargained authoritarianism in China' in *American Journal of Sociology* 118(6): 1475–1508.

Lee, E. (2010) 'Information disclosure and environmental regulation: green lights and grey areas' in *Regulation & Governance* 4: 303–328.

Lee, J. (2014) 'Theory to practice: adaptive management of the groundwater impacts of Australian mining projects' in *Environmental and Planning Law Journal* 31(6): 251–287.

Lee, M. (2005) *EU Environmental Law: Challenges, Change and Decision-Making*. Oxford: Hart Publishing.

Lee, M. (2014) *EU Environmental Law, Governance and Decision-Making*. Oxford: Hart Publishing.

Lee, M. and Abbot, C. (2003) 'The usual suspects? public participation under the Aarhus Convention' in *The Modern Law Review* 66(1): 80–108.

Lee, M., Armeni, C., de Cendra, J., Chaytor, S., Lock, S., Maslin, M., Redgwell, C. and Rydin, Y. (2012) 'Public participation and climate change infrastructure' in *Journal of Environmental Law* 25(1): 33–62.

Leichenko, R. and Silva, J. (2014) 'Climate change and poverty: vulnerability, impacts, and alleviation strategies' in *WIREs Clim Change* 5: 539–556.

Lélé, S.M. (1998) 'Resilience, sustainability, and environmentalism' in *Environment and Development Economics* 3(2): 251–255.

Levin, D. (2015) Fear of Toxic Air and Distrust of Government Follow Tianjin Blasts. *The New York Times* [Online] 18 August [Accessed 28 July 2016] Available from: http://www.nytimes.com/2015/08/19/world/asia/china-identifies-executives-of-company-linked-to-tianjin-explosions.html

Lewis-Lettington R. and Mwanyiki, S. (eds.) (2006) *Case Studies on Access and Benefit-sharing*. Rome: International Plant Genetic Resources Institute.

Li, J. and Gan, N. (2016). China's climate envoy bullish on hitting reduction goal for 2020. *South China Morning Post* [Online] 23 February [Accessed 28 July 2016] Available from: http://www.scmp.com/news/china/policies-politics/article/1916025/chinas-climate-envoy-bullish-hitting-reduction-goal

Li, T., Ng, S. and Skitmore, M. (2012) 'Public participation in infrastructure and construction projects in China: from an EIA-based to a whole cycle process' in *Habitat International* 36: 47–56.

Li, W., Liu, J. and Li, D. (2012) 'Getting their voices heard: three cases of public participation in environmental protection in China' in *Journal of Environmental Management* 98: 65–72.

Lieberthal, K. (1997) *China's Governing System and its Impact on Environmental Policy Implementation*. China Environment Series. Washington, DC: Woodrow Wilson.

Lipton, M. (1977) *Why Poor People Stay Poor – Urban Bias in World Development*. London: Temple Smith.

Liu, L. (2013) 'Geographic approaches to resolving environmental problems in search of the path to sustainability: the case of polluting plant relocation in China' in *Applied Geography* 45: 138–146.

Liu, Y., Li, Y., Xi, B. and Koppenjan, J. (2016) 'A governance network perspective on environmental conflicts in China: findings from the Dalian paraxylene conflict' in *Policy Studies* 37(4): 314–331.

Lixinski, L. (2013) *Intangible Cultural Heritage in International Law*. Oxford: Oxford University Press.

Lloyd's (2015) Lloyd's City Risk Index 2015–2025. [Online]. [Accessed 4 December 2016]. Available from: http://www.lloyds.com/cityriskindex

Lloyd-Bostock, S. (2010) Public perceptions of risk and "compensation culture" in the UK' in B.M. Hutter (ed) *Anticipating Risks and Organising Risk Regulation*. Cambridge: Cambridge University Press.

Lo, C. and Fryxell, G. (2005) 'Governmental and societal support for environmental enforcement in China: an empirical study in Guangzhou' in *The Journal of Development Studies* 41(4): 558–588.

Lo, K. (2015) 'How authoritarian is the environmental governance of China' in *Environmental Science & Policy* 54: 152–159.

Lobel, O. (2004) 'Setting the agenda for new governance research' in *Minnesota Law Review* 89: 498–509.

Lockwood, M., Davidson, J., Hockings, M., Haward, M. and Kriwoken, L. (2012) 'Marine biodiversity conservation governance and management: regime requirements for global environmental change' in *Ocean & Coastal Management* 69: 160–172.

London Sustainability Exchange. 'Definitions of Environmental Justice and Environmental Inequalities'. [Online]. [Accessed 4 December 2016]. Available from: http://www.lsx.org.uk/resources/EJIDefinition_page3198.aspx

López Contreras, J. (2004) *Ecuador – Perú. Antagonismos, Negociación e Intereses Nacionales*. Quito, Ecuador: Ediciones Abya-Yala and FLACSO.

Lora-Wainwright, A. (2013) *Fighting for Breath: Living Morally and Dying of Cancer in a Chinese Village*. Honolulu: University of Hawai'i Press.

Lorenzoni, I. and Pidgeon, N. (2006) 'Public views on climate change: European and USA perspectives' in *Climatic Change* 77(1): 73–95.

Lotspeich, R. and Chen, A. (1997) 'Environmental protection in the People's Republic of China' in *Journal of Contemporary China* 6(14): 33–59.

Ludescher, M. (1997) 'El régimen legal de los recursos naturales en el Perú y sus consecuencias para los pueblos indígenas de la Amazonía' in *Law & Anthropology* 9: 226–243.

Luhmann, N. (1993) *Risk: a Sociological Theory*. New Brunswick, NJ: Aldine Transaction.

Lung, S., Lee, C. and Hu, S. (2014) 'Inequality of Asian-type neighborhood environmental quality in communities with different urbanization levels' in *Environmental Science and Policy* 38: 1–10.

Lyons, M. (2009) 'Building back better: the large-scale impact of small-scale approaches to reconstruction' in *World Development* 37(2): 385–398.

Ma, X. and Ortolano, L. (2000) *Environmental Regulation in China: Institutions, Enforcement, and Compliance*. Lanham: Rowman & Littlefield Publishers.

MacAuslan, P. (1980) *The Ideologies of Planning Law*. Oxford: Pergamon Press.

Macintosh, A., Foerster, A. and McDonald, J. (2014) 'Policy design, spatial planning and climate change adaptation: a case study from Australia' in *Journal of Environmental Planning and Management* 58(8): 1–22.

Mackenzie, D. (2009) 'Making things the same: gases, emission rights and the politics of carbon markets' in *Accounting, Organizations and Society* 34: 440–455.

Macrae, C. (2010) 'Regulating resilience? Regulatory work in high-risk arenas' in B.M. Hutter (ed) *Anticipating Risks and Organising Risk Regulation*. Cambridge: Cambridge University Press.

Macrory, R. (2014) *Regulation, Enforcement and Governance in Environmental Law*. Oxford: Hart Publishing.

Magraw, D. and Hawke, L. (2007) 'Sustainable development' in Bodansky, D., Brunnée, J. and Hey, E. (eds.) *The Oxford Handbook of International Environmental Law*. Oxford; New York: Oxford University Press.

Mallak, L. (1998) Resilience in the Healthcare Industry. 7th Annual Industrial Engineering Research Conference. Banff, Alberta.

Malm, A. and Hornborg, A. (2014) 'The geology of mankind? A critique of the Anthropocene narrative' in *The Anthropocene Review* 1: 62–69.

Manyena, S. (2006) 'The concept of resilience revisited' in *Disasters* 30(4): 434–450.

Marino, E. and Ribot, J. (2012) 'Special issue introduction: adding insult to injury: climate change and the inequities of climate intervention' in *Global Environmental Change* 22: 323–328.

Martin, C. and Peck, H. (2004) 'Building the resilient supply chain' in *The International Journal of Logistics Management* 15(2): 1–14.

McAllister, L. (2008) *Making Law Matter: Environmental Protection and Legal Institutions in Brazil*. Stanford: Stanford University Press.

McCord, C. and Freeman, H. (1990) 'Excess mortality in Harlem' in *New England Journal of Medicine* 322: 173–177.

McCormack, P. and McDonald, J. (2014) 'Adaptation strategies for biodiversity conservation: has Australian law got what it takes?' in *Environmental and Planning Law Journal* 31: 114–136.

McDermott, M., Mahanty, S. and Schreckenberg, K. (2013) 'Examining equity: a multidimensional framework for assessing equity in payments for ecosystem services' in *Environmental Science and Policy* 33: 416–427.

Mcdonald, D. (2002) *Environmental Justice in South Africa*. Athens, OH: Ohio University Press; Cape Town: University of Cape Town Press.

McDonald, J. (2010) 'Mapping the legal landscape of climate change adaptation' in Bonyhady, T., Macintosh, A. and McDonald, J. (eds) (2010) *Adaptation to Climate Change: Law and Policy*. Sydney: The Federation Press.

McDonald, J. (2011) 'The role of law in adapting to climate change' in *Wiley Interdisciplinary Reviews: Climate Change* 2(2): 283–295.

McDonald, J. (2015) 'A short history of climate adaptation law in Australia' in *Climate Law* 4(1–2): 150–167.

McDonald, J. and Styles, M. (2014) 'Legal strategies for adaptive management under climate change' in *Journal of Environmental Law* 26(1): 25–53.

McDonald, J. and Styles, M. (2014) 'Legal strategies for adaptive management under climate change' in *Journal of Environmental Law* 26(1): 25–53.

McDonald, J., McCormack, P., Fleming, A., Harris, R. and Lockwood, M. (2016) 'Rethinking legal objectives for climate-adaptive conservation' in *Ecology and Society* 21(2). 25. [Online]. Available from: http://www.ecologyandsociety.org/vol21/iss2/art25/

McEldowney, J. and McEldowney, S. (2011) 'Science and environmental law: collaboration across the double helix' in *Environmental Law Review* 13: 169–198.

McElwee, C. (2011) *Environmental Law in China: Mitigating Risk and Ensuring Compliance*. Oxford: Oxford University Press.

McKenney, B. and Kiesecker, J. (2010) 'Policy development for biodiversity offsets: a review of offset frameworks' in *Environmental Management* 45: 165–176.

Michel-Kerjan, E. (2015) Rethinking government disaster relief in the U.S.: evidence and a way forward. [Online]. 8 October 2015. [Accessed 4 December 2016] Available from: http://opim.wharton.upenn.edu/risk/conference/pprs/Michel-Kerjan_Rethinking-Disaster-Relief.pdf

Mill, J. (1991) 'On liberty' in John Gray (ed.) *On Liberty and Other Essays*. Oxford: Oxford University Press.

Millennium Ecosystem Assessment (2005) *Ecosystems and Human Well-being: Synthesis*. Washington, DC: Island Press.

Miller, F., Osbahr, H., Boyd, E., Thomalla, F., Bharwani, S., Ziervogel, G., Walker, B., Birkmann, J., van der Leeuw, S., Rockström, J., Hinkel, J., Downing, T., Folke, C. and Nelson, D. (2010) 'Resilience and vulnerability: complementary or conflicting concepts?' in *Ecology and Society* 15(3): 11. [Online]. Available from: http://www.ecologyandsociety.org/vol15/iss3/art11

Milly, P., Betancourt, J., Falkenmark, M., Hirsch, R., Kundzewicz, Z., Lettenmaier, D. and Stouffer, R. (2008) 'Stationarity is dead: whither water management?' in *Science* 319(5863): 573–574.

Ministry of Environmental Protection of the People's Republic of China (2012) Huanjing Baohu Zhuangkuang (Environmental Protection Situation) [Online] 10 April. [Accessed 28 July 2016] Available from: http://www.gov.cn/test/2012-04/10/content_2110072.htm

Minzner, C. (2009) 'Riots and cover-ups: counterproductive control of local agents' in China in *University of Pennsylvania Journal of International Law* 31: 53–123.

Mitlin, D. and Satterthwaite, D. (2012) *Urban Poverty in the Global South: Scale and Nature*. London: Routledge.

Mol, A. and Carter, N. (2006) 'China's environmental governance in transition' in *Environmental Politics* 15(2): 149–170.

Monastersky, R. (2015) 'Anthropocene: the human age' in *Nature* 519(7542): 144–147.

Monbiot, G. (2009) 'Stop blaming the poor. It's the wally yachters who are burning the planet: population growth is not a problem – it's among those who consume the least. So why isn't anyone targeting the very rich?' *The Guardian*. [Online]. 28 September 2009 [Accessed 28 July 2016]. Available from: http://www.theguardian.com/commentisfree/cif-green/2009/sep/28/population-growth-super-rich

Monteriro-Penteado, A. (2012) 'The law of the land: intangible and tangible rights in Aboriginal Australia' in *Revista de Direito Economico e Socioambiental* 3(1): 227–252.

Morgan, J. and Stallworthy, M. (2013) 'Indemnifying against flood loss in a changing environment' in *Legal Studies* 33(2): 239–263.

Morgenson, G. and Story, L. (2011) 'In financial crisis, no prosecutions of top figures' *New York Times.* [Online]. 14 April 2011 [Accessed 27 July 2016]. Available from: http://www.nytimes.com/2011/04/14/business/14prosecute.html

Munich Re. (2012) Severe weather in North America. Knowledge Series.

Munich Re. (2016a) 2015 natural catastrophe losses curbed by El Nino; brutal North American winter caused biggest insured losses.

Munich Re. (2016b) Natural loss events worldwide 2015: geographical overview. [Online]. January 2016. [Accessed 2 June 2016]. Available from: https://www.munichre.com/site/mram-mobile/get/documents_E1656163460/mram/assetpool.munichreamerica.wrap/PDF/07Press/2015_World_map_of_nat_cats.pdf

Murphy, A., Barnet, B., Nikolova, N., Hartell, J. and Skees, J. (2011) State of Knowledge Report-market Development for Weather Index Insurance: Key Considerations for Sustainability and Scale Up. GlobalAgRisk Project Report. Lexington USA: GlobalAgRisk, Inc.

Napier, D. (2002) 'On anthropology and intellectual property' in MacClancy, J. (ed.) *Exotic no More: Anthropology on the Front Lines*. Chicago: University of Chicago Press.

Nathan, A. (2003) 'Authoritarian resilience' in *Journal of Democracy* 14(1): 6–17.

National Academies of Sciences, Engineering and Medicine (2016) Attribution of Extreme Weather Events in the Context of Climate Change. Washington DC: National Academies Press.

National Water Commission (NWC) (2013) Monitoring and evaluation for adaptive water management: issues paper. Canberra: NWC.

National Water Commission (NWC) (2014) Australia's Water Blueprint: National Reform Assessment 2014. Canberra: NWC.

Nelson, D. (2011) 'Adaptation and resilience: responding to a changing climate' in *WIREs Clim Change* 2(1): 113–120.

Nelson, D., Adger, W. and Brown, K. (2009) 'Adaptation to environmental

change: contributions of a resilience framework' in *Annual Review of Environment and Resources* 32: 395–419.
Neumayer, E. and Plümper, T. (2007) The gendered nature of natural disasters: the impact of catastrophic events on the gender gap in life expectancy 1981–2002. *Annals of the Association of American Geographers* 97(3): 551–566.
Newell, P. (2005) 'Race, class and the global politics of environmental inequality' in *Global Environmental Politics* 5: 70–94.
Newman, P. (2006) 'The environmental impact of cities' in *Environment and Urbanization* 18: 275–295.
Nhira, C., Baker, S., Gondo, P., Mangono, J.J. and Marunda, C. (1998) Contesting Inequality in Access to Forests: Zimbabwe country study. Policy That Works for Forests and People. International Institute for Environment and Development.
Nietzsche, F. ([1887] 1996) *On the Genealogy of Morals*. Oxford: Oxford University Press.
Nixon, R. (2011) *Slow Violence and the Environmentalism of the Poor*. Cambridge, MA: Harvard University Press.
Njoka, J. and Macek, P. (2012) 'Natural resources' in Headey, D. and Kennedy, A. (eds.) *Enhancing Resilience in the Horn of Africa: Synthesis of an Evidence*. Washington, DC: US AID and International Food Policy Research Institute (copyright IRPRI).
Njon, A. (2002) 'Barriers to community participation in development planning: lessons from the Mutengene (Cameroon) self-help water project' in *Community Development Journal* 37(3): 233–248.
Nordhaus, W. (2007) 'Critical assumptions in the Stern Review on Climate Change' in *Science* 317: 201–202.
Notre Dame Global Adaptation Index (2014a) 'Disproportionate risk: the world through the lens of climate change vulnerability and readiness' [Online] November 2014. [Accessed 28 July 2016]. Available from: http://gain.org/sites/default/files/Infographics_0.pdf
Notre Dame Global Adaptation Index (2014b) 'ND-GAIN Country Index' [Online]. November, 2014. [Accessed 28 July 2016] Available from: http://www.gain.org/about-the-index
Nourse, V. and Shaffer, G. (2014) 'Empiricism, experimentalism, and conditional theory' in *South Methodist University Law Review* 67: 101–142.
O'Brien, G. and Read, P. (2005) 'Future UK emergency management: new wine, old skin?' in *Disaster Prevention and Management* 14(3): 353–361.
Odemerho, F. (2015) 'Building climate change resilience through bottom-up adaptation to flood risk in Warri, Nigeria' in *Environment and Urbanization* 27(1): 139–160.
Oxford English Dictionary (2010) 'Resilience' in Oxford English Dictionary,

3rd edition [Online]. [Accessed 28 July 2016]. Available from: http://www.oed.com/view/Entry/163619?redirectedFrom=resilience#eid

Office of the United Nations High Commissioner for Human Rights (OHCHR) (2016) '"A deadly undertaking" – UN experts urge all governments to protect environmental rights defenders' [Online] [Accessed 15 July 2016] Available from: http://www.ohchr.org/EN/NewsEvents/Pages/DisplayNews.aspx?NewsID=20052&LangID=E

Okereke, C., Bulkeley, H. and Schroeder, H. (2009) 'Conceptualizing climate governance beyond the international regime' in *Global Environmental Politics* 9(1): 58–78.

Olsson, L., Jerneck, A., Thoren, H., Persson, J. and O'Byrne, D. (2015) 'Why resilience is unappealing to social science: theoretical and empirical investigations of the scientific use of resilience' in *Science Advances* 1(4). e1400217. [Online]. Available from: http://doi/10.1126/sciadv.1400217

Olsson, P., Galaz, V. and Boonstra, W.J. (2014) 'Sustainability transformations: a resilience perspective' in *Ecology and Society* 19(4): 1. [Online]. Available from: http://dx.doi.org/10.5751/ES-06799-190401

O'Malley, P. (2000) 'Uncertain subjects: risks, liberalism and contract' in *Economy and Society* 29: 460–484.

O'Malley, P. (2011) 'Neoliberalism and risk' in *Carceral Notebooks* 7: 41–68.

Orloff, N. and Stedinger, J. (1983) 'A framework for evaluating the preponderance-of-the-evidence standard' in *University of Pennsylvania Law Review* 131: 1159–1174.

Orta-Martínez M. and Finer, M. (2010) 'Oil frontiers and indigenous resistance in the Peruvian Amazon' in *Ecological Economics* 70(2): 207–218.

Osborne, D. and Gaebler, T. (1993) *Inventing Government: how the Entrepreneurial Spirit is Transforming the Public Sector*. New York: Plume.

Oshita, S. and Ortolano, L. (2006) 'Effects of economic and environmental reform on the diffusion of cleaner coal technology in China' in *Development and Change* 37(1): 75–98.

Ostrom, E. (2009) 'A general framework for analyzing sustainability of social-ecological systems' in *Science* 325(5939): 419–422.

Ostrom, E. (2010) 'Beyond markets and states: polycentric governance of complex economic systems' in *American Economic Review* 100: 641–672.

Ostrom, E. (2012) 'Polycentric systems: multilevel governance involving a diversity of organizations' in Brousseau, E., Dedeurwaerdere, T., Jouvet, P. and Willinger, M. (eds) *Global Environmental Commons: Analytical and Political Challenges in Building Governance Mechanisms*. Oxford: Oxford University Press.

Ostrom, V. and Ostrom, E. (1965) 'A behavioural approach to the study of intergovernmental relations' in *Annals of the American Academy of Political and Social Science* 359: 135–146.

Overdevest, C. and Zeitlin, J. (2014) 'Assembling an experimentalist regime: transnational governance interactions in the forest sector' in *Regulation and Governance* 8(1): 22–48.

Oxfam (2013) 'No accident: resilience and the inequality of risk'. Oxfam Briefing Paper 172.

Oxfam America (2012) 'Horn of Africa risk transfer for adaptation: HARITA quarterly report'.

Özkaynak, B., Rodriguez-Labajos, B., Arsel, M., Avcı, D., Carbonell, M.H., Chareyron, B., Chicaiza, G., Conde, M., Demaria, F., Finamore, R., Kohrs, B., Krishna, V.V., Mahongnao, M., Raeva, D., Singh, A.A., Slavov, T., Tkalec, T., Yánez, I., Walter, M. and Živčič, L. (2012) Mining Conflicts around the World: Common Grounds from Environmental Justice Perspective. EJOLT Report No. 7.

Paavola, J. and Adger, N. (2002) Justice and adaptation to climate change. Working Paper 23, Tyndall Centre for Climate Change Research.

Painter, M. and Durham, W. (1995) *The Social Causes of Environmental Destruction in Latin America*. Ann Arbor: University of Michigan Press.

Park, J., Seager, T., Rao, P., Convertino, M. and Linkov, I. (2013) 'Integrating risk and resilience approaches to catastrophe management in engineering systems' in *Risk Analysis* 33(3): 356–367.

Parkins, J., Dunn, M., Reed, M. and John Sinclair, A. (2016) 'Forest governance as neoliberal strategy: a comparative case study of the Model Forest Program in Canada' in *Journal of Rural Studies* 45: 270–278.

Pattberg, P. and Widerberg, O. (2015) 'Theorising global environmental governance: key findings and future questions' in *Millennium – Journal of International Studies* 43(2): 684–705.

Pearce, F. and Tombs, S. (1998) *Toxic Capitalism: Corporate Crime and the Chemical Industry*. Brookfield: Ashgate.

Pedersen, O. (2013a) 'Environmental enforcement undertakings and possible implications: response, smarter or rent seeking?' in *Modern Law Review* 76(2): 319–345.

Pedersen, O. (2013b) 'Modest pragmatic lessons for a diverse and incoherent environmental law' in *Oxford Journal of Legal Studies* 33(1): 103–131.

Pedersen, O. (2015) 'The rhetoric of environmental reasoning and responses as applied to fracking' in *Journal of Environmental Law* 27(3): 325–334.

Pedersen, O. 2011. 'Environmental justice in the UK: uncertainty, ambiguity and the law' in *Legal Studies* 31: 279–304.

Peek, L.A. and Fothergill, A. (2008) 'Displacement, gender, and the challenges of parenting after Hurricane Katrina' in *NWSA Journal* 20(3): 69–105.

Peel, J. (2008) 'Ecologically sustainable development: more than mere lip service?' in *Australasian Journal of Natural Resources Law and Policy* 12(1): 1–34.

Peerenboom, R. (2002) *China's Long March Toward Rule of Law*. Cambridge: Cambridge University Press.

Pellow, D. (2000) 'Environmental inequality formation: toward a theory of environmental injustice' in *American Behavioral Scientist* 43(4): 581–601.

Pellow, D. and Brulle, R. (2005) *Power, Justice, and the Environment: a Critical Appraisal of the Environmental Justice Movement*. Cambridge, MA: MIT.

Petak, W. (2002) 'Earthquake resilience through mitigation: a system approach. International Institute for Applied Systems Analysis'. Paper presented at International Institute for Applied Systems Analysis, Laxenburg, Austria. [Online]. Available from: https://www.researchgate.net/profile/William_Petak/publication/228793628_Earthquake_Resilience_through_Mitigation_A_System_Approach/links/0a85e52fb0bcbda8d1000000.pdf

Peterson, T., Stott, P. and Herring, S. (2012) 'Explaining extreme events of 2011 from a climate perspective' in *Bulletin of the American Meteorological Society* 93(7): 1041–1067.

Phelan, L., Henderson-Sellers, A. and Taplin, R. (2013) 'The political economy of addressing the climate crisis in the Earth system: undermining perverse resilience' in *New Political Economy* 18(2): 198–226.

Phillips, T. (2015) Tianjin blasts: fears of cyanide pollution as Chinese officials lambasted. *The Guardian* [Online] 17 August [Accessed 28 July 2016] Available from: http://www.theguardian.com/world/2015/aug/17/tianjin-explosions-fears-over-pollution-as-chinese-media-lambasts-officials

Pickett, K. and Wilkinson, R. (2010) *The Spirit Level: Why Equality is Better for Everyone*. London: Penguin.

Pidgeon, N. and Butler, C. (2009) 'Risk analysis and climate change' in *Environmental Politics* 18(5): 670–688.

Piguet, E., Laczko, F. (eds) (2014). *People on the Move in a Changing Climate: the Regional Impact of Environmental Change on Migration*. Dordrecht: Springer.

Piketty, T. (2014) *Capital in the Twenty-First Century*. Cambridge. MA: Harvard University Press.

Pinninti, K. (2014) *Climate Change Loss and Damage: Economic and Legal Foundations*. New York: Springer.

Pisano, U. (2012) Resilience and sustainable development: theory of resilience, systems thinking and adaptive governance in ESDN

Quarterly Report No 26, Vienna European Sustainable Development Network.

Plummer, J. and Taylor, J. (2004) *Community Participation in China: Issues and Processes for Capacity-building*. London: GHK.

Plummer, R. and Armitage, D. (2007) 'A resilience-based framework for evaluating adaptive co-management: linking ecology, economics and society in a complex world' in *Ecological Economics* 61(1): 62–74.

Plummer, R., Baird, J., Bullock, J., Dupont, D. and Renzetti, S. (2016) 'Probing the relationship between ecosystem perceptions and approaches to environmental governance: an exploratory content analysis of seven water dilemmas' in *Resilience* 14(1): 1–20.

Porten, S. von der. and de Loë, R. (2014) 'How collaborative approaches to environmental problem solving view indigenous peoples: a systematic review' in *Society & Natural Resources* 27(10): 1040–1056.

Porten, S. von der. and R. de Loë (2013) 'Collaborative approaches to governance for water and indigenous peoples: a case study from British Columbia, Canada' in *Geoforum* 50: 149–160.

Power, M. (2004) *The Risk Management of Everything: Rethinking the Politics of Uncertainty*. London: DEMOS.

Prakash, A. (2002) 'Green marketing, public policy and managerial strategies' in *Business Strategy and the Environment* 11(5): 285–297.

Prüss, A., Kay, D., Fewtrell, L. and Bartram, J. (2002) 'Estimating the burden of disease from water, sanitation and hygiene at a global level' in *Environmental Health Perspectives* 110(5): 537–542.

Quinto, C. (2012) *Insurance Systems in Times of Climate Change: Insurance of Buildings Against Natural Hazards*. Berlin: Springer.

Ragas, A., Huijbregts, M., Henning-De Jong, I. and Leuven, R. (2008) 'Uncertainty in environmental risk assessment: implications for risk-based management of river basins' in *Integrated Environmental Assessment and Management* 5(1): 27–37.

Rajamani, L. (2010) 'The increasing currency and relevance of rights-based perspectives in the international negotiations on climate change' in *Journal of Environmental Law* 22(3): 391–429.

Ran, R. (2013) 'Perverse incentive structure and policy implementation gap in China's local environmental politics' in *Journal of Environmental Policy & Planning* 15(1): 17–39.

Ravallion, M., Chen, S. and Sangraula, P. (2007) 'New evidence on the urbanization of global poverty' in WPS4199. Washington DC: World Bank.

Rawls, J. (1999) *Theory of Justice*. rev. edn, Cambridge, MA: Belknap Press of Harvard University Press.

Raz, J. (1986) *Morality of Freedom*. Oxford: Oxford University Press.
Redman, C. (2014) 'Should sustainability and resilience be combined or remain distinct pursuits?' in *Ecology and Society* 19(2): 37. [Online]. Available from: http://www.ecologyandsociety.org/vol19/iss2/art37/
Reid, M. (2013) 'Disasters and social inequalities' in *Sociology Compass* 7(11): 984–997.
Renn, O. (2011) 'The social amplification/attenuation of risk framework: application to climate change' in *Wiley Interdisciplinary Reviews: Climate Change* 2(2): 154–159.
Revi, A., Satterthwaite, D., Aragón-Durand, F., Corfee-Morlot, J., Kiunsi, R., Pelling, M., Roberts, D., Solecki, W., Gajjar, S. and Sverdlik, A. (2014) 'Urban areas' in Field, C.B., Barros, V., Dokken, D.J., Mach, K.J., Mastrandrea, M.D., Bilir, T.E., Chatterjee, M., Ebi, K., Estrada, Y.O., Genova, R.C., Girma, B., Kissel, E.S., Levy, A.N., MacCracken, S., Mastrandrea, P.R. and White, L.L. (eds) *Climate Change 2014: Impacts, Adaptation, and Vulnerability. Part A: Global and Sectoral Aspects*. Contribution of Working Group II to the Fifth Assessment Report of the Intergovernmental Panel on Climate Change. Cambridge and New York: Cambridge University Press.
Rhodes, R. (1997) *Understanding Governance: Policy Networks, Governance, Reflexivity, And Accountability*. Buckingham, PA: Open University Press.
Richard, M. (2015) 'Anthropocene: the human age' in *Nature* 519(7542): 144–147.
Richardson, B. and Razzaque, J. (2006) 'Public participation in environmental decision-making' in Richardson, B. and Wood, S., eds. (2006) *Environmental Law for Sustainability*. Oxford: Hart Publishing.
Rijke, J., Brown, R., Zevenbergen, C., Ashley, R., Farrelly, M., Morison, P. and van Herk, D. (2012) 'Fit-for-purpose governance: a framework to make adaptive governance operational' in *Environmental Science & Policy* 22: 73–84.
Rittel, H. and Webber, M. (1973) 'Dilemmas in a general theory of planning' in *Policy Sciences* 4: 155–169.
Robinson, L., Gledhill, D., Moltschaniwskyj, N., Hobday, A., Frusher, S., Barrett, N., Stuart-Smith, J. and Pecl, G. (2015) 'Rapid assessment of short-term datasets in an ocean warming hotspot reveals "high" confidence in potential range extensions' in *Global Environmental Change* 31: 28–37.
Rockström, J., Steffen, W., Noone, K., Persson, A., Chapin, F., Lambin, E., Lenton, T., Scheffer, M., Folke, C., Schellnhuber, H., Nykvist, B., de Wit, C., Hughes, T., van der Leeuw, S., Rodhe, H., Sörlin, S., Snyder, P., Costanza, R., Svedin, U., Falkenmark, M., Karlberg, L., Corell, R., Fabry, V., Hansen, J., Walker, B., Liverman, D., Richardson, K., Crutzen,

P. and Foley, J. (2009) 'Planetary boundaries: exploring the safe operating space for humanity' in *Ecology and Society* 14(2): 32. [Online]. Available from: http://www.ecologyandsociety.org/vol14/iss2/art32/

Rogers, P. (2013) 'Rethinking resilience: articulating community and the UK riots' in *Politics* 33(4): 322–333.

Rothstein, H., Borraz, O. and Huber, M. (2013) 'Risk and the limits of governance: exploring varied patterns of risk-based governance across Europe' in *Regulation and Governance* 7(2): 215–235.

Rothstein, H., Huber, M. and Gaskell, G. (2006) 'A theory of risk colonization: the spiralling regulatory logics of societal and institutional risk' in *Economy and Society* 35(1): 91–112.

Royal Society Science Policy Centre (2012) *People and the Planet* London: The Royal Society.

Rubin, O. (2014) 'Social vulnerability to climate-induced natural disasters: cross-provincial evidence from Vietnam' in *Asia Pacific Viewpoint* 55: 67–80.

Ruhl, J. (1997) 'Thinking of environmental law as a complex adaptive system: how to clean up the environment by making a mess of environmental law' in *Houston Law Review* 34(4): 933–1002.

Ruhl, J. (2005) 'Regulation by adaptive management – is it possible?' in *Minnesota Journal of Law, Science, and Technology* 7(1): 21–57.

Ruhl, J. (2010) 'Climate change adaptation and the structural transformation of environmental law' in *Environmental Law* 40: 363–431.

Ruhl, J. (2010) 'General design principles for resilience and adaptive capacity in legal systems – with applications to climate change adaptation' in *North Carolina Law Review* 89: 1374–1403.

Ruhl, J. (2011) 'General design principles for resilience and adaptive capacity in legal systems – with application to climate change adaptation' in *North Carolina Law Review* 89: 1373–1401.

Ruhl, J. and Fischman, R. (2010) 'Adaptive management in the courts' in *Minnesota Law Review* 95(2): 424–484.

Ruhl, J. and Salzman, R. (2007) 'The law and policy beginnings of ecosystem services' in *Journal of Land Use & Environmental Law* 22(2): 157–172.

Rutter, M. (2012) 'Resilience as a dynamic concept' in *Development and Psychopathology* 24: 335–344.

Rydin, Y., Bleahu, A., Davies, M., Dávila, J., Friel, S., De Grandis, G., Groce, N., Hallal, P., Hamilton, I., Howden-Chapman, P., Lai, K., Lim, C.J., Martins, J., Osrin, D., Ridley, I., Scott, I., Taylor, M., Wilkinson, P. and Wilson, J. (2012) 'Shaping cities for health: complexity and the planning of urban environments in the 21st century' in *The Lancet* 379(9831): 2079–2108.

Rydin, Y., Lee, M. and Lock, S. (2015) 'Public engagement in decision-making on major wind energy projects' in *Journal of Environmental Law* 27:139–150.

Sabel, C. and Zeitlin, J. (2011) 'Experimentalist governance' in Levi-Faur, D. (ed.) *The Oxford Handbook of Governance*. Oxford: Oxford Publishing.

Salo, M. and Toivonen, T. (2009) 'Tropical timber rush in Peruvian Amazonia: spatial allocation of forest concessions in an uninventoried frontier' in *Environmental Management* 44(4): 609–623.

Sands, P. and Peel, J. (2012) *Principles of International Environmental Law*. Cambridge: Cambridge University Press.

Sant'anna, A. (2016) 'Land inequality and deforestation in the Brazilian Amazon', in *Environment and Development Economics* 22(1): 1–25.

Santos-Granero, F. and Barclay, F. (2011) 'Bundles, stampers, and flying gringos: native perceptions of capitalist violence in Peruvian Amazonia' in *The Journal of Latin American and Caribbean Anthropology* 16(1): 143–167.

Satterthwaite, D. (2016) 'Missing the Millennium Development Goal targets for water and sanitation in urban areas' in *Environment and Urbanization* 28(1): 99–118.

Satterthwaite, D. and Dodman, D. (2013) 'Towards resilience and transformation for cities within a finite planet' in *Environment and Urbanization* 25(2): 291–298.

Satterthwaite, D. and Mitlin, D. (2014) *Reducing Urban Poverty in the Global South*. London: Routledge.

Satterthwaite, D. and Sverdlik, A. (2012) 'Energy access and housing for low-income groups in urban areas' in Grubler, A. and Fisk, D. (eds) *Energizing Cities*. London: Earthscan Publications.

Savage, M., Devine, F., Cunningham, N., Taylor, M., Li, Y., Hjellbrekke, J., Le Roux, B., Friedman, S. and Miles, A. (2013) 'A new model of social class? findings from the BBC's Great British Class' in *Sociology* 47(2): 219–250.

Savaresi A. (2015) 'The legal status and role of safeguards' in Voigt, C. (ed.) *Research Handbook on REDD+ and International Law*. Cheltenham, UK and Northampton, MA: Edward Elgar Publishing.

Sayer, A. (2015) *Why We Can't Afford the Rich*. Bristol: Policy Press.

Schlosberg, D. (2007) *Defining Environmental Justice: Theories, Movements, and Nature*. Oxford: Oxford University Press.

Schlosberg, D. and Collins, L.B. (2014) 'From environmental to climate justice: climate change and the discourse of environmental justice' in *Wiley Interdisciplinary Reviews: Climate Change* 5(3): 359–374.

Scotford, E. and Robinson, J. (2013) 'UK environmental legislation and its administration in 2013 – achievements, challenges and prospects' in *Journal of Environmental Law* 25: 383–409.

Scott, J. and Holder, J. (2006) 'Law and new environmental governance in the European Union' in De Búrca, G. and Scott, J. (eds) *Law and New Governance in the EU and the US*. Oxford: Hart Publishing.

Scott, J. (1998) *Seeing Like a State*. New Haven: Yale University Press.

Secretariat of the Convention on Biological Diversity (2011) Global Biodiversity Outlook 4.

Sen, A. (1981) *Poverty and Famines: an Essay on Entitlement and Deprivation*. Oxford: Clarendon Press.

Sen, A. (1983) 'Poor, relatively speaking' in *Oxford Economic Papers* 35(2): 153–69.

Sen, A. (1999) *Development as Freedom*. New York: Oxford University Press.

Sexton, K. (2013) 'Evolution of public participation in the assessment and management of environmental health risks: a brief history of developments in the United States' in *Journal of Public Health Research* 2: 106–112.

Shanghai Municipal Government, 2007. Shanghai shi jieneng jianpai gongzuo shishi fang'an [Shanghai municipality energy efficiency and emissions reduction work plan] [Online] [Accessed 28 July 2016]. Available from: http://www.shanghai.gov.cn/shanghai/node2314/node3124/node3177/node3188/userobject6ai1840.html

Shapiro, J. (2016) *China's Environmental Challenges (Second Edition)*. Cambridge: Polity Press.

Shearing, C. and Johnston, L. (2010) 'Nodal wars and network fallacies: a genealogical analysis of global insecurities' in *Theoretical Criminology* 14: 495–614.

Shepherd A. and Bowler C. (1997) 'Beyond the requirements: improving public participation in EIA' in *Journal of Environmental Planning and Management* 40(6): 725–738.

Shi, Y. and Rooij, B. (2015) 'Prosecutorial regulation in the Global South: environmental civil litigation by prosecutors in China compared to Brazil' in *Regulation & Governance* 9: 1–14.

Silver, N. and Dlugolecki, A. (2009) 'The Insurability of the impacts of climate change' in *GIRO Conference Edinburgh*. Edinburgh.

Simonson, S., Biggs, R., Schluter, M., Schoon, M., Bohensky, E., Cundill, G., Dakos, V., Daw, T., Kotschy, K., Leitch, A., Quinlan, A., Peterson, G. and Moberg, F. (2012) Applying Resilience Thinking: Seven principles for building resilience in socio-ecological systems. Stockholm Resilience Centre. [Online]. [Accessed 29 July 2016]. Available from: http://www.stockholmresilience.org/download/18.10119fc11455d3c557d6928/145960241272/SRC+Applying+Resilience+final.pdf

Singer, P. (1993) *Practical Ethics*. Cambridge: Cambridge University Press.
Smit, B. and Wandel, J. (2006) 'Adaptation, adaptive capacity and vulnerability' in *Global Environmental Change* 16: 282–292.
Smith, R. (2003) *Property Law*. Harlow, England: Pearson Longman.
Smith, R. and Wynne, B. (1988) *Expert Evidence: Interpreting Science in the Law*. London: Routledge.
Snow, D., Cress, D., Downey, L. and Jones, A. (1998) 'Disrupting the "quotidian": reconceptualizing the relationship between breakdown and the emergence of collective action' in *Mobilization: An International Quarterly* 3(1): 1–22.
Sofronova, E., Holley, C. and Nagarajan, V. (2014) 'Environmental non-government organisations and Russian environmental governance: accountability, participation, collaboration' in *Transnational Environmental Law* 3(2): 341–371.
Solar, O. and Irwin, A. (2007) 'A Conceptual Framework for Action on the Social Determinants of Health'. Commission on Social Determinants of Health.
Spears, B., Ives, S., Angeler, D., Allen, C., Birk, S., Carvalho, L., Cavers, S., Daunt, F., Morton, R., Pocock, M. and Thackeray S. (2015) 'Effective management of ecological resilience – are we there yet?' in *Journal of Applied Ecology* 52: 1311–1315.
St John, R.B. (1996) 'Conflict in the Cordillera del Cóndor: the Ecuador–Peru dispute' in *IBRU Boundary and Security Bulletin* 4(1) (Spring). America Television Network (Lima), broadcast in Spanish, 7 March 1996, in FBIS-LAT-96-046.
Standard and Poor's Rating Services (2015a) Simulated Natural Catastrophe Impacts.
Standard and Poor's Rating Services (2015b) Climate Change Will Likely Test The Resilience Of Corporates' Creditworthiness To Natural Catastrophes.
Standing, G. (2011) *The Precariat: the New Dangerous Class*. London: Bloomsbury.
Stavins, R. (2003) 'Experience with market-based environmental policy instruments' in Mäler, K. and Vincent, J. (eds.) *Handbook of Environmental Economics*. 1st edition. Amsterdam; Boston: Elsevier.
Steele, J. (2001) 'Participation and deliberation in environmental law: exploring a problem-solving approach' in *Oxford Journal of Legal Studies* 21(3): 415–442.
Steffen, W., Burbidge, A.A., Hughes, L., Kitching, R., Lindenmayer, D., Musgrave, W., Stafford Smith, M. and Werner, P.A. (2009) *Australia's biodiversity and climate change: a strategic assessment of the vulnerability of Australia's biodiversity to climate change*. A report to the

Natural Resource management Ministerial Council commissioned by the Australian Government. Canberra: CSIRO Publishing.

Steffen, W., Richardson, K., Rockström, J., Cornell, S.E., Fetzer, I., Bennett, E.M., Biggs, R., Carpenter, S.R., De Vries, W., De Wit, C.A., Folke, C., Gerten, D., Heinke, J., Mace, G.M., Persson, L.M., Ramanathan, V., Reyers, B. and Sörlin, S. (2015) 'Planetary boundaries: guiding human development on a changing planet' in *Science* 347(6223): 1–10.

Steinhardt, C. and Wu, F. (2016) 'In the name of the public: environmental protest and the changing landscape of popular contention in China' in *The China Journal* 75: 61–82.

Stern, N. (2007) *The Economics of Climate Change: The Stern Review*. Cambridge: Cambridge University Press.

Stern, R. (2010) 'On the frontlines: making decisions in Chinese civil environmental lawsuits' in *Law & Policy* 32: 79–103.

Stern, R. (2013) *Environmental Litigation in China: a Study in Political Ambivalence*. Cambridge: Cambridge University Press.

Stern, R. (2014) 'The political logic of China's new environmental courts' in *China Journal* 72: 53–74.

Stevenson H. and Dryzek, J. (2014) *Democratizing Global Climate Governance*. New York: Cambridge University Press.

Stiglitz, J. (2002) 'Participation and development: perspectives from the comprehensive development paradigm' in *Review of Development Economics* 6(2): 163–182.

Stiglitz, J. (2002) *Globalization and its Discontents*. New York: W.W. Norton & Co.

Stockmann, D. (2012) *Media Commercialization and Authoritarian Rule in China*. Cambridge: Cambridge University Press.

Stoll-Kleemann, S. and Welp, M. (eds.) (2006) *Stakeholder Dialogues in Natural Resources Management: Theory and Practice*. Berlin: Springer.

Stott, P.A., Christidis, N., Otto, F., Sun, Y., Vanderlinden, J., Van Oldenborgh, G., Vautard, R., Von Storch, H., Walton, P., Yiou, P. and Zwiers, F. (2016) 'Attribution of extreme weather and climate-related events' in *WIRES Climate Change* 7: 23–41.

Stromberg P., Dedeurwaerdere, T. and Pascual, U. (2013) 'The heterogeneity of public *ex situ* collections of microorganisms: empirical evidence about conservation practices, industry spillovers and public goods' in *Environmental Science & Policy* 33: 19–27.

Stromberg, P., Pascual, U. and Ituarte-Lima, C. (2012) 'Global environmental governance and payments for ecosystem services. Principal component analysis of bioprospecting agreements' in Rival, L. and Muradian, R. (eds.) *Governing the Provision of Ecosystem Services*. Dordrecht: Springer.

Stuligross, D. (1999) 'The political economy of environmental regulation in India' in *Pacific Affairs* 72: 392–406.
Sturm, S. (2006) 'Gender equity regimes and the architecture of learning' in De Búrca, G. and Scott, J. (eds) *Law and New Governance in the EU and the US*. Oxford: Hart Publishing.
Su, Y. and He, X. (2010) 'Street as courtroom: state accommodation of labor protest in South China' in *Law & Society Review* 44(1): 157–184.
Sunstein, C. (2005) *Laws of Fear: Beyond the Precautionary Principle.* Cambridge, UK; New York: Cambridge University Press.
Surminski, S. and Lopez, A. (2015) 'Concept of loss and damage of climate change – a new challenge for climate decision-making? A climate science perspective' in *Climate and Development* 7(3): 267–277.
Susskind, L., Camacho, A. and Schenk, T. (2010) 'Collaborative planning and adaptive management in Glen Canyon: a cautionary tale' in *Columbia Journal of Environmental Law* 35: 1–55.
Sustainable Development Research Network (2004). Environment and Social Justice: Rapid Research and Evidence Review.
Suttmeier, R. (2008) 'The "Sixth Modernization"?: China, safety, and the management of risks' in *Asia Policy* 6(1): 129–146.
Sverdlik, A. (2011) 'Ill-health and poverty: a literature review on health in informal settlements' in *Environment and Urbanization* 23(1): 123–156.
Svolik, M. (2012) *The Politics of Authoritarian Rule*. Cambridge: Cambridge University Press.
Swingland, I. (ed.) (2003) *Capturing Carbon and Conserving Biodiversity: the Market Approach*. London: Royal Society – Earthscan.
Syme, G. and Sadler, B. (1994) 'Evaluation of public involvement in water resource planning, a researcher–practitioner dialogue' in *Evaluation Review* 18(5): 523–542.
Tamanaha, B. (2001) *A General Jurisprudence of Law and Society*. Oxford: Oxford University Press.
Taylor-Gooby, P. (2012) 'Root and branch restructuring to achieve major cuts: the social policy programme of the 2010 UK Coalition Government' in *Social Policy and Administration* 46(1): 61–82.
Techera, E. (2012) *Marine Environmental Governance: From International Law to Local Practice*. Oxford: Routledge.
The Lancet (2015) [Editorial] 'Urban health post-2015' in *The Lancet* 385(9970): 745.
The National Academies of Sciences, Engineering and Medicine (2016) Attribution of Extreme Weather Events in the Context of Climate Change.
Thomas, C. (1999) 'Linking public agencies with community-based watershed organisations: lessons from California' in *Policy Studies Journals* 27(3): 544–564.

Thrush, S., Hewitt, J., Dayton, P., Coco, G., Lohrer, A., Norkko, A., Norkko, J. and Chiantore, M. (2009) 'Forecasting the limits of resilience: integrating empirical research with theory' in *Proceedings of The Royal Society Biological Sciences* 276(1671): 3209–3207.

Tierney, K. (2012) 'Disaster governance: social, political, and economic dimensions' in *Annual Review of Environment and Resources* 37: 341–363.

Tierney, K. (2014) *The Social Roots of Risk: Producing Disasters, Promoting Resilience*. Stanford, California: Stanford Business Books.

Tobin, B. and Swiderska, K. (2001) *Speaking in Tongues: Indigenous Participation in the Development of a Sui Generis Regime to Protect Traditional Knowledge in Peru*. London: International Institute for Environmental and Development (IIED).

Tombs, S. and Whyte, D. (2015) *The Corporate Criminal: Why Corporations Must Be Abolished*. Abingdon: Routledge.

Trubek, D. and Trubek, L. (2007) 'New governance & legal regulation' in *Columbia Journal of European Law* 13: 540–564.

Tsang, S. (2009). 'Consultative Leninism: China's new political framework' in *Journal of Contemporary China* 18(62): 865–880.

UNEP (2009) *From Conflict to Peacebuilding – The Role of Natural Resources and the Environment*. Nairobi, Kenya: United Nations Environment Programme.

UNESCO (1989) Recommendation on the Safeguarding of Traditional Culture and Folklore. General Conference of the United Nations Educational, Scientific and Cultural Organization.

UN-Habitat (2003) *Water and Sanitation in the World's Cities: Local Action for Global Goals*. London: Earthscan Publications.

United Nations (1969) Vienna Convention on the Law of Treaties. Document A/CONF.39/27.

United Nations (1992) United Nations Framework Convention on Climate Change.

United Nations (2002) Plan of Implementation of the World Summit on Sustainable Development. A/CONF.199/20, Chapter 1, Resolution 2, Johannesburg, September 2002.

United Nations (2007) Declaration on the Rights of Indigenous Peoples, Resolution adopted by the General Assembly on 13 September 2007, A/61/L.67. New York.

United Nations (2015) Transforming our World: the 2030 Agenda for Sustainable Development, Resolution adopted by the General Assembly on 25 September 2015, A/RES/70/1, New York.

United Nations (2015) World Urbanization Prospects: The 2014 Revision, POP/DB/WUP/Rev.2014/1/F09, Population Division, Department of Economic and Social Affairs, New York.

United Nations Economic and Social Council's Sub-Commission on Prevention of Discrimination and Protection of Minorities (1994) Draft Declaration on Discrimination against Indigenous Peoples E/CN.4/ Sub.2/1994/2/Add.1.

United Nations Framework Convention on Climate Change (2015) Report of the Adaptation Committee, Decision 4/CP.21 [Online]. [Accessed 4 December 2016]. Available from: http://unfccc.int/resource/docs/2015/ cop21/eng/10a02.pdf#page=4

United Nations Framework Convention on Climate Change (2016) Green Climate Fund [Online]. 2 December 2016. [Accessed 4 December 2016]. Available from: http://unfccc.int/cooperation_and_support/financial_ mechanism/green_climate_fund/items/5869.php

United Nations Fund for Population Activities (2013) The Demography of Adaptation to Climate Change.

United Nations Fund for Population Activities (2014) State of the World Population 2014. The Power of 1.8 Billion.

United Nations Office for Disaster Risk Reduction (2016) Terminology [Online]. [Accessed 4 December 2016] Available from: https://www. unisdr.org/we/inform/terminology

United Nations University – Institute for Environment and Human Security (2014) World Risk Report 2014. Focus: the city as a risk area.

Urry, J. (2011) *Climate Change and Society*. Cambridge: Polity.

Urteaga-Crovetto. P. (2000) 'Territorial rights and indigenous law: an alternative approach', in Assies W., Van de Haar, G. and Hoekena, A. (eds), *The Challenge of Diversity: Indigenous People and the Reform of the State in Latin America*. Purdue IN: Purdue University Press.

US Senate Homeland Security and Government Affairs Committee (2014) Testimony by Lindene Patton, Zurich Insurance Group, Ltd.

USAID (2014) Resilience and economic growth in arid lands – accelerated growth. USAID/Kenya [Online] November 2015 [Accessed 29 July 2016]. Available from: https://www.usaid.gov/kenya/fact-sheets/resilie nce-and-economic-growth-arid-lands-%E2%80%93-accelerated-growth

Vale, L. and Campenella, T. (2005) *The Resilient City: how Modern Cities Recover from Disaster*. New York: Oxford University Press.

Van Rooij, B. (2006) *Regulating Land and Pollution in China: Lawmaking, Compliance, and Enforcement: Theory and Cases*. Amsterdam: Amsterdam University Press.

Van Rooij, B. (2010) 'Greening industry without enforcement? An assessment of the World Bank's pollution regulation model for developing countries' in *Law & Policy* 32: 127–152.

Van Rooij, B. (2012) 'The People's Regulation: citizens and implementation of law in China' in *Columbia Journal of Asian Law* 25(2): 116–179.

Van Rooij, B. and Lo, C. (2010) 'Fragile convergence: understanding variation in the enforcement of China's industrial pollution law' in *Law & Policy* 32(1): 14–37.

Van Rooij, B., Lora-Wainwright, A., Wu, Y. and Zhang, Y.A. (2012) 'The compensation trap: the limits of community-based pollution regulation in China, in *PACE Environmental Law (PELR) Review* 29(3): 701–745.

Van Rooij, B., Fryxell, G., Lo, C. and Wang, W. (2013) 'From support to pressure: the dynamics of social and governmental influences on environmental law enforcement in Guangzhou City, China' in *Regulation & Governance* 7(3): 321–347.

Van Rooij, B., Stern, R.E. and Fürst, K. (2016) 'The authoritarian logic of regulatory pluralism: understanding China's new environmental actors' in *Regulation & Governance* 10: 3–13.

Van Rooij, B., Stern, R.E. and Fürst, K. (2016) 'The authoritarian logic of regulatory pluralism: understanding China's new environmental actors' in *Regulation & Governance* 10: 3 –13.

Varian, H. (1992) *Microeconomic Analysis*. 3rd edition, New York: Norton.

Vaughan, D. (1997) 'Anomie theory and organizations: culture and the normalization of deviance' in Passas N. and Agnew R. (eds) *The Future of Anomie Theory*. Boston, MA: Northeastern University Press.

Vlahov, D., Agarwal., S., Buckley, R., Teixeira., W. Corvalan, C., Chika, A., Finkelstein, R., Friel, S., Harpham, T. and Hossain, M. et al (2011) 'Roundtable on urban living environment research (RUL)' in *Journal of Urban Health* 88(5): 793–857.

Vlahov, D., Freudenberg, N., Proietti, F., Ompad, D., Quinn, A., Nandi, V. and Galea, S. (2007) 'Urban as a determinant of health' in *Journal of Urban Health* 84(1): i16–i26.

Vogel, D. (2003) *National Styles of Business Regulation: a Case Study of Environmental Protection*. Washington, DC: Beard Books.

von Peter, G., von Dahlen, S. and Saxena, S. (2012) Unmitigated disasters? New evidence on the macroeconomic cost of natural catastrophes. BIS Working Papers No. 394. Basel: Bank for International Settlements.

Walby, S. (2015) *Crisis*. Cambridge: Polity.

Walker, B. and Salt, D. (2006) *Resilience Thinking*. Washington DC: Island Press.

Walker, B. and Salt, D. (2006) *Resilience Thinking: Sustaining Ecosystems and People in a Changing World*. Washington, DC: Island Press.

Walker, B., Holling, C., Carpenter, S. and Kinzig, A. (2004) 'Resilience, adaptability and transformability in social-ecological systems' in *Ecology and Society* 9(2): 5–14.

Walker, G., Mitchell, G., Fairburn, J. and Smith, G. (2005) 'Industrial pollution and social deprivation: evidence and complexity in evaluating and

responding to environmental inequality' in *Local Environment* 10(4): 361–377.
Walker, N. (2006) 'EU constitutionalism and new governance', in de Búrca, G. and Scott, J. (eds) *Law and New Governance in the EU and the US*. Oxford: Hart Publishing.
Walsh, F. (1996) 'Concept of family resilience: crisis and challenge' in *Family Process* 35(3): 261–281.
Wang, A. (2013) 'The search for sustainable legitimacy: environmental law and bureaucracy in China' in *Harvard Environmental Law Review* 37: 365–440.
Wang, Y. and Minzner, C. (2015) 'The rise of the Chinese security state' in *The China Quarterly* 222: 339–359.
Warner, K. and Molotch, H. (2000) *Building Rules: how Local Controls Shape Community Environments and Economics*. New York: Westview.
Weale, A., Pridham, G., Williams, A. and Porter, M. (1996) 'Environmental administration in six European states: secular convergence or national distinctiveness?' in *Public Administration* 74: 255–274.
Weber, M. ([1904–5] 2002). *The Protestant Ethic and the Spirit of Capitalism*. London: Penguin.
Weber, M. ([1922] 1978) *Economy and Society*. G. Wittich and C. Wittich (eds) Berkeley, CA: University of California Press.
Weick, K. and Sutcliffe, K. (2001) *Managing the Unexpected: Assuring High Performance in an Age of Complexity*. San Francisco: Jossey-Bass.
Weir, L., O'Malley, P. and Shearing, C. (1997) 'Governmentality, criticism, politics' in *Economy and Society* 26(4): 501–517.
Weiss, D. and Weidman, J. (2013) Disastrous Spending: Federal Disaster-Relief Expenditures Rise Amid More Extreme Weather. 29 April. Washington DC: Center for American Progress. [Online]. 29 April 2013. [Accessed 4 December 2016]. Available from: https://www.americanprogress.org/issues/green/report/2013/04/29/61633/disastrous-spending-federal-disaster-relief-expenditures-rise-amid-more-extreme-weather/
Weiss, E. (1992) 'In fairness to future generations and sustainable development' in *American University International Law Review* 8: 19–26.
Weller, R. (2008) 'Responsive authoritarianism' in B. Gilley and Diamond, L. (Eds.) *Political Change in China: Comparisons with Taiwan*. Boulder, CO: Lynne Rienner Publishers.
Wesselink, A., Paavola, J., Fritsch, O. and Renn, O. (2011) 'Rationales for public participation in environmental policy and governance: practitioners' perspectives' in *Environment and Planning* 43: 2688–2704.
Whiting, S.H. (2006) *Power and Wealth in Rural China: the Political Economy of Institutional Change*. New York: Cambridge University Press.

Whitmarsh, L. (2008) 'Are flood victims more concerned about climate change than other people? The role of direct experience in risk-perception and behavioural response' in *Journal of Risk Research* 11(3): 351–374.

World Health Organization/UNICEF (2014) Progress on Drinking-Water and Sanitation; 2014 Update, Joint Monitoring Programme. Geneva: WHO and UNICEF.

World Health Organization/UNICEF (2015) 25 Years Progress on Sanitation and Drinking Water; 2015 Update and MDG Assessment. Geneva: WHO and UNICEF.

Wijbenga, B., Ruessink, H., de Wit, A. and P. Kapitein (2008) Environmental Policing in the 21st Century – Background, Organisation & Experience in The Netherlands. Paper presented at the Eighth International Conference on Environmental Compliance and Enforcement, Cape Town, South Africa.

Wildavsky, A. (1988) *Searching for Safety*. Berkeley, CA: University of California Press.

Wolf, J. and Moser, S. (2011) 'Individual understandings, perceptions, and engagement with climate change: insights from in-depth studies across the world' in *Wiley Interdisciplinary Reviews: Climate Change* 2(4): 547–569.

Wong, E. (2013) Cost of Environmental Damage in China Growing Rapidly Amid Industrialization. *The New York Times* [Online] 29 March [Accessed 28 July 2016] Available from: http://www.nytimes.com/2013/03/30/world/asia/cost-of-environmental-degradation-in-china-is-growing.html?_r=0

Woodhill, J. and Roling, N. (2002) 'Guidance for Initiating National and Basin Level Dialogues'. Dialogue Working Paper 5, The Global Dialogue on Water, Food and Environment, Colombo, Sri Lanka: Dialogue Secretariat.

Woods, D. and J. Wreathall (2003) *Managing Risk Proactively: The Emergence of Resilience Engineering*. [Accessed 15 November 2016] Available from: http://s3.amazonaws.com/academia.edu.documents/39750458/Managing_Risk_Proactively_The_Emergence_20151106-1328-u38wae.pdf?AWSAccessKeyId=AKIAJ56TQJRTWSMTNPEA&Expires=1479233830&Signature=nUSTWiwmrZnjAl3DYxFZGr93gNM%3D&response-content-disposition=inline%3B%20filename%3DManaging_Risk_Proactively_The_Emergence.pdf.

World Bank (1996) *The World Bank Participation Sourcebook*. Washington DC: The World Bank.

World Commission on Environment and Development (1987) *Our Common Future*. Oxford: Oxford University Press.

World Economic Forum (2011) A Vision for Managing Natural Disaster Risk. [Online]. Available from: http://www3.weforum.org/docs/WEF_VisionManagingNaturalDisaster_Proposal_2011.pdf
World Economic Forum (2015) *Global Risks 2015*. 10th Edition. Geneva: WEF.
World Economic Forum (2016) *Global Risks Report 2016*. 11th Edition. Geneva: WEF.
World Food Programme and Oxfam America (2016) R4 Rural Resilience Initiative: Quarterly Report October–December 2015. [Online] [Accessed 4 December 2016]. Available from: http://documents.wfp.org/stellent/groups/public/documents/newsroom/wfp281956.pdf
World Health Organization (2014). Burden of disease from Household Air Pollution for 2012. Geneva: WHO.
World Trade Organization (1994) Agreement Establishing the World Trade Organization [Online] [Accessed 27 October 2016] Available from: http://www.wto.org/english/docs_e/legal_e/legal_e.htm
World Trade Organization (1994) Agreement on Trade-Related Aspects of Intellectual Property Rights (TRIPS) 1994, entered into force on 1 January 1995 [Online] [Accessed 27 October 2016] Available from: https://www.wto.org/english/docs_e/legal_e/27-trips_01_e.htm
World Wide Fund for Nature (2014) Living Planet Report.
Wright, E. (ed.) (2005) *Approaches to Class Analysis*. Cambridge: Cambridge University Press.
Wright, E. (1985) *Classes*. London: Verso.
Wurzel, R., Zito, A. and Jordan, A. (2013) *Environmental Governance in Europe: a Comparative Analysis of the Use of New Environmental Policy Instruments*. Cheltenham: Edward Elgar Publishing.
Wyborn, C. (2011) 'Landscape scale ecological connectivity: Australian survey and rehearsals' in *Pacific Conservation Biology* 17(2): 121–131.
Wynne, B. (1989) 'Establishing the rules of laws: constructing expert authority' in Smith, R. and Wynne, B. (eds) (1989) *Expert Evidence: Interpreting Science in the Law*. London: Routledge.
Wynne, B. (1996) 'May the sheep safely graze? A reflexive view of the expert–lay knowledge divide' in Lash, S., Szerszynski, B. and Wynne B. (eds.) *Risk, Environment and Modernity: Towards a New Ecology*. London and Thousand Oaks, CA: Sage Publications.
Wynne, B. (2002) 'Risk and environment as legitimatory discourses of technology: reflexivity inside out?' in *Current Sociology* 50: 459–477.
Xie, Y. (2012) 'The political logic of weiwen in contemporary China' in *Issues & Studies* 48(3): 1–41.
Xu, F. and Webb, J.P. (2015) 'Tianjin chemical clean-up after explosion' in *Canadian Medical Association Journal* 187(13): E404.

Young, O. (2010) 'Institutional dynamics: resilience, vulnerability and adaptation in environmental and resource regimes' in *Global Environmental Change* 20: 378–385.
Zalma, B. (2007) *Insurance: Cases and Materials on Coverage, Claims, and Litigation*. Durham, NC: Carolina Academic Press.
Zhang, A. (2014) 'Rational resistance: homeowner contention against waste incineration in Guangzhou' in *China Perspectives* 2014(2): 45–52.
Zhang, L., He, G., Mol, A.P.J. and Zhu, X. (2013) 'Power politics in the revision of China's Environmental Protection Law' in *Environmental Politics* 22(6): 1029–1035.
Zhang, L., Mol, A.P. and He, G. (2015) 'Transparency and information disclosure in China's environmental governance' in *Current Opinion in Environmental Sustainability* 18: 17–24.
Zhang, L., Mol, A.P.J., He, G. and Lu, Y. (2010) 'An implementation assessment of China's Environmental Information Disclosure Decree' in *Journal of Environmental Sciences* 22: 1649–1656.
Zheng, S., Sun, C., Qi, Y. and Kahn, M. (2014) 'The evolving geography of China's industrial production: implications for pollution dynamics and urban quality of life' in *Journal of Economic Surveys* 28(4): 709–24.
Ziervogel, G., Waddell, J., Smit, W. and Taylor, A. (2016) 'Flooding in Cape Town's informal settlements: barriers to collaborative urban risk governance' in *South African Geographical Journal* 98(1): 1–20.
Zusman, E. (2004) 'Guest editor's introduction' in *Chinese Law and Government* 37(3): 3–7.

CASES

Berkeley v. Secretary of State for the Environment [2001] Env. L.R. 16.
R (Edwards) v. Environment Agency [2008] UKHL 22.
R (on the application of Champion) v. North Norfolk District Council and another [2015] UKSC 52.
R (on the application of ClientEarth) (Appellant) v. Secretary of State for the Environment, Food and Rural Affairs (Respondent) [2015] UKSC 28 and [2013] UKSC 23.
R (on the application of Greenpeace Ltd) v. Secretary of State for Trade and Industry [2007] EWHC 311.
R v. Swale Borough Council, ex parte RSPB [1991] 1 PLR 6.
Walton v. Scottish Ministers (Scotland) [2012] UKSC 44.

LEGISLATION

Climate Change Act 2008.
Environmental Permitting (England and Wales) (Amendment) (England) Regulations 2016.
EU Directive 2014/52/EU of the European Parliament and of the Council of 16 April 2014 amending Directive 2011/92/EU on the assessment of the effects of certain public and private projects on the environment.
EU Industrial Emissions Directive 2010 Directive 2010/75/EU of the European Parliament and of the Council of 24 November 2010 on industrial emissions (integrated pollution prevention and control).

Index